CULTURE AND CUSTOMS
OF ISRAEL

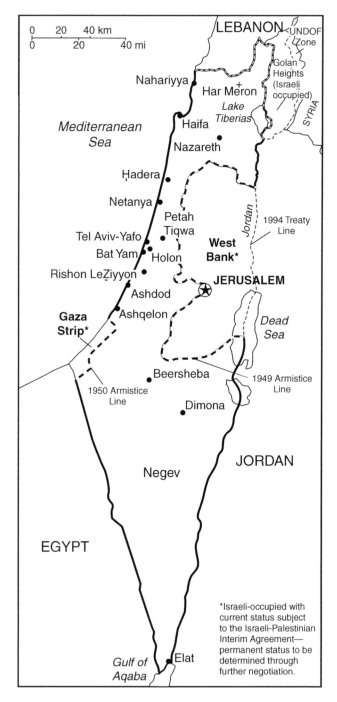

0 20 40 km
0 20 40 mi

LEBANON

UNDOF Zone

Golan Heights (Israeli occupied)

SYRIA

Nahariyya

Har Meron +

Lake Tiberias

Mediterranean Sea

Haifa

Nazareth

Ḥadera

Netanya

Petah Tiqwa

Jordan

1994 Treaty Line

Tel Aviv-Yafo

West Bank*

Bat Yam

Holon

JERUSALEM

Rishon LeZiyyon

Ashdod

Dead Sea

Gaza Strip*

Ashqelon

Beersheba

1949 Armistice Line

1950 Armistice Line

Dimona

JORDAN

Negev

EGYPT

*Israeli-occupied with current status subject to the Israeli-Palestinian Interim Agreement— permanent status to be determined through further negotiation.

Gulf of Aqaba

Elat

Cartography by Bookcomp, Inc.

CULTURE AND CUSTOMS OF ISRAEL

Rebecca L. Torstrick

Culture and Customs of the Middle East

GREENWOOD PRESS
Westport, Connecticut • London

Library of Congress Cataloging-in-Publication Data

Torstrick, Rebecca L., 1954–
   Culture and customs of Israel / Rebecca L. Torstrick.
     p. cm. — (Culture and customs of the Middle East)
   Includes bibliographical references and index.
   ISBN 0–313–32091–8 (alk. paper)
  1. Ethnology—Israel. 2. Israel—Social life and customs.
I. Title. II. Series.
   GN635.I78T67   2004
   306'.095694—dc22   2004004577

British Library Cataloguing in Publication Data is available.

Library of Congress Catalog Card Number: 2004004577
ISBN: 0–313–32091–8

First published in 2004

Greenwood Press, 88 Post Road West, Westport, CT 06881
An imprint of Greenwood Publishing Group, Inc.
www.greenwood.com

Printed in the United States of America

The paper used in this book complies with the
Permanent Paper Standard issued by the National
Information Standards Organization (Z39.48–1984).

10 9 8 7 6 5 4 3 2 1

Contents

Series Foreword

At last! *Culture and Customs of the Middle East* fills a deep void in reference literature by providing substantial individual volumes on crucial countries in the explosive region. The series is available at a critical juncture, with, among other events, the recent war on Iraq, the continued wrangling by U.S. interests for control of regional oil resources, the quest for Palestinian autonomy, and the spread of religious fundamentalist violence and repression. The authoritative, objective, and engaging cultural overviews complement and balance the volley of news bites.

As with the other Culture and Customs series, the narrative focus is on contemporary culture and life, in a historical context. Each volume is written for students and general readers by a country expert. Contents include:

Chronology

Context, including land, people, and brief historical overview

Religion and world view

Literature

Media

Cinema

Art and architecture/housing

Cuisine and dress

Gender, marriage, and family

Social customs and lifestyle

Music and dance

Preface

It is far more common to find the state of Israel excluded when considering the culture and customs of people living in the Middle East than it is to find it included. That is why this volume is so important—because it squarely places Israel within the Middle East. There is good reason why Israel is an anomaly in the Middle East. Its political leaders see themselves as closer to the Western world in values, lifestyle, and political aspirations; at the same time, many of its citizens themselves have or had deep roots in Middle Eastern cultures and values. Where does Israel belong? Is it part of the region, or does it represent a Western outpost, artificially planted in the area? As you will see as you read this book, the question about Israel's place has been a central concern in all forms of cultural productivity in the country since before its founding, and it continues to engage the current creators of modern Israeli culture.

Israel is fascinating to study because it has all the problems of modern industrialized states in a country the size of New Jersey with as many citizens as there are residents of the city of Chicago. It is a country both of and not of its citizens. In its role as the protector of Jewish communities around the world, the Israeli state often acts in ways that do not benefit its current citizens—for example, when scarce national funds are spent to encourage and support new immigration while veteran citizens are suffering from unemployment, cuts in social benefits, and decreases in spending on education. Israel is democratic, but there are limits to the extent of its democracy because it also insists on being a Jewish state. As the heartland for three world faiths—Judaism, Christianity, and Islam—Israel provides the zone at which these three religions come most directly into contact with each other. What makes Israeli culture so vibrant and exciting is this contact, where so many different cultural traditions are brought together. They may mix, merge, and generate new cultural meanings and forms—or they simply coexist side by side, each enriching or challenging the other.

Finally, Israel draws our attention because of the Israeli-Palestinian conflict, one of the more intractable in the world today. It has lasted for more than 50 years and appears to be further from a solution now than it was 50 years ago. The conflict has made a deep imprint on all aspects of Israeli culture. It has tragically been interwoven with the extensive history of Jewish persecution that culminated in the Nazi Holocaust, to the extent that the two events cannot be separated. The Holocaust as well is seared into Israeli culture and continues to exercise an influence to this day as Israelis struggle to come to terms with it.

In this work, I have included as much as possible coverage about the contributions of all Israelis (Ashkenazim, Mizrahim, and Palestinians) to the development of an Israeli national culture. I have limited my discussion to the major themes and highlights of Israeli culture. Entire books have been written on a single aspect (e.g., art or music) and on the works of a single cultural creator (e.g., major Israeli authors or playwrights). For readers who wish to learn more, I suggest starting with sources in the bibliography and expanding out from there. I have concentrated on sources in English that students will be able to find and read on their own. This limited some of my coverage because not much has been written in English (or Hebrew or Arabic for that matter) about some of the communities and their cultural contributions. The book covers the period from the beginnings of Jewish immigration to the country in the late nineteenth century to the present and deals with Israel as a geographic entity within the borders that existed until 1967.

Chronology

1516–1918	Ottoman Empire controls most of the Middle East, including Palestine.
1880s	Rise of Arab nationalism in Ottoman areas.
1881–1903	First wave (aliyah) of Jewish immigration to Palestine.
1894	Alfred Dreyfus, a Jewish French officer, is tried and convicted for selling military secrets to the Germans. The trial unleashes a wave of anti-Semitism in France that continues to reverberate for the next 10 years, until Dreyfus is retried in 1904 and cleared in 1906.
1896	Theodore Herzl, an Austrian journalist and playwright, writes *Der Judenstaat* (The Jewish State), calling for a world council to settle the Jewish question and for Jews to organize as a nation requiring a state of their own.
1897	First Zionist Congress held in Basel, Switzerland. Zionist Organization founded under the leadership of Herzl.
1903–1906	Mob attacks (pogroms) sanctioned by the authorities in southern Russia.
1903	Sixth Zionist Congress. Herzl presents the Uganda Scheme, Britain's offer to make land available in British East Africa for the Jewish homeland.
1904–1914	Second aliyah.

1914–1918	World War I.
1916	Britain and France negotiate the Sykes-Picot Agreement: France will gain control of the areas that become Lebanon and Syria, Britain will get Iraq and Transjordan (later renamed Jordan), and Palestine is to be under international administration.
1917	In Great Britain, Foreign Secretary Arthur James Balfour writes to Baron Lionel Rothschild, a wealthy Jewish banker and member of the British Parliament, that the government of King George V looks with favor on the establishment in Palestine of a national home for the Jewish people. This document comes to be known as the "Balfour Declaration."
1917–1921	More pogroms in eastern Europe and Ukraine.
1918	Ottoman control over Palestine ends, and Great Britain assumes control.
1919	American King-Crane Commission (appointed by U.S. president Woodrow Wilson) recommends against unlimited Jewish immigration and a separate Jewish state in Palestine.
1919–1923	Third aliyah.
1920	Histadrut (Jewish federation of labor unions) and Haganah (Jewish defense organization) founded in Palestine.
1922	League of Nations approves and grants Britain a mandate over Palestine.
1924–1928	Fourth aliyah.
1929	Riots begin in Jerusalem and spread to Hebron and Safed, leaving 120 Jews and 87 Palestinians dead.
1929	Jewish Agency established in Palestine to govern the Jewish community in Palestine, encourage immigration, and raise money for settlements.
1929–1939	Fifth aliyah, mainly refugees from Nazi Germany.
1931	Irgun, a Jewish right-wing underground movement, founded.
1936	Palestinians form the Supreme Arab Committee, later known as the Arab Higher Committee, to protest Jewish immigration and land acquisitions.
1936–1939	The Palestinian Revolt, a grassroots protest against Zionist aspirations in Palestine. The revolt included both violent and nonviolent aspects—riots, strikes, refusal to pay taxes, and

other forms of civil disobedience. By the end of the revolt, 101 British soldiers, 463 Jews, and between 3,000 and 5,000 Palestinians had been killed.

1937   In July, the British Peel Commission report is issued. Declares mandate unworkable and recommends partitioning of country into Palestinian and Jewish states, with British control maintained over Nazareth, Bethlehem, Jerusalem, and a corridor to the sea. In August, the Zionists agree to partition but reject proposed boundaries. Report resparks the Palestinian revolt, and in September, Britain declares martial law in Palestine, the Arab Higher Committee is dissolved, and its leaders are arrested. The Mufti, Haj Amin al-Husseini (supreme Muslim religious leader, appointed by the British), flees the country.

1939   Stern Gang, a more extreme terrorist group, splits off from the Irgun.

1939   Great Britain issues the MacDonald White Paper; it limits Jewish immigration and land purchases in Palestine and promises Arab state within 10 years.

1939–1945   Palestinian Jewish volunteers join British forces to fight in World War II.

1945   Labour government in England continues support for 1939 White Paper and limits immigration and land purchases in Palestine.

1946   Irgun blows up the King David Hotel in Jerusalem, killing 91 soldiers and civilians (British, Arab, and Jewish).

1946   Twenty-second Zionist Congress appoints David Ben Gurion, founder of the Histadrut and president of the Israel Worker's Party, as executive chairman and defense minister of Jewish Agency. Institutes arming and expansion of the Haganah.

1947   Great Britain turns the Palestine Question over to the United Nations for resolution. On November 29, General Assembly approves proposal to partition Palestine into separate Jewish and Palestinian states.

1948–1949   Civil war in Palestine. Fighting begins in April as the Haganah takes the offensive. When the final armistice is declared, the new Israeli state holds 77 percent of Palestine, including large portions that had been designated for the Palestinian state. Gaza is occupied by Egypt, while Jordan takes control of the West Bank. Palestine ceases to exist as a political entity.

1948	Irgun raids Deir Yassin on April 9, killing 254 inhabitants.
1948	Israel declares statehood on May 14.
1948–1958	Massive immigration to Israel from Europe, North Africa, and Asia.
1949	David Ben Gurion, as first prime minister, forms first government.
1956	Suez War begins as Israeli forces invade the Sinai Peninsula. Fifty-one villagers killed by Israeli border police at Kafr Qasim.
1957	Israelis forced to withdraw from Sharm El Sheikh and Gaza Strip.
1964	Palestine Liberation Organization (PLO) formed in Cairo, Egypt, as umbrella political movement for Palestinians throughout the world.
1967	Escalation of clashes on Israel-Syria and Israel-Egypt borders from February to May. President Gamal Abdel Nasser of Egypt requests that United Nations units be withdrawn from the Israel-Egypt border and puts blockade on Strait of Tiran and Gulf of Aqaba while warning he may also close Suez Canal to some or all ships.
1967	On June 5, Israel launches preemptive air strike against Egypt and destroys almost entire Egyptian Air Force on the ground. War is over in six days. Israel conquers and occupies Golan Heights, West Bank, East Jerusalem, Gaza Strip, and Sinai Peninsula. The United Nations issues U.N. Security Council Resolution 242, calling on Israel to withdraw from "occupied territories" and for all parties to agree to secure and recognized boundaries.
1968	Gush Emunim, the new religious-nationalist settlement movement, establishes an Israeli presence just outside Hebron.
1973	Egypt and Syria launch attacks across the 1967 cease-fire lines. Egyptian forces breach Israeli defenses in the Sinai. Syrian attack crushed by October 17, and counterattack launched on Egyptians. By October 24, when cease-fire is declared, Egyptian Third Army is encircled by Israeli forces.
1973	David Ben Gurion dies.
1975	Gush Emunim allowed to move into a former Israeli army camp in the West Bank. Jewish settlement of the West Bank begins.

1976	Six Israeli Palestinians killed during protest against confiscation of Palestinian land in the Galilee. The event comes to be celebrated as "Land Day" in the Palestinian Israeli community.
1977	The Likud Party, under the leadership of Menachem Begin (a former Irgun commander), emerges as the victor in parliament (Knesset) elections. President Anwar Sadat of Egypt visits Israel.
1978	Camp David Accords between Israel and Egypt signed in September. First accord provided for autonomy plan for the West Bank and Gaza Strip to be followed after five years by a permanent settlement. Second accord provided a framework for concluding peace between Israel and Egypt.
1981	Israel bombs and destroys a nuclear reactor being built in Iraq.
1981	President Sadat of Egypt is assassinated, partly for having made peace with Israel.
1982	On June 6, Israel invades Lebanon in Operation Peace for the Galilee and launches the Lebanon War. In September, Israeli military forces allow Christian Phalange troops into the Palestinian refugee camps of Sabra and Shatila, under Israeli control. More than 2,000 people are massacred in the camps, while Israeli searchlights and flares provide light and Israeli soldiers keep the camps sealed off.
1983	Israel withdraws south of the Awali River in Lebanon. The occupation of southern Lebanon begins.
1987	Four Palestinian workers from Gaza are accidentally run over and killed by an Israeli truck driver. Violence breaks out as reports circulate they were deliberately run over. The first popular uprising, the intifada, begins and will last for almost five years.
1991	The Gulf War begins on January 17. Iraq launches Scud missiles at Israel. Forty missiles fall on Tel Aviv, Ramat Gan, and Haifa. Four thousand apartments are destroyed and several hundred people are wounded, but only one person is killed.
1991	Madrid conference opens. Israelis and Arabs are talking directly to one another.
1991	As Soviet Union disintegrates, Soviet Jewish immigration to Israel becomes a flood.
1992	Labor Party regains control of the government. Yitzhak Rabin becomes prime minister.

1993   Secret negotiations between Israel and the PLO are held in Oslo, Norway, between January and August. In September, the Oslo Declaration of Principles is signed in Washington, D.C. Rabin and Yassir Arafat shake hands.

1994   In February, an Israeli settler opens fire on worshipers at the mosque in Hebron, killing 29 people. In May, the Cairo Agreement is signed by Arafat and Rabin. Agreement gives Palestinian Authority full control over internal security, health and welfare, and education in the Occupied Territories. Gaza and Jericho are turned over to the control of the Palestinian Authority.

1995   In September, Rabin and Arafat sign Oslo II, the timetable and framework for Palestinian self-rule in the West Bank. In November, Rabin is assassinated in Tel Aviv by a Jewish religious student from Bar Ilan University who opposes the peace process.

1996   Likud regains power in Knesset as Benjamin Netanyahu is elected prime minister by a narrow margin. He halts implementation of the Oslo Accords and offers a new plan to annex most of the West Bank to Israel. He lifts the freeze on Jewish settlement construction in the occupied territories.

1998   Wye Memorandum signed in United States between Arafat and Netanyahu. Accord spells out steps to be taken to fulfill interim peace agreement and framework for moving to final settlement talks.

1999   In May, Ehud Barak is elected prime minister and the Labor Party regains control of the government. In September, he signs a new peace agreement with Arafat at Sharm El Sheikh that provides for a final peace accord by September 2000.

2000   Israel completes its withdrawal from Lebanon.

2000   In September, Ariel Sharon visits the Temple Mount, a site in Jerusalem that is sacred to Muslims and to Jews. His visit sparks riots. This marks the beginning of the second intifada, which continues to this day.

2001   Ariel Sharon, the Likud leader, is elected prime minister by a wide majority and forms a broad-based, national unity government. Sharon stops negotiating with the Palestinians, demanding complete end to violence before returning to talks.

2002   Labor Party withdraws from the national unity government.

2003   Israeli parliament (Knesset) elections. Ariel Sharon is re-elected and forms a narrow coalition (66 seats) with political parties to the right of center and with Shinui, the moderate party. Under pressure from the United States and Great Britain, he resumes political negotiations with the Palestinians, who are now represented by their newly named prime minister, Mahmoud Abbas. After four months, Abbas resigns in frustration. Ahmed Qureia is named the new prime minister.

2004   Peace talks do not resume, attacks continue on both sides, Israel constructs a fence to separate the West Bank from Israel to halt suicide bombings, and Sharon proposes a unilateral Israeli withdrawal from Gaza.

1

Introduction: Land, People, Education, Economy, and History

The strip of land we call Israel, the size of New Jersey, weighs on the consciousness of the world far more than its size might seem to merit. Located at the junction of the continents of Europe, Asia, and Africa, this strip of land (called variously Canaan, Israel, Palestine, the "Holy Land," and Filastin) has been a natural route for trade and migration since prehistory. Here Neanderthals lived in proximity to more modern humans in the Carmel Mountain ranges. In the Mesolithic era (9000–11,000 B.C.), the Natufians harvested wild grains, using flint sickles, and ground them using stone mortars and pestles. By 8000 B.C. at Jericho, local inhabitants had started to grow their own food and began settling down and building permanent communities. The region was and still is the crossroads of a number of different cultures, as peoples moved into it from both north and south. Army after army swept through this land, leaving behind their traces in artifacts, remains of destroyed towns and villages, and the people themselves, as soldiers settled and remained behind when armies moved on. The region, birthplace of monotheism, is an important religious site for Jews, Christians, and Muslims throughout the world.

LAND

Located on the eastern shore of the Mediterranean Sea, Israel is bordered to the north by Lebanon, to the northeast by Syria, to the east and southeast by Jordan, and to the southwest by Egypt. It covers 7,992 square miles and stretches about 290 miles north to south and 85 miles east to west at its widest point and only 6 miles at its narrowest point.[1] Israel's climate is Mediterranean, with two distinct seasons: a hot, dry summer (May to September), followed by a cool, wet

Busy East Jerusalem street. Photo by the author.

winter (October to April). Despite its small size, Israel can be divided into four distinct ecological zones, each with its own unique physical features and climate. These zones are the coastal plain, the hill regions of central and northern Israel, the Jordan Rift Valley, and the Negev desert region.

The coastal plain is the most intensively developed area of Israel. A narrow strip of land about 115 miles long that widens to about 25 miles wide in the south, this zone is home to most of Israel's population. The two main metropolitan areas in this region, Tel Aviv-Jaffa and Haifa, together account for more than half of Israel's population. From the beaches and sandy shorelines, the plain stretches inland to Israel's most fertile farmlands, where oranges, bananas, and other food crops are grown. Annual rainfall here averages about 20 inches per year. The coastal plain is an area of high humidity, especially during the winter. Temperatures range from 84°F in August to 61°F in January.

The hills region has several distinct mountain ranges. In the northeast, the Golan Heights is an area of about 444 square miles. To the south of the Heights lies the agricultural land; to the north, the rocky foothills of Mount Hermon. The mountains of the Galilee, the north-central part of the country, range from 1,600 to 4,000 feet above sea level. The Carmel range cuts northwest across the highlands of the West Bank near Haifa. The hills region gets ample rainfall compared with other parts of the country, about 44 inches of rain a year on average in the Upper Galilee. Temperatures range from 48°F in January to 84°F in August in

Safad; Tiberias, farther east along Lake Kinneret, gets slightly warmer, at 64°F and 97°F, respectively.

The Jordan Rift Valley is part of the Great Rift Valley, a fissure in the earth's crust that stretches from southern Turkey into East Africa. As the Jordan River flows north to south through the Rift, it passes through the Hula Valley into Lake Kinneret (the Sea of Galilee), winds through the Jordan Valley, and empties into the Dead Sea. South of the Dead Sea, lies the 'Arava Valley, which extends to the Gulf of Eilat. At the north, the Jordan Rift Valley is fertile and well watered. The Israelis drained the Hula Valley swamps in the 1950s for farmland. By the early 1990s, they reversed the process, converting part of the Hula back to wetlands due to the negative environmental consequences. The Kinneret is Israel's largest freshwater lake and provides most of the country's water. Farther south, the land becomes semi-arid and agriculture requires irrigation. The Dead Sea, the lowest point on earth at 1,300 feet below sea level, has water that is the most saline and dense in the world. It is famous for both its density, which means bathers float in its waters, and its salts, as well as the potash, magnesium, and bromine found in its waters.

The Negev region, in the south of Israel, accounts for almost half of Israel's total land area, yet only about 8 percent of the population live there. Triangular shaped, with its apex to the south, the Negev is a semi-arid steppe region of lime-stone and chalks, punctuated by high cliffs and wadis, dry stream beds or shallow, sharply defined depressions that often flood during winter rains. The giant ero-sion craters Maktesh Ramon and Maktesh ha'Gadol found here are spectacular natural landmarks that display a wide variety of rock types. Rainfall varies greatly and ranges from 8 to 12 inches in the north at Beersheva to 3 to 4 inches in the central region to negligible in the south at Eilat. Temperatures range from 61°F in January to over 104°F in August at Eilat (although it can get quite cold at night). An important grain-producing area under the Romans, the Negev has bloomed again through the use of irrigation into a significant agricultural region that produces vegetables, grain, fodder, and fruits. In addition to these products, the Negev also supplies copper, natural gas, phosphates, potash, bromine, and magnesium to Israeli industries.

Israel's different ecological zones are home to many diverse plants and animals. Israel can boast more than 100 species of mammals, more than 500 types of birds, 97 kinds of reptiles, and 7 types of amphibians. The largest land animals are the mountain gazelles in the hills; wild boar, foxes, and—rarely seen—leopards, hye-nas, jackals, and wolves in the wooded areas; and the Nubian ibex in the desert regions. Smaller mammals include hares, badgers, coneys, and tiger weasels. Since the 1960s, the Hai-Bar program of the Nature Reserves Authority has rein-troduced populations of animals native to the region during biblical times and that had disappeared because of habitat destruction; these include Persian fallow deer, roe deer, Asiatic wild asses (onagers), and the Arabian white oryx (an ante-lope). Israel's skies are home to more than 380 kinds of birds, including the com-mon bulbul, partridge, tropical cuckoo, bustard, sand grouse, and desert lark, as

Kibbutznik at work spreading fertilizer. Courtesy of the Government Press Office, State of Israel.

well as a number of raptor species (including imperial and spotted eagles, falcons, hawks, kestrels, and long-legged buzzards). Hundreds of thousands of birds migrate the length of the country twice yearly, which makes for excellent bird-watching opportunities. Among its reptile population, Israel is home to chameleons, snakes such as the carpet viper, and agama lizards and geckos. Because the Hula wetlands had previously been drained for farmland, there are only seven amphibian species in the country today. Finally, Eilat's coral reef is home to corals, sponges, and shellfish. One of the most diverse in the world, the reef is home to 1,270 different species of fish, belonging to 157 families, along with hundreds of species of coral and 1,120 species of mollusk.

More than 2,800 kinds of plants have been found in Israel, ranging from alpine species in the north to papyrus reeds in the desert south. After the first rains begin in October, the countryside blooms, and once-brown fields are covered with a green carpet of flowers. Honeysuckle vines, rockrose and thorny broom, crocus, cyclamen, peonies, anemones, lupine, marigold, and wild relatives of the iris, tulip, hyacinth, and Madonna lily color the landscape. Atlantic pistachios, date palms, plane trees, and calliprinos oaks dot the hillsides, valleys, and streams of the country—along with groves of orange trees and ancient olive trees. The sabra cactus also dots the landscape, marking places of human disturbance and the ruins of old villages and settlements.

Water is the most vital resource in Israel; Israel has suffered from chronic water shortages for years. The main sources for fresh water are the Kinneret, the coastal aquifer, and the mountain aquifer (under the Carmel Mountain range).[2] Water is pumped via the national water carrier from the north to all areas of the country, including the arid south. The agricultural sector uses about 60 percent of the available water (down from 77 percent in the 1960s). Overall, Israel uses more than 95 percent of its total freshwater; with the recent drought, the aquifers did not adequately replenish themselves and the government was forced to initiate cutbacks to the agricultural sector and the general public. As demand for water increases due to population increases and future agricultural and industrial demands, Israel faces the prospect of even more severe water shortages. Scientists in the country have devised a number of measures to conserve water and make do with less, but Israel will need to find further sources of water in order to prevent a future crisis.

PEOPLE

Israel has a population of more than 6.5 million people; 81 percent are Jewish (mainly immigrants), and 19 percent are Palestinian Arabs (the original native population).[3] Jews have immigrated to Israel since its founding in 1948 from more than 120 different countries in Europe, Africa, Asia, the Middle East, and North and Latin America. The country is thus culturally quite heterogeneous. Israel's Jewish residents are often categorized according to their place of birth. *Ashkenazim*, Israelis who emigrated (or whose parents emigrated) from countries in Europe, Russia, or the Americas, make up 41 percent of Israeli Jews. *Mizrahim*, whose parents emigrated from countries in the Middle East, Africa, and Asia, make up 30 percent of the Jewish population. *Sabras* were born in Israel and now make up 29 percent of Israeli Jews. About 91 percent of Israeli Jews live in 200 urban centers, with another 5 percent living in agricultural settlements. The Palestinian population, once largely rural, has shifted as Arab villages have urbanized over the years. Today 60 percent of Palestinians live in villages in the central and western Galilee, 30 percent in the area called the Little Triangle (between the villages of Et Tira and Et Taiyiba near the Jordanian border), and 10 percent in the Negev. Those who live in urban areas tend to be concentrated in the major Arab cities of Nazareth and Shfar 'Amr and in the "mixed" cities of Acre, Haifa, Lod, Ramleh, Tel Aviv-Jaffa, and Jerusalem (cities with both Jewish and Palestinian residents).

Most Jewish Israelis would say that they are secular and not particularly religious, although the state religion of Israel is Orthodox Judaism.[4] Among Orthodox Jews, there are a number of different factions, each of which follows a different rabbi as their spiritual leader. Best known are the Hasidic groups, which trace their roots to former Jewish communities in eastern Europe, many of which were annihilated during the Nazi Holocaust. The Palestinian Arab population is Sunni Muslim (82 percent); more than 30 different denominations of Christians, including Roman Catholics, Greek Catholics, Greek Orthodox, Russian Orthodox, Maronites, Copts, Armenian Catholics, and Protestants (9 percent); and Druze (9 percent). All Israeli citizens carry identity cards, which include a listing

Father and sons in the Arab community of Um El Fahem. Photo by Nati Harnik. Courtesy of the Government Press Office, State of Israel.

of their nationality. For Jews and the Druze, their nationality is the same as their religion, respectively, "Jew" and "Druze." For Christian and Muslim Israelis, their nationality is listed as "Arab." The fact that the Israeli state does not recognize one single nationality—Israeli—for all Israeli citizens has been a major point of contention in Israel's political affairs.

LANGUAGES

Israel, the country of immigrants, is also a country of many languages. The official languages are Hebrew and Arabic, although English is widely taught and understood. Since only about 60 percent of Israeli Jews were born there, Hebrew is still not the mother tongue for a significant portion of the population, who may speak Arabic or Judeo-Arabic (the 20 percent who are Palestinians or Mizrahi Jews not born in Israel), Russian (over a tenth of the Jewish population), or Yiddish (about 5 percent, mainly older people), as well as French, Romanian, Hungarian, Polish, Persian, English, Amharic and Tigrinia, Spanish, or German. Hebrew itself was brought back to life as a modern, spoken language through the efforts of early immigrants, led and inspired by Eliezer Ben Yehuda, who compiled a massive 17-volume Hebrew dictionary and founded the Hebrew Language Council. The fact that Hebrew was still actively taught so a large number of Jewish men could understand biblical passages and prayers in Hebrew helped these pioneers in their effort to make Hebrew a modern language. Israeli educators developed an intensive language program, the *ulpan*, for the purpose of teaching Hebrew to new immigrants. Students learn basic speaking, writing, and comprehension skills through actively and intensively practicing the language.

EDUCATION

School attendance in Israel is free and required for students ages 5 to 13. The earliest schools were closely linked to the major political parties, so they were often used as vehicles for gaining the votes of the students' parents. That practice was stopped in 1953, when the state passed a new law that established the Ministry of Education and made it responsible for all schools and their curricula. The 1953 law established three different school systems: a Hebrew-language, secular, state-funded track (*mamlakhtī*); a Hebrew-language, religious, state-funded track (*mamlakhtī-dāti*); and an Arabic-language, state-funded track. The law also provided for "nonofficial recognized" schools and "exempt, unofficial, and unrecognized" schools (such as different types of Orthodox Jewish religious schools, as well as foreign and missionary schools).[5]

Since 1968, the Israeli schooling system has consisted of a primary level of six years, a middle school level of three years, and a secondary level of three years. Students attend elementary and junior high schools based on their place of residence. For high school, however, parents can, and often do, send their children to schools in other locations. The major limiting factor is the cost of transporta-

Arab high school students in Kalansuwa. Photo by Moshe Milner. Courtesy of the Government Press Office, State of Israel.

tion. State schools make up 95 percent of formal education (*mamlakhtī* 75 percent; *mamlakhtī-dātī*, 20 percent), with private religious schools accounting for most of the remaining 5 percent. State schools are divided into separate Hebrew and Arab systems, each with its own curricular requirements.[6] High schools offer either an academic, a vocational/technical, or a low-level vocational focus, although some schools (the *māqīf*, or comprehensive) provide more than one track from which their students may choose. Within the academic track (similar to the American college-preparatory), secondary students select their program of study, choosing those subjects and areas for which they have both ability and interest. At the completion of their secondary studies, students sit for either final exams or matriculation exams. Students who wish to continue to university studies or to get a job in various occupations must sit for and pass matriculation exams (*bagrūt*). In recent years, about a half million jobs in Israel have required successful completion of the *bagrūt* examination as one of the minimum qualifications to enter that job; this is approximately one-third of the Israeli job market.

Responsibilities for the educational system in Israel are divided between the Ministry of Education and the local authorities. In practice, since the municipalities also receive most of their budgets from the central state, schools are financed by the national government. Funding levels for the schools vary widely from place to place depending on the strength of the local government and its ability to get more money for their schools.[7] The Arab schools do not receive the same level of funding as do Jewish schools. For example, over the years, the Arab school system in Acre, a mixed city, has struggled with lack of space, equipment, playground facilities, and books, while Jewish schools in the same community have been comparatively well provided for. Part of the funding difference arises from the role of external Jewish institutions such as the Jewish Agency, which partners Israeli Jewish schools with American Jewish congregations who provide additional financial support for the school.

Except for some religious schools, most Israeli schools are coeducational. In the classroom, relations between teachers and pupils are relaxed. Classroom style is correspondingly raucous, and one might be tempted to believe there are discipline problems in Israeli schools. The Arab school system maintains more formal relations between students and teachers, and the classroom atmosphere is accordingly more disciplined. In the Jewish system, a great deal of attention is paid to "social education," or education for citizenship. School newspapers, student government, class trips lasting several days, celebrations, parties, field trips, sports days, concerts, and performances are all organized to encourage students to be involved in their school and in their country. Students in the Jewish system are encouraged to develop critical-thinking skills; teachers tend to lecture less and to devise more hands-on learning activities. In recent years, teachers in the Arab system have also come to rely less on lecturing and more on promoting critical thinking. In addition, only within the last 10 years have teachers within the Arab system been able to discuss current events and politics in their classrooms with their students. Prior to this, such discussions might have caused a teacher to lose his or her job.

Teens are tracked in junior and senior high school in Israel. The tracking is based on elementary grades, recommendations from counselors, and family variables. Once on a track, students tend to remain there. Although in principle they are free to choose their high school and track, in practice students and their parents are counseled about what is available given the student's achievements.[8] Teachers and counselors have a powerful position in determining a student's life chances. In 1993, 47 percent of Jewish high school students were on the vocational track. Since the early 1990s, only about one-third of Jewish teens have been entitled to the *bagrūt* at the end of high school. In the Palestinian sector, matters are even worse. For example, in 2000, only 18.4 percent of Palestinian Arab 17-year-olds, compared with 40.4 percent of Jewish 17-year-olds, were eligible to attend university.[9]

Higher education in Israel is divided into six distinct subsystems. One subsystem includes six top universities authorized to grant undergraduate and graduate degrees (Hebrew University in Jerusalem, Tel Aviv University, the Technion-IIT, University of Haifa, Ben Gurion University of the Negev, Bar Ilan University) while the other five subsystems include specialized institutions for distance and regional undergraduate education, varied professional training, and teacher education.[10] The typical age of attendance for Jewish Israeli university students is 20 to 29 due to the mandatory army service required of them after high school. Palestinian students, who are not drafted, follow the typical age pattern found in U.S. and other Western university systems. Except for the Open University, Israel does not have liberal arts colleges. University students apply for admission to faculties such as humanities, social sciences, sciences, business, medicine, or law. An undergraduate humanities or social sciences degree typically takes three years, whereas professional degrees in law, medicine, or engineering may take three-and-a-half to five years. In 2002, there were 73,904 students studying for first degrees at the universities, 30,992 students studying for second degrees, and 7,020 studying for third degrees. Palestinian students accounted for 10 percent of first-degree enrollments, 5 percent of second-degree enrollments, and only 3 percent of third-degree enrollments. Among Jewish Israelis, Ashkenazi students are the largest sector at all degree levels (38 percent, 44 percent, and 57 percent, respectively), and Mizrahi students are underrepresented (24 percent, 24 percent, and 16 percent, respectively).[11]

THE ECONOMY

In the years after its founding in 1948, Israel faced difficult economic times. The new state had a bare-bones economic infrastructure, with little in the way of monetary reserves, natural resources, or public services. The new immigrants who flooded into the country had to be fed, housed, clothed, educated, and employed. The state took on these tasks, leading to the development of a quasi-socialist economy. From 1948 to 1972, the Israeli economy experienced rapid growth in gross national product (GNP), with average yearly increases of more than 10 percent. Israel's rapid growth owed a great deal to both the human and the financial capital that flooded into the country during these years. In its first year, the new state took over the property (lands, houses, shops, and factories) and assets (furnishings, equipment, commodities, and money) of the Palestinian refugees, as well as any property and assets left by the British government. The government obtained additional capital through active charitable appeals to Jews throughout the world (through the Jewish Agency and the World Zionist Federation), through German reparations payments made to Israeli Holocaust survivors and the Israeli government, through U.S. foreign aid in the form of grants-in-aid, military assistance, and loan guarantees, and through the capital that immigrants brought with them. These forms of revenue were supplemented with loans, commercial credits, and foreign investment.

Beginning in the early 1970s, the state began to increase spending on social welfare, in response to protest movements such as the Israeli Black Panthers, who drew attention to the discrimination faced by Mizrahi Jews in Israeli society. The state developed programs for education, housing, and welfare for the urban Mizrahi poor. The government also faced higher military spending and increased oil costs due to Arab embargoes in 1973 and 1979. The result was that from 1973 to 1988, the economy slowed dramatically, with the GNP increasing only about 2 percent on average annually. Inflation soared, reaching 445 percent in 1984. The decline in the GNP, high inflation rate, and lower rates of immigration combined to drive Israel's economy down. In 1985, the government initiated an emergency program

Shops at the central bus station in Beersheva. Photo by the author.

to halt hyperinflation and eliminate the budget deficit. Within a year, they succeeded in balancing the budget. Israel has experienced favorable economic growth
in the years since, especially between 1994 and 1996 (the peace dividend years),
although the economy has struggled since the end of 2000, due in part to the general slowing of the U.S. economy and to local declines in tourism and construction
due to political unrest. In 2001, Israel experienced a drop in gross domestic product.
By early in 2002, Israel was in the midst of a recession. Unemployment rates are
skyrocketing as foreign investment has slowed and the government's budget deficit
continues to grow because of increased military spending and construction of Jewish settlements in the West Bank and Gaza.

From 1948 to the 1970s, three different sectors held ownership of the means of
production in Israel: the government, private enterprises, and the Histadrut, the
powerful labor federation. The government and the Histadrut dominated the
economy, especially the service sector. Histadrut-affiliated companies controlled
much of public transport, agricultural production and marketing, insurance,
banking, and other industries. The government controlled military industries,
such as Israel Aircraft Industries and Israel Military Industries, as well as El-Al,
the refineries, Israel Electric, and Zim Shipping. Since the 1970s, however, the
government is privatizing the economy. Movement in that direction greatly
accelerated in the 1980s and 1990s. Israel's telecommunications company, Bezeq,
was privatized in 2001–2002. The Histadrut has sold off companies as part of its
reorganization efforts and completed its privatization by the early 1990s.

Israel's natural mineral resources are limited: potash; bromine and magnesium
(from the Dead Sea); copper ore from the 'Arava; phosphates, small amounts of
gypsum, and natural gas reserves from the Negev; a little marble in the Galilee;
and small oil deposits in the northern Negev. Israel depends on imports to fuel
energy production in the country. They import oil from Mexico and Egypt and
coal from Australia, South Africa, and Britain to produce needed electricity.
Israel is a world leader in the development of solar power. Most large apartment
buildings get hot water during the summer from solar water heaters located on
the buildings' roofs.

Historically, agriculture plays an important symbolic role in Israeli national
life. For those settlers who entered the country after 1905, cultivation of the land
was a sacred duty. As Amos Elon noted in his book *The Israelis: Founders and
Sons*, "The pioneers believed that nations, like trees, must be 'organically' rooted
in the soil and that anti-Semitism was a result of the 'unnatural' occupational
structure of Jews in Eastern Europe."[12] Those immigrants who established themselves as farmers came to be called *halutzim* (pioneers). Two innovative types of
farming communities developed in Israel—the kibbutz (a collective settlement
whose residents pool labor and resources and share equally in profits) and the
moshav (a settlement whose residents individually own land but collectively purchase supplies and market produce). Over the years, Israeli farms have employed
fewer people (from 17.4 percent in the 1950s to 1.9 percent of employed persons
in 2001) while increasing the amount of commodities they produce by using

modern industrial farming technologies—specialized equipment, improved crop varieties, pesticides, and fertilizers.[13] With only 17 percent arable land, irrigated land expanded considerably over the years until the mid-1980s, when farmers had to cut back on irrigating because of water shortages. In the year 2000 alone, the amount of fresh water made available to farmers was reduced by 50 percent.[14] Israeli farmers cultivate about 1.1 million acres, a half million of which are irrigated. Israel produces most of its own food (about 70 percent), needing to import only some grains, oilseeds, meat, coffee, cocoa, and sugar. The main agricultural products are poultry and dairy products, fruits (bananas, grapes, apples, citrus), vegetables (avocados, olives, tomatoes, and cucumbers), and hothouse flowers (carnations, roses, and other flowers). During the winter months, Israel exports flowers, fruits, and vegetables to European markets.

Until the 1970s, Israel depended on the traditional branches of food processing, textiles and fashion, furniture, fertilizers, pesticides, pharmaceuticals, chemicals, rubber, plastic, and metal products for most of its industrial output. Traditional industries have been hurt by competition and industrial growth in countries with lower wage rates. Israel has instead turned to high-technology manufacturing to continue developing. The massive influx of highly educated immigrants from the former Soviet Union in the late 1980s and early 1990s helped in the development of sophisticated high-technology ventures. Intel, Motorola, IBM, Microsoft, Alcatel, and 3Com all have research and development facilities in Israel. Israel invests 2.2 percent of its gross domestic product in research and development (the third highest level in the world, after Japan and Sweden, and on par with Germany). In 1999, direct investment in Israeli companies—virtually all in the high-technology sector—reached a record $3.7 billion, up from $2.4 billion in 1998.[15] Israel is a world leader in fields as varied as computerized printing technologies, advanced computer and communications systems, genetic cross-breeding of plants and animals, software, weaponry, and diamond cutting and polishing.

In more recent years, Israel has turned to tourism to develop its economy. Besides sites sacred to three of the world's major religions (Judaism, Christianity, and Islam), Israel can boast a wealth of archaeological and historical sites, places of great natural beauty and wide ecological diversity, and numerous resort areas. Tourism is an important component of Israel's economy because it brings much-needed foreign currency into the country. In 2000, tourism's high point, almost 2.5 million tourists visited the country, coming from Europe, North America, Asia, Latin America, Africa, and Oceania. However, due to ongoing political violence, the tourist industry has been heavily affected. In 2001, fewer than 1.2 million people came to the country, for a drop in tourism revenues of 47 percent. This trend continues as many foreign tourists have decided to stay clear of Israel for personal safety reasons.

Israel enjoys an enviable position in terms of foreign trade. Israel joined the General Agreement on Tariffs and Trade (GATT), established a free trade area for industrial products with the European Community in 1975 (signing an association agreement in 2000), and established a free trade area for all products with the United States in 1985. Thus Israeli products can enter European and U.S. markets duty-free. The Free Trade Area agreement with the United States grants Israel preferential "rules of origin" benefits; for example, a garment could be cut in Israel but assembled in a low-cost country and still enter the United States duty-free. Combined with the North American Free Trade Agreement (NAFTA), Israel's Free Trade Area agreement with the United States gives it duty-free access to Canadian and Mexican markets as well. Israel continues to struggle with a large annual balance of trade deficit ($6.8 billion in 2001, $6.7 billion in 2002).[16] Israel imports mainly raw materials, capital goods, and food and exports high-technology products (e.g., telecommunications equipment, software, semiconductors, biotechnology, and medical electronics, as well as polished diamonds) and fruit, vegetables, and flowers to Europe.

THE GOVERNMENT

Israel is a parliamentary democracy along the model used in many western European countries. Its political structure consists of a 120-member elected parliament (the Knesset), the office of the president, and the offices of the prime minister with a cabinet. The president is elected by the Knesset and serves as a ceremonial head of state; the prime minister serves as chief executive. Elections in Israel focus on the political parties and their platforms, not the candidates. Israel has a multiparty system dominated by two main parties, Labor and Likud. The Labor Party represents center-left, socialist Zionist tendencies; Likud represents Zionist center-right tendencies. The two main parties create governments by entering into coalitions with smaller parties or by forming unity governments in alliance with each other. From 1948 to 1977, the Labor Party controlled the Knesset; since 1977, the Likud has been (and is currently) the dominant power (except the periods 1992–1996 and 1999–2001, when Labor returned to power). Since no party has ever been able to earn a majority of seats in the Knesset, smaller parties have wielded considerable influence in governing because major parties needed their seats to create a government. Religious parties in Israel, especially, can benefit by joining coalitions with either Labor or Likud. They use the influence of their Knesset seats to ensure that Orthodox Judaism is the law of the land.

A major problem in the political system is its claim to be both a democratic state and a Jewish state; these principles contradict each other when they are put into practice. Israelis have never adopted a constitution. Instead, the country operates under a system of Basic Laws. As of 2002, there were 11 Basic Laws that dealt with the Knesset, Israel lands, the president, the government, state economy, the army, Jerusalem, the judiciary, the state comptroller, human dignity and liberty, and freedom of occupation. In addition, a number of ordinary laws govern areas of life, such as nationality, the Law of Return, the education system, women's rights, and the courts. While Israel's Declaration of Independence asserts that all Israeli citizens will be treated equally, in practice Palestinians have a second-class status and are often harmed by ordinary laws that give Jewish citizens rights and benefits not available to Palestinian citizens.

To further complicate matters, the state has turned over a number of governmental functions to entities called "national institutions"—public-sector organizations such as the World Zionist Organization, the Jewish Agency, and the Jewish National Fund. These entities raise funds from Jewish communities outside Israel that are then invested within Israel in housing, social programs, educational enrichment, immigrant resettlement, and community development. Very little of this money supports the needs of Israel's Palestinian citizens; in some cases, these organizations have rules that prevent them from assisting non-Jewish populations. Finally, Israel has no civil code regulating marriage, divorce, alimony, child custody, or inheritance. These matters fall under the jurisdiction of religious courts established for Jews, Muslims, Druze, and Christians, although the recent creation of family courts has allowed matters of alimony and child custody to be settled outside the jurisdiction of the religious courts.

HISTORY

Pre-1948: Laying the Groundwork for a State

Supporters of the state often see Israel as fulfilling the charter God gave the Israelites in the Hebrew Scriptures, but the modern state of Israel has its origins in distinctly modern historical processes and political events. The rise of nationalist movements in Europe in the late nineteenth century and a marked increase in anti-Semitism in western Europe and persecutions and pogroms in eastern Europe and the Russian Empire led many Jews to believe that the only way they would ever live free of persecution would be to have a state of their own. This movement, which came to be called Zionism, sponsored emigration of Jews from different parts of Europe to Palestine, then a province of the Muslim Ottoman Empire. Contrary to a popular Zionist slogan, Palestine was not "a land without people for the people without a land." The Arab population of Palestine experienced its own nationalist awakening as local peoples attempted to replace Turkish Ottoman control with their own local Arab political leaders. The resultant clash between these two nationalist movements over the land of Palestine is the root of today's ongoing political struggles.

Immigration to Palestine by eastern European and Russian Jews was small at first, about 25,000 people between 1881 and 1900. These first settlers blended in with the native population quickly. During World War I, the Jewish population of Palestine actually decreased by about 15,000 people as settlers either returned home or moved to the United States. The individuals who came in the second (1904–1914) and third (1919–1923) waves of Jewish immigration to Palestine (called *aliyot* in Hebrew) had a different vision of settlement. These immigrants eventually became the founding fathers of the new state of Israel. They brought with them a brand of Zionism that aimed to create a Jewish state in Palestine, and they quickly began to establish the economic, political, and bureaucratic basis for that state.

With the fall of the Ottoman Empire at the end of World War I, the British government was awarded a mandate over Palestine from the League of Nations that took effect in 1923. According to the census of 1922, Jews in Palestine numbered 84,000, or 11 percent of the population. The British government, however, had earlier indicated support for the creation of a "Jewish homeland" in Palestine in the Balfour Declaration of 1917. Under the terms of their mandate, the British pledged to "secure establishment of the Jewish National Home" in Palestine. Under British control, Palestine absorbed more and more Jewish immigrants. The British authorities allowed Jewish immigrants to set up their own independent economic and political infrastructure, while maintaining tight control over the Palestinian population. Friction with the Palestinians was inevitable as the arrival of new Jewish immigrants began to have negative effects on Palestinian lives. Displaced by Jewish land purchases, with Jewish industries closed to them (under the policy of Jewish-only labor), more and more Palestinians began to protest Jewish immigration as it was destroying their way of life. Early clashes in the 1920s escalated into the riots of 1929 (which left 120 Jews and 87 Palestinians dead) and eventually into the Palestinian Revolt of 1936–1939. The revolt, a grassroots movement with both violent and nonviolent dimensions, succeeded in convincing the British to scrap a plan to partition the country into two states. In the MacDonald White Paper of 1939, the British government also imposed restrictions on Jewish immigration and Jewish land purchases in Palestine. In this document, they also promised to create self-governing institutions with the aim of moving Palestine to independent statehood within 10 years, to a state that would be shared by its Jewish and Palestinian inhabitants.

The Zionists responded to the MacDonald White Paper by launching a campaign of sabotage and attacks to drive the British out. While such attacks were muted in the early years of World War II, once the German threat to the Middle East ended in 1942, the attacks escalated. The Palmach (the elite branch of the Haganah, the pre-state defense force of the Jewish community in Palestine, which became the army of the state of Israel) and right-wing paramilitary groups such as the Irgun and the Stern Gang (Lehi) carried out bombings (such as the King David Hotel attack in 1946), hostage taking, attacks against railroads and communication lines, and political assassinations.[17] These attacks bore fruit when Britain turned Palestine over to the fledgling United Nations in 1947. On November 29, 1947, U.N. member-nations decided to partition the territory into two states—one Jewish and one Palestinian. At this time, there were about 650,000 Jews and 1.3 million Palestinians in Palestine; Jews owned 7 percent of the land. Palestinians did not accept the U.N. decision. In the ensuing turmoil, the Zionists moved to consolidate their control over parts of Palestine they judged to be essential, and the Haganah went on the offensive. From early April to mid-May, they carried out a series of operations that extended their control and the borders of the new state. One of the more infamous actions was the Zionist assault on the Palestinian village of Deir Yassin, which had signed a nonbelligerency agreement with its Jewish neighbors. Irgun and Lehi forces slaughtered more than 200 men, women, and children, whose bodies were mutilated and thrown into a well for disposal. As news of the massacre spread, Palestinians began to flee before advancing Zionist forces, fearing they and their families would also be killed.

David Ben Gurion, head of the provisional government, declared the establishment of the state of Israel on May 14, 1948. Britain relinquished its mandate the next day, and war broke out in Palestine. To Israeli Jews, this was their War of Independence; for Palestinians, it was *al-Nakbah* (the catastrophe). The ragtag, ill-equipped, and inexperienced Palestinian and Arab fighting forces (numbering about 55,000) were no match for the well-equipped and well-organized Israeli army of approximately 100,000 (which included an estimated 20,000 to 25,000 European World War II veterans). Only the Arab Legion of Jordan, which was British armed and trained, could have effectively taken on the Haganah. King Abdullah kept them out of the fighting because he had reached an agreement with the Zionists that they would split the country between them.

When an armistice was finally declared in 1949, the new state of Israel controlled 77 percent of Palestine. Israel existed; the Palestinian state was never created. More than 780,000 Palestinians found themselves refugees in nearby countries. More than 100,000 Palestinians remained within the borders of the new Israeli state and became Israeli citizens. Jordan controlled East Jerusalem and the Old City, as well as the West Bank. Egypt occupied Gaza. The country of Palestine ceased to exist in the world's consciousness.

State and Society Building, 1948–1966

The new Israeli government turned its attention to the challenges of creating a Western-style state in the Middle East. The government immediately removed restrictions on immigration that had been imposed by the British authorities. With the 1950 passage of the Law of Return, which gives any Jew anywhere in the world the right to come to Israel and become a citizen, Israel's Jewish population rapidly increased as immigrants arrived from all over the world, 900,000 of them in the first 10 years alone. The earliest immigrants came from the displaced-persons camps of Europe, which were set up at the end of World War II to house the former residents of Nazi concentration and forced labor camps until they could be returned home or resettled elsewhere. Many Jewish displaced persons chose to immigrate to Israel. Between 1950 and 1956, immigrants began to arrive from North Africa and Asia. The early state had to provide housing, employment, health care, and education to these new citizens. In addition to immigrants, the new state also had to absorb between 120,000 and 150,000 Palestinians as citizens. From 1948 to 1966, Israel's Palestinian citizens lived under military rule and were subject to many restrictions.

The Labor Party, under David Ben Gurion, consolidated its control over the new government and began the process of state building. The government initially controlled the production and distribution process for food, housing, and clothing and instituted rationing in order to provide for the needs of citizens. Austerity did not last long, as money poured into the country from German Holocaust reparation payments, from overseas Jewish communities, and from loans and new investments. By 1954, the country was experiencing rapid economic growth, which continued throughout this period. To forge an Israeli national identity, Ben Gurion used the new army, the Israel Defense Forces (IDF), as the unifying symbol for the country. It was established not only to defend the country but also to serve as a significant institution for assimilating new immigrants.

Many of the tensions present in Israeli society today date to the beginnings of the state and this early period. Tensions between Israeli Jews and Israeli Palestinians, between veteran settlers and new immigrants, between Ashkenazi and Mizrahi Jews, and between secular and religious Israelis all have their roots in this era. Ben Gurion compromised with Orthodox religious parties to create the "status quo," a political arrangement that left personal and family law in Israel under the control of religious authorities and imposed Orthodox religious practice on the entire population in exchange for the religious parties' support of his Labor government. Veteran Israelis and political elites quickly stigmatized the new Mizrahi immigrants as primitive people who threatened Israeli cultural life. The Mizrahis were reduced to the status of second-class citizens. The new Israel was a Western country—there could be no room in it for the Arab culture of these new immigrants. Tremendous pressure was brought to bear on them to leave their Arab cultures behind and assimilate into a new, Western, Israeli identity. Mizrahi immigrants found themselves relegated to the margins of the country, to low-skilled jobs in factories or settled as farmers in front-line communities. The same political elites embraced new immigrants from more Western countries and made sure they were settled in the core of the country and given adequate housing and good jobs. Israeli Palestinians worked to rebuild their lives in the aftermath of the catastrophe of 1948. The community was subject to property seizures, land confiscation, tight military control over their movements, and denial of their Palestinian identity by a state that relabeled them as "Israeli Arabs." On October 29, 1956, the community was again reminded of its vulnerability, when Israeli border guards shot down in cold blood 49 men, women, and children from the village of Kafr Qasim who were returning home from work that evening, unaware that a curfew had been imposed. Although sentenced to prison, the soldiers responsible had their sentences overturned. No one served more than three-and-a-half years in jail.

The 1956 Suez War punctuated this period. After President Nasser of Egypt nationalized the Suez Canal in July, Britain enlisted the aid of France and Israel to restore British control over the canal. In October 1956, Israel attacked Egypt to put the plan into motion and occupied Gaza and Sharm el-Sheik. By November, the United Nations imposed a cease-fire, but Israel refused to withdraw. They only withdrew when it became clear in February 1957 that the United States would vote to support a U.N. resolution that called for the end of all military, economic, and financial assistance to Israel until they complied. After this abortive military exercise, the next 10 years passed relatively quietly.

Entrance to Empire, 1967–1977

By the early 1960s, tensions once again began to mount in the region. Beginning in 1965, Palestinian guerrilla groups organized attacks against Israel. Over time, Israel had gradually annexed the demilitarized zone separating Israel and Syria by building fortified settlements and basing military personnel there. In 1964, Israel began to divert water from the Jordan River in the Golan Heights to its new National Water Carrier. When Syria built its own facility in response, the IDF launched frequent attacks against it. In April 1967, Israel announced it would begin cultivating the entire demilitarized zone, prompting clashes with Syrian forces. Responding to reports that Israel would invade Syria, President Nasser of Egypt requested U.N. withdrawal from the Israeli-Egyptian border. He closed the Strait of Tiran to Israeli ships and sent two divisions to the Sinai at the same time (much of Egypt's army was tied up in the Yemeni civil war). Israeli leaders, citing Nasser's actions as evidence he was planning to attack Israel, struck preemptively on June 5, 1967. The war lasted only six days. Israel defeated the Egyptian army and seized Gaza and the Sinai, captured the West Bank and East Jerusalem and the Old City from the Jordanians, and seized control of the Golan Heights from the Syrians in the north. A stunning victory, it initiated a new era in Israel's national development, with lasting consequences for Israel and the Palestinians who came under its control.

The 1967 victory unleashed a surge of religious nationalism among Israeli Jews, almost messianic in its fervor, the goal of which was to retain Israeli control over all this territory, if not to expand Israel's borders further. The new territories more than doubled Israel's size and placed more than an additional 1 million Palestinians under Israeli control. The 1967 defeat radicalized the Palestinian resistance forces, with the Palestine Liberation Organization (PLO), an umbrella organization composed of the Fatah movement (the guerrilla group formed by Yasir Arafat) and other groups, becoming dominant.

The Israeli cabinet voted unanimously on June 19, 1967, to give the Sinai back to Egypt and the Golan Heights to Syria in exchange for demilitarization and peace. From Jordan, they demanded territorial concessions and refused to return any part of Jerusalem. All three Arab countries refused to negotiate until Israel withdrew, so Israel retained the territories it had conquered. Although the United Nations issued Resolution 242 in November 1967, calling on Israel to withdraw from all territories occupied during the war, Israel refused. In fact, the

When Israelis went to the polls in 1977, other long-standing frustrations welled up—anger over the 1973 war, disgust with the Labor Party scandals, and Mizrahi frustration with their continued second-class citizenship. When the results were counted, the Labor alignment lost a third of its seats in the Knesset. The Likud Party, greatly strengthened by a strong crossover vote from Mizrahi Israelis who were tired of broken Labor Party promises, formed the new government. For the first time in Israel's history, Labor no longer controlled the political process. Israel had swung to the right and would remain there throughout the decade.

One outcome of the change in government was a change in policies concerning settlement in the territories Israel conquered in 1967—Gaza and the West Bank (also called the Occupied Territories). Until 1977, only about 5,000 settlers had moved to these areas. However, the Likud government supported the goals of the Israeli settlers' movement, Gush Emunim. For the members of Gush, it was their national and religious obligation to settle in and eventually annex the Occupied Territories to Israel, as Greater Israel. To facilitate this outcome, the Gush, with government support, began a massive settlement drive in the territories, such that by 1987, there were approximately 175,000 Jewish Israelis living in 130 settlements in the West Bank and another 2,500 people living in 19 settlements in Gaza. While many of the earliest settlers were ideologically motivated, later settlers were urban professionals attracted by the spacious housing and low mortgage terms that the government offered to entice Israelis to live there.

The same government that believed in the vision of a Greater Israel was also, however, the government that reached a peace settlement with Egypt in 1979, the Camp David Accords, brokered by U.S. president Jimmy Carter. While the accords contained provisions for dealing with the Israeli-Palestinian conflict, the Likud government never seriously intended to implement them. They moved throughout the decade to more closely tie the territories into Israel's infrastructure and economy. The Likud government replaced democratically elected Palestinian mayors and municipal councils in the territories with their own chosen, "more moderate" candidates. Eventually, the Likud government decided to strike at the PLO leadership then based in Lebanon. In 1982, Israel invaded Lebanon under the pretense of securing the northern Galilee from attacks across the Lebanese border, in what came to be called "Operation Peace for Galilee." However, the IDF quickly overran the initial 25-mile limit they had announced for their invasion and ended up encircling and bombing Beirut in order to force Yasir Arafat and the PLO to evacuate. On September 16–18, 1982, the IDF, which controlled access to the Sabra and Shatilla Palestinian refugee camps, allowed Lebanese Phalangist forces into the camps, where the Phalangists spent 40 hours massacring the camps' residents—men, women, and children. Total estimates of those killed were as high as 1,500 to 2,000. The Israeli Kahan Commission found Minister of Defense Ariel Sharon "indirectly" responsible for the massacre because he had given the go-ahead to allow the Phalangists into the camps; Sharon resigned as defense minister but remained in the government. The International Commission of Inquiry went even further and found the Israeli authorities involved in the planning and preparation for and facilitating of the massacre. In the fall of 1983, Prime Minister Menachem Begin also resigned.

That Israeli forces could stand by and let the massacre happen under their watch was more than many Israelis could bear. The peace movement, particularly Peace Now, was reinvigorated, and new groups came into existence, such as Parents Against Silence, Yesh Gvul, and Women Against the Invasion of Lebanon. Israelis took to the streets to protest against their government's actions, with 400,000 people demonstrating when the camp massacres were revealed.

In the 1984 Knesset elections, neither Labor nor Likud won a decisive victory. The two parties agreed to form a national unity government, with the prime ministership held first by Shimon Peres (Labor) for 25 months and by Yitzhak Shamir (Likud) for the remainder of the term. Yitzhak Rabin (Labor) served as defense minister for both men. Under Peres, in 1985, the IDF withdrew from most of Lebanon, keeping troops in an area called the "security zone," which they ruled with support from the South Lebanon Army (SLA), which they financed.[18] The government also initiated a recovery plan to radically alter Israel's economic structure and rein in rampant inflation. In October 1986, Shamir took over as prime minister and began ramping up settlement activities in the Occupied Territories again, with Ariel Sharon as his housing minister.

Uprisings and Peace Processes, 1987 to the Present

On December 8, 1987, an Israeli army tank transporter ran into a line of cars filled with Palestinian workers at a military checkpoint in the north of Gaza. Four Palestinians died, and seven were seriously injured. Rumors began to spread that the collision had been deliberate, in revenge for the death of an Israeli in Gaza a few days earlier. As police put down demonstrations in force, harming more Palestinians, the unrest spread. So began a massive, grassroots campaign of civil disobedience that lasted from 1987 to 1991—what has been termed the intifada (in Arabic, this translates as "shaking off").

By 1987, the Palestinian population of the territories had lived under military occupation and administration for 20 years. Israeli officials controlled where or whether Palestinians could build a house, study at schools, work, or even travel freely about. In the uprising, the Palestinians used a number of nonviolent strategies of resistance to Israeli rule: refusing to pay taxes, boycotting Israeli goods, closing their businesses in strikes, demonstrating in the streets, and establishing agricultural cooperatives and alternative education centers. They also threw stones and Molotov cocktails and erected barricades to slow the movement of the Israeli army.

The Israeli government was again caught off guard and responded to the uprising with what Defense Minister Rabin called "the iron fist" policy of beatings to break bones. Israeli troops used live ammunition and tear gas to disperse street demonstrations and also tried water cannons, plastic, and rubber bullets. The government moved to more drastic measures: curfews, cutting off water and elec-

On the Ben Yehuda pedestrian mall in Jerusalem. Photo by Moshe Milner.
Courtesy of the Government Press Office, State of Israel.

tricity, collective punishment, arrests, and expulsions of people assumed to be
leaders. By 1994, more than 1,250 Palestinians had been killed, and 172 Israeli
civilians and 80 Israeli soldiers had been killed.[19]

The Gulf War in January and February 1991 pushed the uprising to the background on the international scene. In the aftermath of that conflict, the international community focused on resolving the Israeli-Palestinian conflict. An
international peace conference held at Madrid in October 1991 was followed
quickly by the dissolution of the Soviet Union in December 1991 and a Labor
victory in Israel in the June 1992 elections. Secret meetings to negotiate a settlement began in Norway in January 1993; in September 1993, Arafat and Prime
Minister Yitzhak Rabin signed the Oslo Accords in Washington, D.C. The next
day, Israel and Jordan signed a peace treaty.

The Israelis withdrew from Jericho and Gaza according to schedule. On July 1,
1994, Yasir Arafat returned to Palestine. In the early days, there was considerable
euphoria on both sides. Palestinians and Israelis alike were tired of the conflict and
ready to reap their own peace dividend. The accords were an agenda for negotiations
to produce a final peace treaty. Those negotiations quickly ran into trouble. In October 1995, the Israeli army withdrew from Palestinian cities in the West Bank, and
the Palestinian Authority took control. Right-wing religious and extreme nationalist Israeli groups began to demonstrate against Rabin, going so far as to call for his
death. On November 4, 1995, they got what they wanted when Rabin was assassinated by a Jewish zealot while attending a peace rally in Tel Aviv. Rabin's death at
the hands of an Israeli Jew stunned Israeli society. Within the Palestinian commu-

nity, members of Hamas (the Islamic Resistance Movement) and Islamic Jihad (a small, highly militant faction funded by Syria and Iran that sought to overthrow Israel and establish an Islamic state) opposed any peace settlement with Israel; they used suicide bombings to derail the process. Although Shimon Peres took over as prime minister and vowed to continue the process as outlined in the Oslo Accords, he could not hold the government together. In May 1996, the first-ever direct election of the prime minister, Israelis elected Benjamin Netanyahu by a margin of less than 1 percent of the popular vote and put the Likud back into power. The Oslo Accords were effectively dead, although the process they started would limp along for another four years before everyone accepted their demise.

Netanyahu pursued a policy of "peace with security," with the stress on security. Heavy pressure on the part of then U.S. president Bill Clinton led to the signing of the Wye Memorandum on October 23, 1998. This agreement provided detailed steps to be taken by Israel and the Palestinians to complete the interim peace deal negotiated over the previous five years. It also laid the groundwork for negotiations to permanently settle the Israeli-Palestinian conflict. Each side pledged action: Israel was to carry out further troop redeployments, and the Palestinians were to crack down on Hamas and Islamic Jihad. Almost immediately, the agreement began to fall apart. Netanyahu faced major opposition to the agreement by his own governing coalition. After his efforts to create a national unity government came to naught, he joined the majority in the Knesset and voted to dissolve his government. New elections were scheduled for May 17, 1999.

In those elections, Ehud Barak, running as the candidate for the One Israel Party (an alliance of Labor, the left-leaning Orthodox Meimad Party, and the Mizrahi Gesher Party) won the election for prime minister by a margin of 12 percent. Barak called his government the "coalition for peace." Barak fulfilled a campaign promise and finally withdrew Israeli soldiers from Lebanon. He reinvigorated the peace negotiations with the Palestinians and entered new peace negotiations with the Syrians. Negotiations with the Palestinians failed in July 2000 over the issue of the holy sites and Jerusalem, although efforts to find a solution continued into September. On September 28, 2000, Ariel Sharon, accompanied by police, visited the Temple Mount to assert Israeli control over the site. His visit sparked widespread rioting and was the flashpoint that set off a new uprising, the Al-Aqsa Intifada.

Relations between Israeli Palestinians and Israeli Jews hit an all-time low in early October 2000; during demonstrations in the Galilee in support of Palestinians in the West Bank and Gaza, 13 Palestinian Israelis were shot dead by Israeli policemen. Fighting broke out in the mixed cities of Acre, Upper Nazareth, Haifa, and Jaffa between Palestinian and Jewish residents. The events of October 2000 shattered any appearance of peaceful coexistence in these areas. Barak's government could not survive the aftermath of these events, and once again, Israelis went to the polls to determine the future of their country.

On February 6, 2001, Ariel Sharon swept to power in Israel, defeating Barak by a margin of 62.4 percent to 37.6 percent. Sharon set up a unity government with

Labor and announced that there would be no more negotiations with the Palestinians. By mid-June 2002, the Israeli army had reoccupied much of the West Bank and Gaza. On January 28, 2003, Ariel Sharon was reelected prime minister when the Likud party won more than twenty percent of the votes in the elections for the 16th Knesset. Sharon formed a coalition government with the centrist Shinui Party and the right wing National Religious Party and the National Unity Party. The country has descended into a widening cycle of violence, as Israeli attacks in the camps have generated suicide bombings, which are then used to justify further Israeli attacks. Since September 29, 2000, 941 Israelis have been killed (665 civilians, 276 soldiers) and 6,260 have been injured (4,431 civilians and 1,829 soldiers).[20] Of those killed, 449 died at the hands of suicide bombers, with another 99 dying as a result of other forms of bombing. During this same time period, 2,771 Palestinians have been killed and a further 25,146 have been injured.[21] Of those killed, 152 were women and 477 were children under the age of 18 (118 of whom were under the age of 12).

After the September 11, 2001, attacks in the United States, Ariel Sharon was able to further marginalize Yasir Arafat, who has been kept a virtual prisoner in his compound. Under U.S. pressure, the Palestinians selected Mahmoud Abbas as their new prime minister in March 2003, but he served only four months before resigning in frustration on September 6, 2003. Arafat chose Ahmed Qureia as the new prime minister on September 8, 2003, and Qureia has attempted to get the peace process restarted. However, peace talks have been hampered by actions on both sides: an increase in the number of suicide bomb attacks within Israel and increased Israeli raids and targeted assassinations in the Occupied Territories, as well as Israeli construction of a fence to separate the West Bank from Israel. Prime Minister Sharon has broached the idea of a unilateral Israeli withdrawal from Gaza, while some Palestinians have begun to speak of the death of the two-state solution and to call for the establishment of a single, binational, secular, democratic state. What the outcome will be is anyone's guess.

NOTES

1. All references to Israel refer to the pre-1967 boundaries of the country, an area often referred to as "inside the Green Line." For a discussion of Palestinian life in Gaza, the West Bank, Golan Heights, and East Jerusalem, see the forthcoming book in this series, *Culture and Customs of the Palestinians*.

2. Israel and the Palestinians in the West Bank share two main water sources, the mountain aquifer and the Upper Jordan River and its tributaries. All the running water in the West Bank comes from the aquifer; Palestinians receive no water from the Jordan. Since 1967, Israel has also controlled the water in the eastern aquifer in the West Bank and the Gaza aquifer.

3. Israel Central Bureau of Statistics, "The Population, by Religion and Population Group," Table 2.1, *Statistical Abstract of Israel 2002.* http://www.cbs.gov.il/shnaton53/st02_01.pdf.

4. Several small Conservative and Reform congregations now exist and hold services, but they are not recognized or supported by the state.

5. See Lynne Franks, *Israel and the Occupied Territories: A Study of the Educational Systems of Israel and the Occupied Territories and a Guide to the Academic Placement of Students in Educational Institutions of the United States* (Washington, D.C.: American Association of Collegiate Registrars and Admissions Officer, 1987), 10.

6. The Arab system teaches in Arabic, although students also learn Hebrew and English. Students who plan to attend university must master Hebrew (and English), since there are no Israeli Arabic-language universities. Arab students at all levels have units on Arabic language and literature and Arab history, in addition to Jewish/Israeli studies.

7. Since the early 1990s, the Israeli government has acknowledged it spends more on educating Jewish students than it does on Palestinian students. Palestinian students are allocated only 60 percent of what Jewish students receive.

8. Nura Resh, "Track Placement: How the 'Sorting Machine' Works in Israel," *American Journal of Education* 106, no. 3 (1998): 416–438.

9. From Human Rights Watch, "Second Class: Discrimination against Palestinian Arab Children in Israel's Schools," September 2001. http://www.hrw.org/reports/2001/israel2/.

10. Yaacov Iram and Mirjam Schmida, *The Educational System of Israel* (Westport, Conn.: Greenwood Press, 1998), 65–68.

11. Israel Central Bureau of Statistics, "Students at Universities by Degree, Field of Study, Sex, Age, Religion, and Origin," Table 8.35, *Statistical Abstract of Israel 2002*. http://www.cbs.gov.il/shnaton53/st08_35x.pdf.

12. Amos Elon, *The Israelis: Founders and Sons* (New York: Penguin Books, 1971), 111.

13. Israel Central Bureau of Statistics, "Employed Persons and Employees, by Industry, Religion, and Sex," Table 12.11, *Statistical Abstract of Israel 2002*. http://www.cbs.gov.il/shnaton53/shnatone53.htm.

14. Jon Fedler, *Israel's Agriculture in the 21st century*. http://www.mfa.gov.il/mfa/go.asp?MFAH00l70.

15. Simon Griver, *Facets of the Israeli Economy: The High-Tech Sector*. http://www.mfa.gov.il/mfa/go.asp?MFAH0jdq0.

16. See Israel Central Bureau of Statistics, "Foreign Trade Balance, Net," Table H/1, *Monthly Bulletin of Statistics, H. Foreign Trade, 2002*. http://www.cbs.gov.il/yarhon/h1_e.htm.

17. According to Howard Sachar (*A History of Israel: From the Rise of Zionism to Our Time* [New York: Alfred A. Knopf, 1979], 265), Lehi alone carried out more than 100 acts of sabotage and murder between September 1946 and May 1948. After June 1946, the Irgun also turned to violence, using it as a weapon against Palestinians, the British, and Jewish informers.

18. A low-level war of attrition with Hezbollah, the Party of God, a Lebanese radical Islamic movement aligned with Iran whose goal was to drive Israel out of Lebanon, continued until Labor prime minister Ehud Barak finally withdrew the last Israeli forces from Lebanon in 2000.

19. B'Tselem, the Israeli Information Center for Human Rights in the Occupied Territories, *Statistics on Total Casualties*. 9 December 1987 to end of May 2003. http://www.btselem.org/.

20. Israel Defense Forces Web site, *Casualties Since 29.09.2000 Updated 18.03.2004*. http://www.idf.il/daily_statistics/english/1.doc.

21. Palestinian Red Crescent Society Web site, March 15, 2004. http://www.palestin ercs.org/crisistables/table_of_figures.htm   and   http://www.palestinercs.org/Latest_Crisis Updates_Figures&Graphs.htm. The Middle East Policy Council has a good database about the conflict that includes both Israeli and Palestinian losses. It provides graphs and a news context for the deaths from September 29, 2000, in half-month increments. It also has a U.S. equivalent feature. Go to http://www.mepc.org/public_asp/resources/ mrates. asp.

2

Religion and World View

Why is Israel such a focus for world attention, given its small size and population? The answer becomes clearer when one realizes the central position that the land of Israel plays in three of the world's major religions—Judaism, Christianity, and Islam. Modern Israel contains within its borders many of the landscapes of the Old and New Testament; others are in the West Bank, which Israel currently controls. Israel is the "Holy Land" for over half the religious adherents in the world (about 3 billion people). Jerusalem's status as a sacred city has led many officials to propose that it be placed under international jurisdiction or given a status similar to that of Vatican City. Religion does not play a major role in the lives of most Israelis, who see themselves as secular. However, it plays a major role in the political affairs of the country. Israel is by law a Jewish state, and this union of state and religion has left its mark on Israeli life.

JUDAISM

Approximately 4.7 million Jews live in Israel, making it the second-largest community in the world behind the Jewish community of North America (which numbers more than 6 million). Worldwide, the Jewish community has more than 14 million adherents, or about .2 percent of worldwide adherents of a religion. Although Judaism might seem insignificant, it is at the heart of both the Christian and Muslim traditions, which together account for almost 53 percent of the world's religious believers.

Forty percent of Israelis describe themselves as secular (*Hiloni*), with another 40 percent seeing themselves as traditional (*Masorti*).[1] About 15 to 20 percent describe themselves as Orthodox (*Dati*) or ultra-Orthodox (*Haredi*). The differences between the two groups have to do with the levels of observance of the commandments set forth in the Hebrew Scriptures. Even secular and traditional Israelis tend to be more observant than their counterparts in the United States. A secular Israeli may light Shabbat (the Jewish Sabbath, or day of rest) candles or keep kosher to an extent. Such practices are rare among Reform Jews in the United States; secular Jews may not even be aware of how to perform these rituals. The religious-secular cleavage is one of the major fault lines in Israeli society. Orthodox religious authorities in Israel are constantly struggling to impose more rigorous observance of Jewish law on Israeli society. Secular Israelis chafe at and resist these attempts to control their lives. Some Israelis now advocate the separation of synagogue and state in Israel as it exists in the United States.

History

The Jewish faith developed over a 4,000-year period. Over that span of time, it has demonstrated a remarkable capacity to adapt and persevere, to absorb elements from the civilizations and cultures with which it has come into contact, but to also retain its own unique identity and heritage. Certain key elements of the faith remained constant. The fundamental teaching of Judaism is belief in one, and only one, God. Thus Judaism represents the first manifestation of a monotheistic religious belief system. By its very nature, monotheism leads to religious universalism—if there is only one God, then this God is the God of all humans. However, Judaism combined monotheism with a specific type of particularism. The One God chose the Jewish people among all humans to be his people and to set an example for the rest of humankind. He bound the Jewish people to him by a covenant that spelled out the terms for life as a chosen people. Failure to live up to this covenant had severe consequences. Obedience to the covenant meant obedience to the laws as given by God, the Ten Commandments. These beliefs continue to inform Jewish life in Israel in modern times.

The Hebrew Bible (the Christian Old Testament)—which consists of the first five books known as the Torah, the books of prophets (neviim), and other writings—sets out the early history of the Jewish people.[2] God—Yahweh—made a covenant with the patriarch Abraham and his descendants to obtain for them the land of Canaan. In exchange, Abraham agreed to worship Yahweh, the one God, and to follow his laws. Abraham led his nomadic group and their flocks of sheep, goats, and cattle from Mesopotamia south into the land of Canaan. There he settled and his descendents flourished. In the late sixteenth or early fifteenth century B.C., Abraham's descendant Jacob fled to Egypt with his family to escape drought and famine in Canaan. They remained in Egypt until Egyptian oppression drove them to revolt and escape, the Exodus led by the prophet Moses, who led them to freedom in the land of Israel.

Under Moses, the religious practices of the Israelites shifted dramatically. God made a covenant with Abraham but gave little in the way of laws to follow. At

View of the Western Wall and the Dome of the Rock in Jerusalem's Old City. Photo by the author.

Mount Sinai, God handed down a new covenant to Moses and the Jewish people. The Mosaic Code, consisting of the Ten Commandments and hundreds of other laws (613 in total), provides the moral framework that has guided the Jewish people. From this point, under the command of Joshua, they conquered the land of Canaan, which confirmed their status as a chosen people. Under King David's leadership, they moved from a loosely knit tribal confederation to a united kingdom of Israel and Judah, with a capital in Jerusalem. David's successor, Solomon, embarked on an ambitious building campaign and centralized spiritual authority in Jerusalem. To construct palaces and monuments, he imposed forced labor and taxes on Canaanites and his citizens in the northern part of the kingdom. Upon his death, the northern 10 tribes broke away to form the kingdom of Israel, which prospered until its destruction by the Assyrians, who exiled its people between 740 and 721 B.C. The southern kingdom of Judah remained independent until the Babylonians conquered Jerusalem, destroyed the First Temple in 586 B.C., and exiled its people. Since this time, the majority of Jews have lived outside the Holy Land. The Babylonian exile inaugurated a new period in the religious development of Judaism.

Living in exile (Diaspora), the Jews needed new ways to preserve their unique identity. They did so by turning to the laws and rituals contained in the Mosaic Code. They codified these into the Talmud, which contains two parts: the Mishnah (rabbinic commentary on the Torah laws) and the Gemara (legal and philosophic debates and stories). Together, the Torah and Talmud became the new basis for Jewish communal identity and cohesion. To these writings were added the Shulchan Aruch, a medieval law code of 1565. As new conditions raised questions for Jewish communities concerning appropriate responses, the rabbis generated a further legalistic literature—the *responsa*—as they published answers to congregants' questions.

The Persian emperor Cyrus allowed the Israelites to return to the Holy Land in the mid–sixth century B.C. Many Jews chose to remain in Babylon, which was a great center of Jewish learning for more than a thousand years. Judah was a small province within the Persian Empire. Its people rebuilt Jerusalem and the Temple. The province passed into the control of Alexander the Great and his successors, the Seleucids. Efforts by the Seleucid rulers to control and Hellenize (make more Greek) the Jewish faith sparked a revolt led by the Maccabee brothers. With success, they founded the Hasmonean dynasty and restored Judah's control over the whole of Palestine, the Golan, and the east bank of Jordan. While religious life remained untouched, Jewish social life became Hellenized. Urban residents adopted Greek as their language, sponsored games and sports, and took Greek names. Greek influence even filtered into philosophical debate and literary traditions. Eighty years of Jewish independence ended when contenders for the throne appealed to the Roman general Pompey for support. In 65 B.C. he seized Jerusalem and installed a high priest. The period of Roman rule in Judah had begun.

Under Roman rule, the Jews retained religious autonomy and some limited rights to rule their own internal affairs through the Sanhedrin (Jewish supreme council with civil, religious, and criminal jurisdiction over the community). It was a time of tremendous turmoil, the period in which Jesus was born and began his ministry. The turmoil eventually erupted into outright revolt under the Zealots, a Jewish nationalist movement. Jerusalem fell to the Romans in A.D. 70. It was completely destroyed (including the Second Temple), and its residents were sold into slavery or exiled overseas. Three years later, the last Zealot survivors perished at Masada. Jewish life in Palestine continued through the rabbinical center established by Rabbi Yohana Ben-Zakki at Yibna. The attempt by the Roman emperor Hadrian to stop the practice of circumcision (which he viewed as mutilation of the body) sparked a final revolt in A.D. 132–135, led by Simon Bar Kochba. The Romans again defeated the Jewish forces. The Romans chose to make an example of what happens to those who revolt. They put to death Jewish leaders and elders, broke up communities, and leveled the ruins of Jerusalem to build a new city, Aelia Capitolina, as capital of the new province of Palestine. Jews were forbidden to come within sight of the city.

The center of Jewish life now passed to communities living in the Diaspora. Jewish life in the Diaspora was a cycle of persecution and prosperity. Generally, the communities flourished, particularly under Islamic rule. Maimonides, a highly respected Jewish scholar of the twelfth century, was personal physician to Egypt's ruler. In Islamic Spain, Jewish culture flowered and experienced a renaissance of its own. As a protected people, Jews were free to travel throughout the Islamic Empire. Many took advantage of trade opportunities and established themselves as merchants; others entered finance and became advisors to rulers.

There were still periodic cycles of persecution, and Jews never forgot they were a subject people, but they experienced a degree of religious and cultural freedom that was lacking in Jewish life under Christendom.

In Europe, the Christian Church made Jewish life precarious by sponsoring and encouraging anti-Jewish activities and purges. In the Middle Ages, as they moved through Europe on their way to the Holy Land, the Crusaders periodically massacred Jewish communities in order to rid Europe of "Jesus killers." Once they drove the Muslims out of Spain, Christian rulers there gave the Jewish community the choice of conversion or death. Christian rulers learned that they could divert their subjects' attention away from their own faults by blaming problems on the Jews and turning their subjects' anger to destroying local Jewish populations. Anti-Semitism in Europe was deeply rooted and was to bear terrible fruit in the twentieth century.

The Jewish Enlightenment, or *Haskalah* (awakening), was an intellectual movement in Europe that lasted for more than 100 years, from the 1770s to the 1880s. Jewish communities in the Diaspora valued education and learning greatly, but the focus was on religious education. The *Haskalah* movement encouraged Jews to study secular subjects, such as literature, science, arts, and crafts, and to learn European languages as well as Hebrew and Yiddish (a Jewish-German dialect). Its followers sought to assimilate into the societies in which they lived, to cease dwelling as a separate community. They wanted to move Jews from traditional jobs such as money lending and trade to more skilled jobs such as crafts and agriculture. Large numbers of Jews assimilated and stopped adhering to Jewish religious law. Some went even further and converted to Christianity. Reform Judaism began at this time in an effort to stop such conversions. When the movement ended, it left a Jewish world that was more secular, more educated, and more nationalistic as it became clear to the "awakened" that assimilation would not bring them the equal status they desired. These individuals turned once again to the Holy Land to bring them what they perceived to be the right of all people—to dwell as a nation within their own state. The Nazi effort to exterminate the Jewish population during World War II, the Holocaust, reinforced for the surviving Jews the necessity for Jews to have a state of their own that would protect them from future attacks. The stage was set for the birth of the modern country of Israel and a new phase in Jewish life.

Central Beliefs

Like the other great monotheistic traditions, Christianity and Islam, Judaism has faced its own reform movements. What marks the movements off from each other is their vision of whether Judaism is evolving and how Judaism should interact with changes in the world. There are four trends worldwide: the Orthodox (including the ultra-Orthodox), the Conservative, the Reconstructionist, and the Reform. Orthodox refers to a wide variety of different Jewish communities who adhere to traditional Jewish practice as proclaimed in the Torah. They believe that the written and oral Torah are the word of God and that Jews must obey the commandments as set down in the Torah. The Orthodox community holds the monopoly over religious practice in Israel, even though they have few adherents there. Reform Judaism's followers do not believe the Torah was written by God. They retain the values and ethics of Judaism but do not obey all the commandments. They are the largest movement worldwide but have few adherents in Israel. The Conservative movement grew out of the tension between Orthodoxy and the Reform movement. Conservative Jews acknowledge that the Hebrew Scriptures and writings contain truths that come from God but that humans transmitted them and that they contain a human component. They accept Jewish law but believe it must evolve and adapt. They are strong within the United States but have no real presence in Israel. The Reconstructionist movement, the smallest segment, is an outgrowth of the Conservative one. They do not believe God chose the Jewish people, but they may observe Jewish law if they so choose as a way of preserving Jewish culture and identity.

Jews believe in one God, a single, whole, indivisible entity. He is the only God, and only he can be worshiped. God created everything in the universe (including evil). He has no body, and it is forbidden to represent him in any physical form. Since he has no body, he is neither male nor female. Because Hebrew has no neutral gender, the male forms are commonly used to refer to God but at times, female forms are used, as with the *Shechinah,* God's presence in the universe. God is at all places at all times and can do anything. He knows all. He has no beginning and no ending and is both just and merciful.

The commandments (mitzvoth) in the Torah are at the heart of Jewish law and religious practice. Many of them are not observed today because it is not possible to do so. For example, those that refer to sacrifices or offerings in the Temple can-

Orthodox Jews in the Mea She'arim neighborhood of Jerusalem. Photo by Nati Harnik. Courtesy of the Government Press Office, State of Israel.

not be performed because there is no Temple. Others apply to the former kingdom of Israel, its king, and priests, which no longer exist. One controversial provision of Jewish law is the question, "Who is a Jew?" A Jew is someone who is born to a Jewish mother or who converts to Judaism under proper rabbinical supervision. A child born to a Jewish father and a non-Jewish mother is not Jewish, even if raised in the traditions of Judaism. This reading of the law has generated a great deal of tension in countries like the United States, where high rates of intermarriage have meant that large numbers of children are born to Jewish fathers and non-Jewish mothers. The Reform movement accepts these children as Jewish if they are raised to see themselves as Jewish. In Israel, these children are not Jewish and would need to formally convert in order to be registered as Jews under the Law of Return, legislation that spells out the right of an individual anywhere in the world to become an Israeli citizen automatically by virtue of being Jewish.

Judaism teaches that human life has inherent dignity and value and that all humans, as created in the image of God, are equal. Unlike Christianity, Judaism does not posit man's original sin. In Jewish teachings, humans are inherently pure and good. They may be tempted to sin but can resist temptation and remain in God's favor. The Torah contains no clear reference to the afterlife, and fear of punishment in an afterlife has never been a motivating factor in a Jewish person leading a good life. One leads a good life because God demands of one that one lead a good life. "Love your neighbor as yourself is the greatest principle in the Torah," said Rabbi Akiva (Palestinian Talmud, Nedarim 9:4). And the great Rabbi Hillel when asked by a pagan to summarize Judaism while standing on one leg, responded, "What is hateful to you, do not do to others; the rest is commentary now go and study" (Babylonian Talmud, Shabbat 31a).

The imperative to behave ethically toward others can be seen as being in conflict with the notion that Jews are a chosen people, and it has produced major paradoxes in modern Jewish thought and practice. Thus, for example, by privileging the chosen people frame of reference, some rabbis in modern Israel claim that the imperative to behave ethically applies only with fellow Jews. The majority of rabbis reject this argument as they stress that Judaism above all values ethical, moral behavior for its own sake. This is at the very heart of what it means to be Jewish.

The Jewish tradition includes belief in a Messiah. He will be a descendent of King David, he will gain power over the land of Israel and gather Jews there from all parts of the world, he will restore them to full observance of the Torah, and he will bring peace to the entire earth. Throughout Jewish history, different individuals have claimed to be the Messiah, but so far, none have fulfilled these prerequisites. The messianic idea is strong within modern religious Zionist (Jewish nationalist) circles because they believe they have seen some of these prophecies come to pass with the establishment of the Israeli state and the ingathering of Jews from different parts of the world. Some religious Zionists believe that for the Messiah to come, all Jews must move to Israel and must become Orthodox in their observance. The messianic ideal can be taken overboard, as when a Jewish terrorist underground group plotted in 1984 to destroy the Muslim holy sites on the Temple Mount in Jerusalem, the location of the Al-Aqsa Mosque and Dome of the Rock, to clear the way for rebuilding the Jewish Temple, which it is believed stood there (and thus forcing the Messiah to return to save the Jewish people).

Sacred Days and Places

The Jewish calendar is based on a lunar cycle, so Jewish holidays move around during the regular calendar year. The most important holidays are the High Holidays of the New Year (Rosh Hashanah) and the Day of Atonement (Yom Kippur), which occur in the seventh month of Tishri. Rosh Hashanah serves as a time of reflection on the year that has passed and of making changes for the year to come. During this day, Jews may walk to flowing water and empty their pockets into it, symbolically casting off their sins (called *tashlikh*). The 10 days that follow are known as the Days of Awe, which end at Yom Kippur. People seek forgiveness and reconciliation with those they have wronged during this time. In some Orthodox communities, the ritual of *kapparot* is still practiced. During this ritual, one swings a live fowl over the head while praying that the fowl be accepted as atonement for sins. The bird is slaughtered and given to the poor. Yom Kippur is the most important holiday of the year. On this day, God's judgment of an individual, first inscribed on Rosh Hashanah, is sealed and can no longer be changed. It is a day of complete fasting, beginning before sunset the evening before and lasting through sundown that day. Most of the day is spent in the synagogue at prayer.

On the fifth day after Yom Kippur, the harvest festival of Sukkoth begins and lasts for seven days. It is followed immediately by Shemini Atzeret (on which the annual cycle of Torah readings is completed) and Simchat Torah (rejoicing in the Torah). Hanukkah, the festival of lights, is an eight-day festival that occurs in the ninth month of the Jewish year. It celebrates the miracle of the temple oil that lasted until a new supply was available. The New Year for Trees, Tu B'Shevat, occurs in the eleventh month. Purim, in the twelfth month, celebrates Esther, who saved the Jewish people from genocide at the hands of the Persian Haman. The Passover holiday (Pesach) in the first month of the year celebrates a different episode of redemption—Moses bringing the Jewish people out of Egypt and into the Promised Land. In the third month, the Festival of Weeks, Shavu'ot, celebrates the giving of the first fruits at the temple as well as the giving of the Ten Commandments on Mount Sinai. In the fifth month, Tisha B'Av is a day of fasting to commemorate all the tragedies that have befallen the Jewish people, especially the destruction of the First and Second Temples.

The entire land of Israel is sacred space for Jews, with Jerusalem holding special status. Every year, Jews pray to hold Pesach "next year in Jerusalem." Within Jerusalem, the most sacred site is the Western Wall (*HaKotel*). The wall is part of

Women praying at the Western Wall in Jerusalem's Old
City. Photo by Nathan Alpert. Courtesy of the Government Press Office, State of Israel.

the retaining wall built by King Herod in 20 B.C. at the top of which stood the
Second Temple. The Romans destroyed that temple in A.D. 70, but the wall has
remained a place of pilgrimage for Jews throughout the ages. At Hebron in the
West Bank, the Cave of Machpelah, burial site of Abraham and the other patri-
archs, is second in importance only to the Western Wall. Rachel's Tomb in Bethlehem is another important site, attracting women who pray for fertility and a
safe birth. Other sites include the Tomb of Rabbi Shimon Bar Yochai, author of
the *Zohar* (the major work of Jewish mysticism) at Meron and the more modern
site of pilgrimage to the tomb of the Moroccan-born Baba Sali, Rabbi Yisrael
Abuhatzira in Netivot.

Judaism and the Life Cycle

One of the most important duties in Judaism is the commandment to be fruit-
ful and multiply. Having children is a sacred duty, and children are cherished.
Ritual events around birth serve to bring the newborn child into the Jewish fold,
through naming, circumcision, and redemption of the first born. The ceremonies
surrounding the birth of a male child are more elaborate than those for a female
child, in keeping with the patrilineal (tracing descent through men only) and
patriarchal (male rule) character of Judaism.

All male children undergo circumcision (*brit milah*) in Judaism (even adult male converts must do this). On the eighth day after birth, the foreskin is removed. Circumcision serves as a sign of the covenant between God and the people of Israel. There are four elements in the traditional ceremony, which is performed by a specially trained individual, the mohel. He must cut off the foreskin (*milah*), tear off and fold back the mucous membrane to expose the glans (*periah*), and suck the blood from the wound (*metzitzah*). The mohel is assisted in his efforts by the baby's father, an individual designated to hold the infant (*sandek*), and other guests whom the family wants to include in the ceremony. At the end of the ceremony, the baby is named. Girl infants are usually named on the first Shabbat (Jewish day of rest) after their birth. The father is called to the Torah to read, and after he completes the reading, he recites a blessing for the mother and the newborn and publicly names the child.

If the child is the firstborn son, an additional ritual is required. The Jewish scriptures dedicate the firstborn of humans and animals to God's service. Hence, a firstborn son must be redeemed (*pidyon haben*) from his prescribed duty to serve God. The ceremony is usually performed on the thirty-first day after the child's birth. The ceremony occurs at a festive meal, the *seudat mitzvah*. After washing the hands and breaking bread, the child is brought in, often on a tray. A Kohen, member of the priestly caste, asks if the father will give away the child or redeem him for five shekels (Israel's currency; one shekel is equivalent to a quarter). The father indicates the latter, recites the appropriate blessings, and gives the Kohen the money. While swinging the money over the baby's head, the Kohen recites a formula to release the child. He blesses the baby, hands him back to the father, and blesses the wine. The ceremony concludes with a meal and grace after the meal.

The next major rite of passage in Judaism occurs as children become subject to the commandments of Judaism, the bar mitzvah (for boys) or bat mitzvah (for girls). This ceremony occurs at the age of 12 for girls and 13 for boys. Once they have become bar or bat mitzvahed, these children are now responsible for fulfilling all the commandments and are subject to punishment or sanctions for failure to follow through with their religious obligations. The ceremony for boys has been used since the fourteenth century, while that for girls dates to 1922. The ceremony consists of three parts: (1) a blessing recited by the father, and the son's or daughter's first call to participate in reading the Torah (*aliyah*); (2) a discourse on a portion of the Talmud (*derashah*), which in less Orthodox communities has become a more general speech; and (3) the festive meal and communal celebration that follows to honor the bar or bat mitzvah (*seudah*).

The burial service in Judaism is very simple. Burial occurs as soon after death as is possible. Members of a burial society (*hevreh kadisha*) prepare the body and clothe it in a simple shroud. In Israel, no coffin is used. Jews do not embalm or cremate their dead, nor do they permit autopsies or organ donations. The body must be returned to God in the best condition possible. Mourning practices apply to seven specific categories of relatives of the deceased—his or her father, mother,

Boy celebrates his bar mitzvah ceremony. Photo by Yuval Marcus.
Courtesy of the Government Press Office, State of Israel.

son, daughter, brother, sister, and husband or wife. The rabbi will tear the shirt or
blouse or a black ribbon worn by mourners to symbolize their grief; the left side is
ripped for a parent (whose loss is deeper); the right side for all others. Once the
casket is lowered into the grave, a prayer for peace for the departed (*El Maley
Rachamim*) is recited. Mourners then shovel earth (*kevorah*) onto the casket as
their final act, often using the back of the shovel to signify their reluctance to do
so. At the graveside, the mourners recite the special memorial prayer (*Kaddish*), a
prayer affirming life and faith in God.

Bereaved family members observe three separate phases of mourning: the first
week (shivah), the first 30 days (*sheloshim*), and the first year (*avelut*). When they
return from the graveyard, it is customary to have a bowl of water with a cup at
the door, to symbolize cleansing from a place of death to a place of life. A special
candle, the shivah candle, is lit upon returning from the cemetery, marking the
beginning of the seven days of mourning. The candle represents the soul of the
deceased. During shivah, the family gathers at a central location and holds an
open house so friends and acquaintances can come to pay respects and share sto-

ries and remembrances of the deceased. Visitors bring donations of food for the mourning family so that the family does not have to work to prepare food for their guests. Friends and neighbors prepare the first meal that the mourners eat after the funeral, the meal of condolence (se'udat havra'ah). It may feature round foods such as hard-boiled eggs or lentils to symbolize the cycle of life. During this time, mourners sit low (to symbolize being brought low with grief), engage in no luxurious bathing or cutting of hair and cover mirrors (all signs of vanity), and remove leather shoes and wear cloth slippers. Sexual relations are forbidden, and mourners conduct no business during this time. Mourning is not allowed on Shabbat and holidays.

During *sheloshim*, mourners return to their normal routine. They avoid events such as celebrations or weddings or places where music or dancing might occur. They may go to synagogue services either every day or every Shabbat to say *Kaddish*. During the 11 months following the death (*avelut*), family members continue to recite *Kaddish* during synagogue services. During this time as well, a tombstone will be placed and dedicated in an unveiling ceremony. Visitors to the gravesite leave pebbles on the grave as tokens of remembrance (a custom with roots in the biblical tradition of burial under piles of stones). At the one-year anniversary (*yahrzeit*, a Yiddish word), the family will again observe a day of remembrance, lighting a candle (the *yahrzeit* candle) which burns for 24 hours. Family members attend the evening, morning, and afternoon synagogue services to recite *Kaddish*. Deceased family members continue to be remembered every year on the anniversary of their death (*yahrzeit*) and at special memorial services (*yizkor*) held on Yom Kippur and at the end of Sukkoth, Passover, and Shavu'ot.

The Legal System

Religious institutions in Israel have their basis in the practices of the Ottoman Empire and its *millet* system—a form of self-government by which each religious community was allowed autonomy to run its own communal affairs under a recognized community leader. Personal status law—marriage, divorce, inheritance, child custody—was left to the control of the community as long as no Muslim was involved. In Ottoman-controlled Palestine, therefore, the Sephardi chief rabbi, the *Rishon Le'Tzion* (First in Zion), represented the Jewish community. When the British assumed their mandate over Palestine, they retained the system of religious courts. With the increase in size of the Ashkenazi community in Palestine, the British pushed the formation of a joint chief rabbinate and a joint rabbinical council. They implemented this system in 1921, with a corresponding structure of local courts, regional appellate courts, and the joint Supreme Rabbinical Court of Jerusalem.

The Israeli government maintained this structure after independence. Thus the state has given religious courts a monopoly over marriage, divorce, child custody, and inheritance. There is no civil code for these matters that applies to all Israeli citizens. For the Jewish community, these matters are settled according to

Jewish religious law, the halakah. Judges of religious courts (*dayanim*) are appointed by the president of the state, on the recommendation of nominating committees, chaired by the minister of religious affairs. Besides the chief rabbis and rabbinical council in Jerusalem, the larger cities have their own chief rabbis (Ashkenazi and Sephardi) and their own local religious council. The councils are responsible for registering marriages and divorces, supervising dietary laws in public institutions, inspecting slaughterhouses, maintaining ritual baths, and supporting synagogues and their staff.

The ultra-Orthodox have formed their own system of courts since they do not recognize the authority or legitimacy of the official Israeli state institutions. Agudat Israel (the non-Zionist ultra-Orthodox) and its community are guided by the Council of Torah Sages, which functions as their supreme rabbinical court. Members of this council are among the most learned men in their community. They oversee dietary law inspections, ritual slaughterers, ritual baths, and schools.

In practice, all Israeli Jews, regardless of whether they personally are religiously observant, must follow Orthodox Jewish law when they go to marry or divorce. To marry, individuals must be able to prove they are Jewish (i.e., born to a Jewish mother or having undergone a religiously valid, halakic conversion). Using Jewish religious law for marriage and divorce imposes a number of restrictions on the freedom of women, especially, to determine their own lives. In Israel, the levirate is still practiced. The levirate is a biblical custom whereby a childless widow might be married off to one of her brothers-in-law. Should she wish to marry someone else, she first had to be ritually repudiated by her brother-in-law in the presence of the rabbis. In modern Israel, widows may face extortion on the part of their in-laws in order to gain this release; they may have to forfeit inheritances or pensions, or pay off their brother-in-law to gain release. It is the man's prerogative to grant his wife a divorce; he can refuse to grant his wife her freedom to remarry. Should the woman pursue other relationships anyway, any child born of those relationships will be labeled illegitimate (*mamzer*) and will never be able to get married in Israel; the husband, meanwhile, is free to father children legally. Married women who are abandoned by their husbands, called *agunot*, can never remarry until either the husband reappears and files a proper divorce or until his death can be established to the satisfaction of the religious court. Wives of soldiers who are missing in action may thus never be able to remarry legitimately. Many secular Israelis choose to circumvent these provisions by marrying outside of the country (Cyprus is a popular spot) and then registering their marriage with the civil authorities upon their return. However, should those marriages later fail, the couple may still find itself forced to resolve the situation in a religious court.

Other Communities: The Karaites, Samaritans, and Black Hebrews

The Karaites broke away from mainstream rabbinic Judaism in the eighth century. Karaites hold the Torah as the authentic source of religious doctrine and practice. They repudiated the oral law and the authority of rabbis to interpret the Torah. In practice, Karaites observe some provisions of Judaism more stringently, and others more leniently. They strictly interpret the provision about not kindling a fire on Shabbat and will sit in the dark. Their dietary practices, however, are much less rigid than Orthodox ones. Some Karaites eat milk and meat together as long as they come from different sources. They do not require separate sets of dishes for meat and milk, arguing that it creates an economic hardship. For the purposes of ritual purification, Karaites simply shower at home instead of visiting the ritual bath, or *mikveh*. In Israel, Kariates are recognized as Jews under the Law of Return, and they serve in the IDF, but the rabbinic authorities refuse to recognize them as Jews, and they are forbidden to intermarry with other Jews. Today, there are 30,000 Karaites all over Israel, with the largest of their 11 synagogues in Ashdod.

The Samaritans are thought to be descendants of the northern tribes of Israel—Levi, Menashe, and Ephraim—who remained in Palestine at the time of the Babylonian exile, beginning in 722 B.C. In the fourth century, they numbered 1 million adherents, living from southern Syria to northern Egypt. Over the years, their community was decimated by conquest and forced conversion, first by the Byzantines and then the Arabs. Today, they number about 654 individuals, split between settlements in Nablus in the West Bank and in Holon in Israel. Thus some Samaritans are Israeli citizens, while others are viewed as Palestinian residents of the West Bank. Arabic is their mother tongue, although they pray in Hebrew.

The Samaritans' faith, which closely resembles Judaism, is based solely on the first five books of the Hebrew Bible (the Torah). Their religious observance is even stricter than the most ultra-Orthodox Jews. Once an individual stops practicing any part of their religion, they are no longer accepted by the Samaritan community. It is also not possible to convert into the religion. Samaritans call themselves the *Shamerim*, those who guard the tradition. They are guided by high priests who trace their lineage from the tribe of Levi. They observe the Sabbath and the following holy days: Passover, Shavu'ot, Seventh Month (New Year), Day of Atonement, Sukkoth, and Shemini Atzeret. They keep the laws of purity and impurity, and their sons are circumcised. On Passover, they still perform the required animal sacrifice. Jewish religious authorities through the ages reviled the Samaritans as heathens and infidels, and the community in Israel today is not recognized as Jewish by rabbinical authorities.

The Black Hebrews, whose full name is "The Original African Hebrew Israelite Nation of Jerusalem," have their roots in the Civil Rights era in the United States. Founded in Chicago by a steelworker named Ben Carter (who changed his name to the Hebrew Ben Ammi Ben Israel), the Black Hebrews first migrated to Liberia in 1967. In Liberia, they developed the practices of their faith—a vegan diet that prohibits all animal byproducts, the wearing of only natural fibers (cotton, wool, linen, silk), abstinence from smoking, alcohol (except their own wine), and medicines, and isolation from the world. A small group of

Black Hebrew men entered Israel in 1969 and 1970 and took up temporary residence. They began studying in order to convert, but that process was stopped by Ben Ammi. Others soon trickled in to join them. The Black Hebrews claim to be the one and only original Hebrew Israelite community. They applied for Israeli citizenship under the Law of Return but were denied. Rather than deport them and risk being labeled racist by the world community, the Israeli government instead steered them toward the towns of Dimona, Mitzpe Ramon, and Arad in the Negev Desert. From 1973 to 1992, the Black Hebrews lived illegally in Israel as their tourist visas and temporary residency permits had long since expired. Since 1992, they have registered 1,500 of their members as temporary residents. On July 29, 2003, the Israeli government granted community members permanent resident status, which brings community members even closer to their goal of becoming full-fledged Israeli citizens.

ISLAM

Islam came to Palestine in the seventh century A.D., with the Arab invaders from Arabia. Except for the brief period of Crusader control over the Holy Land, from 1099 to the fall of the last stronghold at Acre in 1291, Palestine remained under Islamic control until the nineteenth century, when Great Britain assumed its mandate. Today, 901,000 Muslims live in Israel, the remnants of the once-great Islamic Empires that controlled this land for more than a thousand years. There are more than 1 billion Muslims, or 19.8 percent of all religious adherents, worldwide. The Muslims living in Israel are Sunni, the main branch of Islam from which other sects, such as the Shiites, have deviated based on disagreements over leadership of the faith.

History

The word *Islam* means submission—submission to the will of God. A believer in the faith of Islam is known as a Muslim. As a faith, Islam draws on the traditions of Judaism and Christianity. Adherents of these religions are seen as People of the Book and as such, were not subject to the choice of converting or dying that was the lot of people who were nonbelievers or pagans. God's will was made known to man through the words of the prophets, the first of whom was Abraham and the last of whom, and most perfect, was Muhammad.

Muhammad was born into the Quraysh tribe of Mecca in central Arabia around A.D. 570. His mother, Aminah, who came from Medina, died when he was six years old; his father, Abd 'Allah, had died before he was born. He was raised by his grandfather, 'Abd al-Muttalib, who died when Muhammad was eight, and then by his paternal uncle Abu Talib, a wealthy merchant and head of the prestigious Hashim clan. Muhammad traveled with his uncle's caravans on trading expeditions and acquired a reputation as a skilled mediator of disputes.

About A.D. 595, he was in charge of a caravan owned by a wealthy widow, Khadijah. She was so impressed with him that she married him; he was 25, she was 40. Khadijah bore him two sons (who died young) and four daughters.

Due to his own life circumstances, Muhammad was aware of the tensions in Meccan society. Mecca had a certain stability because of its local shrine, the Ka'bah, a sanctuary built around the Black Stone of Mecca. The sanctuary was sacred to many different tribes—no blood could be shed there, and it was a popular site for the swearing of oaths. When the tribesmen came to worship at the Ka'bah, they would trade in Mecca's markets, or *suqs*. Mecca was a major trade center on the prosperous caravan route that ran along the western coast of Arabia, from Yemen to the Mediterranean. Its merchants supplied goods to both the Persians and the Byzantines and grew wealthy from trade. Only a few people had wealth, however, and they no longer fulfilled traditional tribal obligations to aid those less fortunate.

Muhammad would spend the nights in solitary, thinking in a hill cave near Mecca, where he began to receive revelations, starting in 610. Uncertain of the meaning of his visions at first, he soon became convinced he was God's messenger. He gathered followers around him, mainly young men from some of the mightiest Meccan families. He did not begin to preach publicly until 613, and he faced little opposition once he began to do so. Opposition to his teaching began to mount after 615, as the wealthy merchants became more concerned about Muhammad's critiques of their lifestyles. Other clans may also have used Muhammad's activities as a pretext for initiating a boycott of his clan. Both his wife, Khadijah, and his uncle Abu Talib died in 619. The new leader of the clan withdrew its protection from Muhammad, who was forced to leave Mecca for a brief time until he secured protection from another clan. Harassment of Muhammad and his followers continued, culminating in a plot to assassinate him. Warned of the plot, he fled to Medina in 622 with his followers (the celebrated hegira [*hijrah*], the basic meaning of which is the severing of kinship ties).

In Medina, Muhammad established the *umma*, the commonwealth of Muslims. Initially, membership in the *umma* did not require acceptance of Muhammad's religious claims. Over the next eight years, Muhammad built his community, leading his allies in attacks on Meccan caravans and repulsing forces sent from Mecca to teach him a lesson. He strengthened his position by making strategic marriage alliances and forming alliances with other tribes in the area. As his fame grew, the prestige of Mecca's leaders fell. In 630, Mecca's leaders were forced to accept Muhammad's terms for his return to Mecca. Muhammad assumed control over the Ka'bah and cleared it of idols. Henceforth, the terms of membership in the *umma* changed. To belong, the group had to accept Islam. Muhammad moved quickly to solidify his control over all of Arabia. By his death in 632, the peninsula was united and poised to expand outwards. Muhammad died without appointing a successor; this oversight would eventually provoke a split in Islam into Sunni and Shiite factions, the most important schism in the religion. Under his successors, the followers of Islam expanded out of Arabia to conquer widely. Palestine was in Muslim hands completely by A.D. 640. Under the Umayyad dynasty (661–750), Palestine served as one of the major bastions of their power and they built the Dome of the Rock and the al-Aqsa Mosque.

Central Beliefs

The central belief of Islam is the oneness of God. The Quran (also spelled Koran), the set of revelations made to the prophet Muhammad, preaches strict monotheism. The most important duties of a believer are the following acts, known as the Five Pillars of Islam: *shahada*, the profession of faith; *salat*, daily prayers; *zakat*, almsgiving; *sawm*, fasting; and *hajj*, the pilgrimage to the holy city of Mecca. In the *shahada*, the believer states that there is no god but God and Mohammed is his messenger. Spoken in the presence of a religious authority who can vouch that the recital was sincere, saying the *shehada* formally converts the speaker to Islam. Muslims pray five times a day, at dawn, midday, midafternoon, sunset, and nightfall. A member of the community, called the muezzin, calls Muslims to prayer by chanting aloud from a raised place (often the tower, or minaret, of the mosque) When praying, they face the direction of Mecca and go through the prescribed positions of the prayers, after completing the ritual washing of hands, head, and feet. The most important prayers are those that occur midday on Fridays at the mosque. The congregants stand facing the mihrab, a niche that indicates the direction of Mecca. The leading religious official in attendance usually delivers a sermon (*khutba*) after the prayers that may deal with contemporary topics affecting the community. Religious officials have used the sermons as vehicles for political announcements, even calls for revolt.

The *zakat* was an obligatory tax levied on food grains, cattle, and cash after one year's possession. The amount of the tax varied according to different categories. It was collected by the state to be used primarily for supporting the poor, although it could also be used to ransom Muslim war captives, for education or health, or to redeem debts. After the breakup of the last Muslim empire, the *zakat* became a voluntary charitable donation. Many Muslims continue to practice the *zakat* by looking after less-fortunate family members, friends, or neighbors in times of need.

Fasting (*sawm*) during the month of Ramadan (the ninth month of the lunar calendar) is the fourth pillar. The fast is observed from dawn to sunset, during which time Muslims cannot eat, drink, or smoke. Everyone except children under the age of puberty is expected to fast. Pregnant women, the sick, military personnel on active duty, and travelers are exempt from the fast but are expected to make up the missed days later. After sunset, it is permitted to eat. Nights during Ramadan usually turn into festive occasions with much visiting and exchange of hospitality.

The final pillar is the annual pilgrimage to Mecca, which all Muslims should do once in their lifetime if they are able to afford to do it. The pilgrimage takes place during the twelfth lunar month. Pilgrims converge from all over the world on Mecca to perform the complex ritual, which involves circumambulating the Ka'bah seven times. While on pilgrimage, Muslims dress in two seamless white garments, refrain from sexual intercourse, and do not cut their hair or nails, among other provisions.

Like Jews, Muslims follow a strict set of dietary rules. Only animals who have been ritually slaughtered (with the throat cut) are considered edible. Muslims do not eat pork or other carnivorous animals, or drink alcoholic beverages. They avoid using the left hand for passing food or eating from a common pot because that hand is associated with the performance of washing and using the bathroom.

Sacred Days and Places

The two major sacred days are the Id al-Fitr and the Id al-Adha. Id al-Fitr occurs at the end of the fasting month of Ramadan and lasts for three days. People celebrate by buying new clothes, giving gifts, entertaining, and visiting family graves at cemeteries. On the last day of the pilgrimage, the Id al-Adha, Muslims throughout the world offer sacrifice (a sheep, goat, camel, or cow) in remembrance of Abraham's willingness to sacrifice his son Ishmael (to Muslims, Abraham's oldest son from whom Muhammad is descended). The animal's meat is divided equally among the pilgrims, the poor, and friends and neighbors. Muhammad's birthday (Mawlid al-Nabi) ranks third in importance after the Ids. Lailat al-Miraj commemorates the ascension of the prophet Muhammad to heaven following his night journey from Mecca to Jerusalem. While on this journey, Muhammad was commanded by God to have Muslims pray five times a day. The Night of Power (Lailat al-Qadr) commemorates the first revelation of the Quran. The first of Muharram, New Year's Day, marks the flight (hegira) of Muhammad from Mecca to Medina. The tenth of Muharram, Ashura, is celebrated by Shiite Muslims to commemorate the martyrdom of Husayn.

The most sacred spot for Muslims is the Ka'bah in Mecca. The Prophet's mosque in Medina comes next, followed by the Haram as-Sharif in Jerusalem, venerated as the place from which Muhammad ascended into heaven. For Shiite Muslims, Karbala in Iraq (site of Husayn's martyrdom), Meshed (site of the tomb of Imam Reza), and Qom in Iran (site of the tomb of Fatima, Imam Reza's sister) are places of special importance and pilgrimage. The tombs of Sufi saints or other descendants of the prophet Muhammad have also become popular spots for pilgrimage.

Islam and the Life Cycle

Birth rites in Islam are recommended (sunna) rather than obligatory. Children born to Muslim parents are Muslim; therefore there is no need of a ceremony to make them Muslim. When the birth is announced to the father, celebrations and gift giving often occur. If the child is a male, the celebration will be grander than if the child is a female. Special foods may be cooked for the mother and child. One birth rite (the *tahnik*) calls for the parent or a pious person to chew a bit of date until soft and place it in the mouth of the newborn.

On the seventh day, an additional rite may be carried out, a ritual substitution (*aqiqah*). The child's head is shaved, and money the weight of the hair is distributed to the poor. The call to prayer is recited in the infant's right ear, and the second call, the summons to prayer, is recited in the left ear. Children are named at this time. It is common practice to give the child a name of a family member or of a saint or of a hoped-for characteristic, such as Faysal (peacemaker) or Sa'id (happy). Sometimes parents delay naming a child in order to determine what name to choose—a male child might be called Muhammad and a female Fatima in the meantime. If a family has previously lost boys, they might give a new son the name of a girl in order to mislead evil powers and ensure his life. The parents also sacrifice a young animal in the name of the child—two goats for a boy and one goat for a girl.

The next rite of passage is circumcision (*khitan*). The practice receives little mention or justification in Islamic texts. It is a popular practice rather than a religious one and as such, varies from region to region. The circumcision occurs at an age where the child is aware and will remember it, anywhere between age 2 and 12. Rituals are commonly held during the month of the Prophet's birthday and will be performed by the barber. Before the operation, the boy is bathed, dressed in special clothes, and paraded through the neighborhood or village. The ceremony is preceded or followed by a long festive meal and gift giving. The young boy will be watched closely after the operation to ensure that there are no complications. Once circumcised, the young boy will be expected to enter the world of men. Female circumcision is not practiced among Palestinian Muslims in Israel, however it does continue to be practiced among some Bedouin tribes living in the Negev. Girls are circumcised between the ages of 12 and 17. The more educated a woman is, the less likely she will be to circumcise her own daughter.[3] The equivalent rite of passage for a young girl is the onset of menstruation. Girls' movements may be restricted after they begin menstruating in order to protect their virginity and the family's honor.

Muslim death rites are simple. Normally, a dead person is to be buried on the day of death. First, the corpse is bathed (*ghusl*) by persons of the same gender, to remove any impurities. The corpse is then wrapped in a white shroud of three pieces for a man and five pieces for a woman to cover the body completely. The funeral prayer for the dead is performed in the mosque. The corpse is carried to the graveyard for burial by a procession of relatives, friends, and other community members. The corpse is placed in the grave with its face turned toward Mecca and the Ka'bah. Each person in attendance throws three handfuls of earth in the grave. On the third day after the burial, relatives visit the grave and recite passages from the Quran. The bereaved family is paid visits of condolence before and after the burial.

The Legal System

The body of laws that govern all aspects of a Muslim's life is known as the Sharia. Muslims hold the Quran to be the literal word of God, so it cannot be translated into any other language and retain its validity. Besides the Quran, Muslims draw upon the sayings of the prophet Muhammad (the Hadith), which provide anecdotes about the proper way to live (Sunna, "the path"). The Quran and the Hadith are the major sources for Islamic law. Over the years, Islamic judges have built up a body of opinions based on analogy (*qiyas*) as they interpreted the Quran and Hadith to deal with changing lifestyles. Four major schools of Islamic law (Hanafi, Shafi'i, Hanbali, and Maliki) developed in different parts of the Muslim world. In Israel, Hanafi law is the formal foundation for the courts, even though many Muslims in the rural areas are Shafi'i. Hanafi law, developed in Iraq under the Abbasids and found primarily in areas of former Ottoman rule, is a relatively liberal law code that emphasizes the use of reason in making decisions. Shafi'i law is also more liberal, relying on consensus and the decisions of the judges. In Israel, Muslim religious courts have exclusive jurisdiction over all matters concerning Muslim personal status. The judges (*qadis*) apply the Ottoman Law of Family Rights 1917 (as amended by the British in 1919) and also have jurisdiction, with consent of parties involved, over adoption and inheritance. The courts themselves are organized at two levels: Sharia courts of first instance and a Sharia Appeals Court.

The British also established the Supreme Council for Moslem Religious Matters in 1921 to administer communal affairs, such as property owned by the religious endowment funds set up to support particular mosques or other religious institutions (*waqfs*). In 1937, the British removed the council's jurisdiction over the endowments to place them in the hands of a special committee. After 1948, the new Israeli government seized *waqf* property as "absentees' property" to be administered by the Custodian of Absentee Property. In 1965, members of the Knesset, Israel's parliament, amended the Absentees' Property Law to allow trustee committees in seven towns to administer *waqf* property for the benefit of their communities. Trustees could use the resources for aiding the poor, vocational training, health, religious studies, or funding religious ceremonies. While they established some committees, most of the property remains in the hands of the Israeli government.

Other Islamic Communities: The Circassians and the Druze

The Circassians, who are Sunni Muslims, came to Israel from the Caucasus in the 1870s to serve the Ottoman sultan, who used them to prevent the spread of the Bedouin. Today they number some 4,000 inhabitants living in two main Galilean villages, Rihania, north of Tzafat, and Kfar Kama in the lower Galilee, near Yavne, as well as Afula, Hadera, Tzafat, Eilat, and other cities and towns. In Israel, the men serve in the IDF, or work in the border guard or police force. Kfar Kama, the larger village of the two, is surrounded by Jewish communities, and the children from the village attend mainly Jewish schools once they complete their studies in the village. Rihania is closer to Arab communities, and its students are sent to both Arab and Jewish schools. They have preserved their native language and traditions. Circassian young people respect their elderly, no matter what differences there may be between them in terms of education, literacy, or social status. They are known as generous hosts, who will give away anything they own to a guest who admires it.

Druze are a minority community found in modern times in Lebanon, Israel, and Syria. The community worldwide numbers about 1 million, with 104,000 living in Israel in the Galilee (86,000) and the annexed Golan Heights (18,000). In the Galilee, the Druze live in 17 villages, some of which are all Druze, the rest of which are mixed, mostly with Christian Arabs. Less than 10 percent of Druze in Israel lived in cities in the 1980s—compared with more than 60 percent of Christians. The Druze religion is an eleventh-century offshoot from Shiite Islam, through the Isma'ili line.[4] It developed in Egypt around the Islamic Fatimid ruler, Al-Hakim, who ascended to the throne at the age of 11. Al-Hakim, also known as the Mad Caliph, swung between arbitrary and brutal policies (such as killing all dogs because he disliked their barking) and tolerance (distributing food during famines). He encouraged the teachings of Isma'ili missionaries who saw him as the Imam, a divinely appointed and authoritative spokesman for Islam. As the sect developed, he claimed divinity for himself. Al-Hakim vanished mysteriously while taking a walk on February 13, 1021. His disappearance only reinforced the belief of his followers that he was indeed divine. In Egypt, the cult ceased to exist, but it spread, through missionary activities, to communities in Lebanon and Syria, where it took root. The period of missionary activity was brief, and since 1050, the community has been closed to outsiders.

The Druze call themselves monotheists (*muwah hidun*). They permit no conversion, either to or away from their religion, and they allow no intermarriage. The dominant Sunni Muslim rulers have persecuted them over the years because they viewed the Druze as heretics. Because of this, Druze practice dissimulation in hostile environments (*taqiya*). Druze may deny their faith publicly if their life is threatened. In practice, this has meant that Druze communities at times appear to worship like the dominant group, while hiding their faith. Keeping their religion secret has meant that the Druze themselves are divided into different classes of believers, based on their access to the religious teachings and practices. Most Druze are uninitiated (*juhhal*) and thus ignorant of their own doctrines. Uninitiated Druze must obey the moral principles of respecting the elderly and honoring women. A smaller, more elite group, the knowers ('*uqqal*), is fully initiated into the faith. Women are seen as more spiritually prepared than men to enter the ranks of the initiated because they are less likely to be exposed to immoral practices such as murder. The initiated male and female Druze members of the community can be recognized by their dark clothing and white head coverings. The most devout and knowledgeable people among the initiated, the *ajaweed*, hold a place of particular esteem, and they serve as informal leaders of the community.

Druze believe that rituals and ceremonies caused the Jews, Christians, and Muslims to turn away from the true faith. Therefore, they have no ceremonies or rituals, no fixed daily liturgy, no defined holy days, and no pilgrimage obligations. They perform their spiritual accounting with God on a daily basis. The main pillars of their faith are love of truth, loyalty to other Druze, abandoning all other religions, avoidance of evil and evildoers, accepting the unity of God, and submitting to the will of God. Druze are forbidden to eat pork, smoke, or drink alcohol. They believe in the transmigration of souls; at death, one's soul is reincarnated in time and space and reborn into a new life. Through successive reincarnations, the soul eventually unites with the Cosmic Mind, God's will.

In Israel, the Druze community has gathered at particular sites at times to discuss community affairs. Over time, these gatherings have taken on the aura of holidays. Most of the sites are tombs located in or near Druze villages in upper and western Galilee, Mount Carmel, and the Golan. They include: the Jewish prophet Jethro's Tomb (*Nebi Shu'eib*) overlooking the Kinneret where they gather every April 25; the Druze prophet Sabalan's tomb, above the village of Hurfeish, site of an annual festive pilgrimage on September 10; the Jewish prophet Elijah's tomb (*Nabi al-Khadr*) in Kafr Yasif, where they gather on January 25; the Druze prophet Al-Ya'afuri's tomb near Majdal Shams in the Golan; the Jewish prophet Zechariah's (*Nabi Zakarya*) tomb in Abu Sinan; and the tombs of Abu Ibrahim in Daliyat el-Carmel and Abu Abdallah in Isfiya.

CHRISTIANITY

Christians have lived in Israel since the beginnings of that faith. Christianity began as a reform movement within Judaism. The earliest church did not reach out to non-Jews. It was the apostle Paul who took the message of Christianity to non-Jews, in the 40s of the first century A.D. From that point on, Christianity became a movement open to all of humankind. The early church faced considerable persecution at the hands of Roman emperors, until the Roman emperor Constantine converted to Christianity in A.D. 312. After a family tragedy in 326, Constantine's mother, Helena, traveled to what was then Palestine. She is credited with building churches at the sites of Jesus' Nativity and Ascension, as well as with discovering Jesus' cross. Constantine constructed a great basilica, the Church of the Holy Sepulchre, at the site of her discovery.

Jerusalem fell to the advancing Muslim armies in A.D. 614. The Holy Sepulchre was destroyed and the cross carried off to Ctesiphon, in Persia. The church was rebuilt and destroyed several more times, until it was generally restored by the Crusaders in the twelfth century. Regaining the cross was the rallying cry for the Crusaders (1095–1291). The Crusading movement came at a time when relations between the eastern and western Christian churches, which had experienced a de facto schism, were improving. The movement rallied western Christendom to come to the defense of eastern Christians and the Christian holy places that were under Muslim control. By 1099, Jerusalem had fallen to the invading armies. In the general slaughter that followed, all Muslims and Jews there were put to death (despite promises to the contrary). Parts of the Holy Land remained under the control of the Latin states until the last kingdom fell to the Mamluks of Egypt at Acre in 1291.

Today, about 113,000 Arab Christians live in Israel, living mainly in urban areas such as Jerusalem, Nazareth, Haifa, and Shfar'Am. The Israeli government has granted formal recognition to the Greek Orthodox, the Armenian Orthodox, the Syrian Orthodox, the (Latin) Roman Catholic, the Maronite, the (Melkite) Greek Catholic, the Syrian Catholic, the Armenian Catholic, the Chaldean Catholic, and, since 1970, the Anglican (Episcopalian) churches. Many of these churches had earlier received formal recognition and limited autonomy from the Ottoman government under its *millet* system.

The Greek Catholic and Greek Orthodox churches are the largest denominations, mainly located in Jerusalem, followed by the Roman Catholic and Uniate churches. One major difference in the Christian churches in Israel concerns whether they accept the spiritual authority and leadership of the Roman Catholic pope. The Roman Catholic and Uniate churches accept Rome's leadership. The Orthodox churches (Greek, Russian, Romanian, Syrian, Armenian, Coptic, and Ethiopian) do not, although relations have improved in recent years.

The Greek Orthodox Church is the oldest denomination in Israel, granted its authority by the Council of Chalcedon in 451. At the time of the Crusader conquest of Jerusalem in 1099, the patriarchate was removed to Constantinople. The Greek Orthodox Patriarch reestablished residency in Jerusalem in 1845. The Armenian Orthodox Church also has deep roots in Jerusalem, with its first community established there during the fifth century. It is widely believed that an Armenian community has persisted in the city since then. The Armenian Quarter of the Old City of Jerusalem, centered around the St. James Monastery, has existed since at least the fourteenth century. The massacre of 1 to 2 million Armenians between the 1890s and 1920s in Turkey brought new immigrants to the Jerusalem quarter, fleeing for their lives.

The status of the Church of the Holy Sepulchre is a telling example of how the various Orthodox and Catholic churches interact in the Holy Land. Over the years, fighting has erupted over which denomination will control the church. In 1757, the Ottoman authorities drew up rights of possession for nine of the important shrines—an agreement known as the Status Quo. At that time, they also handed the keys to the church to a Muslim family whose job it has remained to open and lock the church each day. The fights over the building have been so protracted that it took until 1959 for the various denominations to agree to a plan to repair damage caused by a fire in 1808 and an earthquake in 1927. The Greek Orthodox Church has rights to more than half of the church. The Armenian Church owns one-third of Jerusalem's holy sites. The Roman Catholics administer only a fraction of Jerusalem's holy sites, including parts of the church. The Copts have a monastery upstairs at the back of the church, as well as a small chapel. The Ethiopians have the Chapel of St. Helena in the church, as well as a monastery located on the roof of the church. The Syrians also have a small chapel in the church. The Uniate churches have no rights to any of the holy places.

The Protestant communities in Israel date from the early nineteenth century, when Western countries began to establish diplomatic outposts in Jerusalem. Missionaries came to Israel to convert the Jews and Muslims there but succeeded only in attracting away Orthodox Christians. The Protestant churches channeled money into Palestine to establish schools, hospitals, and clinics that benefited local residents. European governments, in turn, used the presence of the religious communities as an excuse to involve themselves in the affairs of the Ottoman Empire, which controlled Palestine at this time. Religion and politics were intertwined.

Missionary activity continues to play a major role in the work of many Protestant churches around the world today. Proselytizing in Israel, however, is frowned upon, especially when it is targeted at Jews. For millennia, Jews were the targets of Christian missionary activity in Europe. Israel represents their haven from such pressures. Hence missionary activity is more tolerated when it targets the non-Jewish population. A 1977 Israeli law prohibits any person from offering or receiving material benefits as an inducement to convert. Some Christian groups, such as the Mormons, have made agreements with the Israeli government that they will refrain from trying to seek converts in return for being able to maintain a presence in the country. Missionaries who refuse to comply with the unspoken ban on proselytizing among Jews may find themselves unable to renew their visas.

A joint Anglican–Prussian Lutheran bishopric was established in Jerusalem in 1841. While the joint venture ended in 1886, the Anglicans maintained a presence in the city through the years. In 1976, they created the new Protestant Episcopal Church in Jerusalem and the Middle East and elected and consecrated its first Arab bishop in Jerusalem. The Anglicans are the largest Protestant community in Israel. The Lutheran community established its own independent presence in the Holy Land once the joint venture with the Anglicans ended in 1886. Arabs were attracted to the schools and other institutions run by the church and its affiliated societies. Besides the Arabic-speaking congregation, the Lutherans are represented in Israel by German, Danish, Swedish, and English-speaking congregations with their resident clergy.

The Baptists began their activities in Israel in 1911 when they formed their first congregation in Nazareth. Today, they have 10 churches or centers in Israel, in Acre, Cana, Haifa, Jaffa, Jerusalem, Kfar-Yassif, Nazareth, Petah Tikva, Rama, and Tu'ran. The majority of the congregants are Palestinian Arabs. The Presbyterian Church of Scotland first sent a delegation to Galilee in 1840. Today they maintain facilities in Tiberias and Jerusalem that mainly serve pilgrims and other visitors. There are also small communities of other Christian groups, including Pentecostalists, Quakers, Mormons, and Adventists. Recently, the Jehovah's Witnesses have increased their missionary activities in Israel.

The Christian holy sites in Israel include the Via Dolorosa—Jesus' route to the cross—the Holy Sepulchre, and the Room of the Last Supper in Jerusalem, the Basilica of the Annunciation in Nazareth, and the Mount of Beatitudes at Capernaum near the Kinneret. Other important sites are located in the West Bank, over which Israel holds control. These include the Mount of Temptation near Jericho and the Church of the Nativity and Manger Square in Bethlehem.

More recently, Israel's Christian population has grown because of a new factor: immigration of Jews from the former Soviet Union. Since 1989, more than 800,000 immigrants have arrived from the former Soviet Union. Almost 40 percent of these immigrants cannot be registered as Jews in Israel because they are not Jewish; they are the non-Jewish spouses and children of Jewish immigrants, who are allowed into the country to preserve family unity. They register as either Orthodox or as persons of no religion. These Russian Christians today outnumber the indigenous Arab Christians. They represent the fastest-growing Israeli religious community and account for 8 to 9 percent of the non-Arab population of the state. To accommodate them, new Russian Orthodox churches are being built.

BAHA'ISM

The Baha'i faith has its roots in a Muslim mystical movement founded in Persia (modern Iran) in 1844. A young man, known as the Bab, announced that soon the hidden *imam*, the "Messenger of God" awaited by all the peoples of the world, would arrive. He himself was charged by God with preparing humankind for the messenger's arrival. For his heresy, the Bab was arrested, beaten, imprisoned, and finally executed on July 9, 1850. Twenty thousand of his followers throughout Persia were also put to death. One of the Bab's earliest and strongest followers was Mirza Hoseyn 'Ali Nuri, who took the name Baha'u'llah. Baha'u'llah was born into a wealthy, noble Persian family, but he turned his back on his family's position. Once the persecution of the Bab's followers began, his family could not protect Baha'u'llah. He was arrested in 1852 and jailed in Tehran. While in jail, he became aware that he was the Messenger of God whose coming the Bab had foretold. Released in 1853, he was exiled to Baghdad, where he helped revive the Babi community there. In 1863, shortly before being exiled to Constantinople (Istanbul), he announced to the Babi community that he was the expected Messenger of God. The community accepted his claim and became known as Baha'is. The Ottoman government finally exiled and imprisoned Baha'u'llah in Acre, Palestine (now Israel), to avoid factional violence. Baha'u'llah died there in 1892.

From Acre, Baha'u'llah developed the teachings of the Baha'i faith. He wrote to the leaders of the world of the coming unification of humankind. He called for world leaders to leave behind their differences and work together for world peace. The Baha'i faith promotes the following principles: (1) the elimination of all forms of discrimination, (2) full equality for women, (3) the elimination of extremes of poverty and wealth, (4) universal education, (5) the establishment of a global commonwealth of nations, (6) the recognition of the unity of religious truth, (7) the responsibility of each person to search for the truth, and (8) the recognition that religion is in harmony with reason and scientific knowledge.

Baha'ism has gained a worldwide following, numbering 7 million followers. There are no clergy in the religion. The scriptures have been translated into 800 different languages. The religion's affairs are administered by elected councils at both local and national levels. Israel holds a special place for Baha'is because the properties associated with the religion's founder are located there, in and near Acre. To the south, Haifa is home to the Baha'i World Center, seat of the Universal House of Justice (the supreme elected body that administers affairs of the international community) and the Shrine of the Bab, which sit perched on Mount Carmel overlooking Haifa Bay.

RELIGION AND POLITICS

Religion exerts an influence on politics in Israel in very fundamental ways. Israel is by law a Jewish state. How a person's nationality is listed on identity cards depends on religious definitions of who is a Jew. Identity cards contain separate entries for religion and nationality, but for the Jewish citizens of the state, religion and nationality are one and the same: Jewish. There is no such thing as "Israeli" nationality. It is legally not possible to register a political party that includes in its platform the proposal that Israel should be a secular state or a binational state. Political parties that seek to invalidate the Jewish character of the state are illegal under the same amendment to the elections law that invalidates a party or candidate who challenges the democratic nature of Israel.

The government is involved in religious matters in a variety of ways. It allocates budgets to religious entities, provides funding for religious schools, and sets the legal frameworks for the religious councils. There was a Ministry for Religious Affairs until it was formally disbanded on March 7, 2004, and its functions divided among other ministries. Government facilities and the Israeli army keep kosher. The parliament passes laws that are religious in nature, such as those limiting the raising of pigs or regulating what public services will be available on Shabbat. No bill of rights or civil alternative to the religious institutional control over matters of personal status law (marriage, divorce, or inheritance) exists.

Religious political parties have exerted and continue to exert tremendous influence over governing because they are often sought as coalition partners in forming Israeli governments. The religious parties—Agudat Israel, Degel Hatorah, Shas, the National Religious Party (Mafdal), United Torah Judaism (the union of Agudat and Degel Hatorah), and Yahadut Hatorah—have played major roles in every government from the first to the most recent. From their 16 seats in the First Knesset to their current 22 in the Sixteenth Knesset, the religious parties have held large enough blocs of seats that they could help ensure the formation of Israeli governments. The price for doing that has been to retain the prominent place of Orthodox Jewish law in the land and generous state support of Orthodox religious institutions.

NOTES

1. Ephraim Tabory, "The Influence of Liberal Judaism on Israeli Religious Life," *Israel Studies* 5 (2000): 185.

2. Israel Finkelstein and Neil Asher Silberman, *The Bible Unearthed: Archaeology's New Vision of Ancient Israel and the Origin of Its Sacred Texts* (New York: Free Press, 2001), challenge the version of Jewish history found in the Jewish Scriptures, based on findings from archaeological research in Israel, Jordan, Egypt, Lebanon, and Syria. They demonstrate that there is no evidence for the Exodus, for Joshua's conquest of Canaan, or for the powerful united monarchy of David and Solomon.

3. United Nations, Committee on the Elimination of Discrimination Against Women, *Initial and Second Periodic Reports of State Parties: Israel*, 8 April 1997, 240–241. http://ods-dds-ny.un.org/doc/UNDOC/GEN/N97/096/08/IMG/N9709608.pdf

4. The Isma'ilis broke off after the death of the sixth Imam; they followed the eldest son Ismail as leader, while the majority of Shiites accepted Musa al-Kazim.

3
Literature, Media, and Cinema

LITERATURE

Literature provides a window into the heart and soul of another people. Israelis used literature to create that heart and soul, to constitute a new Israeli national identity and national culture. At various times, Israeli literature supported the state-building mission of the new government only to turn around and critique that same government and its policies as the political context shifted. Israeli literature must come to terms with its place: Is it an outgrowth of Jewish life in the Diaspora or its negation? Is it of the East or of the West? Will it serve the state or serve as the moral conscience of the nation?

Israelis are readers. Every spring, the Book Publishers' Association organizes Hebrew Book Week. They arrange book fairs in 30 cities and towns, and almost half the population visits these fairs. In May in Haifa, Bet Hagefen stages an Arab book fair as part of its Arab Culture Month celebrations. Israeli publishers produce 4,000 new titles and sell 13 million Hebrew books each year, which places Israel among the top 10 countries, worldwide, in per capita book sales.

Prose

Entire volumes have been devoted to the literature of Israel,[1] and even more books to works of particular authors within the genre of modern Israeli literature. It would be impossible to cover every Hebrew author in the space of this chapter. Instead, this section focuses on the major trends within Israeli literature, featuring a few key, well-known authors in each period.

Yosef Haim Brenner (1881–1921) and Shmuel Yosef Agnon (1888–1970) are considered to be the fathers of modern Hebrew prose. Brenner came to Israel in

1909 after having traveled from his native Ukraine to Warsaw and then London. Brenner was vehement about the need for an open-ended, secular Hebrew identity, and he sharply criticized rabbinic Judaism, which he felt had stifled Jewish creativity. In his writing, he struggled with his desire to see Zionism realized and his pessimism that the enterprise would fail. He wrote using realistic and authentic detail and integrated medieval and rabbinical Hebrew to create new idioms. Brenner saw life as a struggle for existence, filled with pain and hardship. Through his writing, he turned the center of Hebrew prose from the Diaspora to Palestine. He was killed in May 1921 in rioting in Jaffa.

Agnon, the other founding father, established himself as an international writer. In 1966, he received the Nobel Prize in literature, the first and only one ever granted to an Israeli writer. He immigrated to Palestine in 1880 but returned to live in Germany between 1913 and 1924, when his home was destroyed by fire. He returned to Palestine and lived the rest of his life there. He began to publish at age 15. Agnon has been called one of the greatest storytellers of our time. His writing is rich in capturing the lives and traditions of a lost time. But he did not simply record those lives. He delved into the important philosophical and ethical issues of his times, fusing experimentalism, surrealism, irony, and religious storytelling in his works. He published 24 volumes of novels, novellas, and short stories.

Brenner and Agnon were followed by the generation *in* the land (*dor ba-aretz*), writers who had been born or educated in Israel and whose complete body of works was conceived while they lived in Palestine/Israel.[2] Prominent names here are S. Yizhar (1916–), Moshe Shamir (1921–), Hanoch Bartov (1926–), and Benjamin Tammuz (1919–1989). This generation put in place a tradition of social realism in Hebrew literature, a tradition that would play an important role from the 1940s through the 1970s. Their basic problem was how to write realistic fiction in times that were so fantastic.[3] This generation sought to merge with local culture, and they produced the image of the native-born Israeli (the sabra) that would come to dominate Israel's creative imagination for years to come.

Yizhar was born in Rehovot to a family of writers. He fought in the 1948 war and then served in the Israeli parliament with the Labor Party until 1967. He writes about Israel just before and after the creation of the state, primarily focusing on what was involved in settling the land. A repeated theme in his work is the conflict that arises when the individual confronts a society with which he does not agree and yet finds himself going along with the collective against his own better moral judgment. His writing is also characterized by detailed descriptions of the physical landscape, often framed as interior monologues. In these descriptions, he rewrites the land of Israel into the collective consciousness, thus fulfilling one of the goals of Zionism—to return Jews to the land.

Shamir grew up in Tel Aviv, was active in Hashomer Hatzair, and lived on a kibbutz for six years. He provided the Ur-sabra in his character, Uri, in the novel *He Walked through the Fields* (1947). Uri was the perfect new national man. His dysfunctional family has no effect on him, he puts his country before his true love, and he is killed trying to save his comrades. Uri and others in his image have continued to cast their shadow over all of Israeli creative life. Shamir's works draw on his own biography. They follow one of two plot patterns: an immigrant family settling the land or preparing the young generation to conquer the land.[4] Shamir eventually turned from these themes to historical writing, turning to the Bible to find his plots. Shamir broke with the Israeli left after 1967 and joined the right-wing Greater Israel movement, helping to found the Tehiya Party (which advocates transferring the Palestinians out of Israel).

Bartov's works concern people coming to terms with new identities—the immigrant and the Israeli, both of whom had to decide who they were. For Bartov, the central literary question is, What would Israeli identity be? In *The Dissembler* (1975), one of his characters is a Holocaust survivor who is pretending to be a sabra but who also at times disguises himself as a German and a Frenchman. He is eventually killed in his sabra role in one of Israel's wars. Tammuz walked his own path in his writing, as do the characters in his novels. In his writing, Tammuz brought forth well-developed individuals, whose paths through life were not necessarily true to the prevalent Israeli mythologies. In his trilogy, *The Life of Elyakum* (1965), *Castle in Spain* (1966), and *Hallucinations* (1969), his main character starts as a naive, exploited innocent, who becomes a bit wiser and ends a raving lunatic. Tammuz's novel *Minotaur* (1980) contains a character who feels no connection to Israel and who falls in love with a foreign woman he never met—the two ultimate betrayals.[5]

The next generation of writers have been called the generation *of* the land (*dor ha'medina*). It includes three Israeli writers who have made names for themselves beyond Israel's borders: A. B. Yehoshua (1936–), Amos Oz (1939–), and Yaacov Shabtai (1934–1981). It is this generation that begins to examine, deconstruct, and critique the Hebrew nation and culture as constructed by previous generations. These authors began to explore new literary styles—such as psychological realism, symbolism, and allegory—and to move their focus from the collective to the individual. They took as their model the modernist writer, a "critical-oppositional intellectual voice."[6] Yehoshua, considered by some to be the Israeli Faulkner, produces richly textured works that peel off the layers to expose the inner animal instincts that threaten to destroy the civilized exterior. In *Mr. Mani* (1990), he explores the history of five generations of a family, through a series of conversations with only one speaker present, until he reveals the dark secret that spans every generation. In *A Journey to the End of the Millennium: A Novel of the Middle Ages* (1997), he traces the journey of a Sephardic merchant, married to two women, into the heart of Europe in order to convince his nephew's wife that his marriages are legal and permissible. In the process, Yehoshua explores the differences between the Ashkenazi and Sephardi traditions, religion, law, and human relationships.

Amos Oz in his fiction and nonfiction has unflinchingly explored the modern landscape of Israel and its people. His novels are intense examinations of human nature, not to denigrate it or glorify it, but rather to see it as it is. *The Same Sea*

(2002) combines prose and poetry in its exploration of the complexities of human relationships after a loved one has died. A widowed accountant finds himself lusting after his son's girlfriend (who moved in), who is sleeping with the son's best friend, while the son himself remains in self-imposed exile, in grief over the loss of his mother. As the characters try to regain control over their lives, one can read into it Oz's own desire for a different future for his country.

Shabtai's writing introduced the vernacular into the Hebrew novel. His major work, *Past Continuous* (1977), hailed as one of the high points of modern Hebrew prose, consists of a spiraling narrative that follows three friends, Goldman, Israel, and Caesar, as they wander through their life in Tel Aviv. One name leads to another story, which leads to another name, as Shabtai weaves a grand panorama of life, in the tradition of Joyce.

Other new voices have arisen in Hebrew literature. Aharon Appelfeld (1932–) reintroduced into Hebrew literature the figure of the Old Jew, by incorporating into his fiction refugees, the elderly, women, children, and people who were persecuted, broken, and terrified.[7] Appelfeld is one of the foremost Israeli writers tackling the subject matter of the Holocaust, in works such as *For Every Sin* (1989) and *The Iron Tracks* (1991). David Grossman (1954–) is noted for his innovative prose technique and his unflinching exploration of social injustice. He has become known for both his novels, *Smile of the Lamb* (1983), *See Under: Love* (1986), *The Book of Intimate Grammar* (1991), and *Be My Knife* (1998), and his nonfiction, *The Yellow Wind* (1987) and *Sleeping on a Wire* (1992); the last two explore Palestinian life in the territories and in Israel, respectively. David Shahar (1926–1977) is best known for his seven-volume series *The Palace of Shattered Vessels* (1969–1994), which brings to mind Marcel Proust's *Remembrance of Things Past*. Through the shifting memories of the narrator, Shahar brings to life Jerusalem in the 1930s. Yoram Kaniuk (1930–) has produced masterful works such as *Confessions of a Good Arab* (1983), which explores where and how Israeli Palestinians could fit into Israeli society, and *Adam Resurrected* (1969), one of the most powerful works of Holocaust fiction ever written.

Mizrahi writers in Israel had to decide in which language they would write—Arabic, their mother tongue, or the new Hebrew. Two Iraqi Jewish writers, Yitzhak Bar Moshe (1927–) and Samir Naqqash (1936–), continue to write in Arabic only. Three other Iraqi Jewish writers, Sami Michael (1926–), Shimon Ballas (1930–) and Eli Amir (1937–), began writing in Arabic in Israel but shifted their work to Hebrew in the early 1960s. The fiction of all three explores the lives and problems of Mizrahi immigrants in Israel, among other themes. The first work that Ballas published in Hebrew was *The Transit Camp* (1964). His more recent novel *He Is Different* (1991) explores literary, political, and intellectual life in Iraq through three different Jewish characters whose lives go different directions. Michael explores relationships between Jews and Arabs (Muslims and Christians), nationalists and communists, and men and women in novels set in both Israel and Iraq. In *Trumpet in the Wadi* (1987), set in Haifa prior to 1982, Michael tells the story of impossible love (Huda the Arab and Alex the Jew) and the importance of family.

In *Scapegoat* (1984), Amir presented a semi-autobiographical novel about a young Iraqi boy integrating into a transit camp after he immigrates to Israel. An even younger generation of Mizrahi writers, born in Israel, is now enjoying popularity with the Israeli public. Ronit Matalon (1959–) and Dorit Rabinyan (1972–) both write novels that explore Jewish life in other lands. Matalon's *The One Facing Us* (1995) explores life over several generations in an Egyptian Jewish family, from central Africa to Israel. Her second book, *Bliss: A Novel* (2000), about two female friends, is set in Paris and Tel Aviv. Rabinyan's *Persian Brides* (1995) and *Our Weddings* (also published as *Strand of a Thousand Pearls;* 1999) look at life within the Persian Jewish community.

Women's voices were scarce in the early years of Israeli literature. Amalia Kahana-Carmon, born on Kibbutz Ein Harod, served as a wireless operator in the Negev during the 1948 war. She published her first collection of stories, *Under One Roof,* in 1966. Her works, which set the pattern for the women writers who would follow her, explore the tensions between the daily ordinary lives her characters lead and the life they dream about. In her novels, characters experience some sort of self-awakening (that results from a love encounter, a creative activity, or some other mystical experience) that allows them to recapture the dreamed-of world and regain self-expression and meaning in their lives. Shulamit Hareven (1930–) immigrated to Palestine in 1940 from Warsaw Poland. She served in the Haganah underground and was a medic during the 1948 war. Many of her novels are set in the desert as she explores different facets of the Hebrew exodus from Egypt in *The Miracle Hater* (1983), *Prophet* (1989), and *After Childhood* (1994) (collected together in one volume *Thirst* [1996]). She recently published a collection of essays, *The Vocabulary of Peace* (1996). Ruth Almog (1936–), an explicitly feminist writer, focused on autobiography in her early stories as she describes life in a settlement. In her later work, she turned to explore the lives of refugees and other traumatized people. *All This Overflowing Bliss* (2003) is a collection of stories that span her career. Shulamit Lapid (1934–), another writer with strong progressive values, is known for her detective fiction as well as her more serious works, such as *Chez Babou* (1998), which explores the lives of foreign workers in Israel. In her earlier *Gai Oni* (1982), Lapid provides a strong feminist fable about life in the settlement that would become Rosh Pina. Orly Castel-Bloom (1960–), Efrat Stieglitz (1961–), and Leah Aini (1962) represent the newest trends in Israeli narrative—*Inniut* and *Kooliut* (or being in and cool)—as Israeli literature comes to resemble the writings of the Post-Generation X in the United States.[8]

The best-known works by Israeli Palestinians consist of three novels, *The Secret Life of Saeed, the Pessoptimist* (1982) by Emile Habibi (1922–1998), *In a Different Light* (1969) by Atallah Mansour (1934–), and *Arabesques: A Novel* (1986) by Anton Shammas (1950–), and an autobiography, *To Be an Arab in Israel* (1975), by Fouzi el-Asmar (1937–). As a young man of 17, Mansour had spent a year living on a kibbutz, and Mansour's novel was written to take revenge on this Israeli institution. His book had the opposite effect, garnering praise from Israeli

Jewish critics.[9] Habiby's novel is the fantastic tale of Saeed, a Palestinian who has remained in Israel and is forced into becoming an informer for the state. A tragic-comic figure, Saeed moves from one absurd episode to another, trying to find a way out. Shammas's work weaves together the tales of two narrators, one story of the village that was, one story of the world that is. The two tales interweave to create an arabesque, a pattern that turns back upon itself. The book created an uproar in Israel when it was published because of Shammas's flawless use in it of Hebrew and Hebrew literary metaphors. He was seen as crossing a boundary line, violating a cultural norm that Hebrew was reserved for Israeli Jewish writers only. El-Asmar's book is the story of his personal ordeals dealing with Israeli authorities and the military government, including his 15 months under administrative detention.

Detective fiction (*sipur habalash*) had become very popular in Israel by the 1980s. The works are quite sophisticated mysteries and well written. Most write only in Hebrew, but a few writers have managed to cross over into English translations. One of the latter, Batya Gur (1947–) has written a superb series of books featuring Michael Ohayon, a Mizrahi policeman. Her titles include *The Saturday Morning Murder: A Psychoanalytic Case* (1988) and *Murder Duet: A Musical Case* (2000). Other writers include Shulamit Lapid, *Local Paper* (1989) and *Bait* (1991); Ora Shem-Or, *Murder in the Singles Club* (1991) and *Murder on Sheinkin Street* (1992); Yoram Kaniuk, *Tigerhill* (1995); and Ruth Almog and Esther Ettinger, *A Perfect Lover* (1995); all of these works are only available in Hebrew. The science-fiction genre is almost completely limited to books for children, with no serious adult science-fiction produced.

Poetry

For both Jewish and Palestinian Israelis, poetry has been an integral part of their cultural heritage and literary tradition from the beginnings of their existence as a people. Poetry holds a special place in the traditions of both peoples. Poetry has always been written in Hebrew, and the 2,000 years of exile did not stop production of Hebrew poetic works. For Palestinians, as Arabs, poetry has been the one art form through which "the Arab genius found its fullest expression."[10] Israelis buy more poetry volumes per capita annually than any other nation in the world. There are 12 different Israeli periodicals that publish poetry, including *Helicon*, *Apiryon*, and *Carmel*.

The two major poets who emerge from that generation of Jewish writers who moved from the Enlightenment to Zionism were Haim Nachman Bialik (1873–1934) and Saul Tchernichovsky (1875–1943), both of whom immigrated to Palestine. Bialik is Israel's national poet. Born in Russia, he studied at a yeshiva (an Orthodox religious school) but was pulled away from that life by the lure of the Enlightenment. He eventually founded a publishing house, Dvir, in Berlin in 1921, moving it to Tel Aviv in 1924. His poems reflect his generation's struggle— how to combine Zionism with Jewish tradition. Bialik produced poems that sought to stir European Jews to create a new destiny, nature poems, love poems, and more personal poems dealing with the conflicts of modern life. He sought in his poetry to combine more biblical Hebrew idioms with the emerging spoken Hebrew of Palestine. His poetry remains widely read and taught.

Tchernichovsky also grew up in Russia in a religious home, but one that was open to more modern ideas. He moved to Israel in 1931. His works include lyric poetry, epics, ballads, and allegories. He wrote about life in the places he knew best—the Crimea, Germany, and Palestine—and his poems dealt with love and beauty, personal pride, and dignity.

The next generation, the émigré poets, were born in the Diaspora, where they had absorbed the culture and ethos of their countries of birth. Transplanted to Palestine, they were the transition generation that had to come to terms with life in the new country. Each approached this transition in a different way. Abraham Shlonsky (1900–1973) embodied this spirit of transition in his work. Shlonsky turned away from Bialik's style of poetry to create new verse traditions. His poems were flooded with images of pioneering—clearing swamps, building roads, putting up new settlements—and with new linguistic inventions. His later poetry, written after witnessing the horrors of the Holocaust in postwar Europe and the alienation of the modern city, was filled with despair, fear, grief, and terror,

Haim Nachman Bialik, the father of Israeli poetry. Photo by Zoltan Kluger. Courtesy of the Government Press Office, State of Israel.

expressed in sharp images. He influenced a whole generation of young writers. Natan Alterman (1910–1970) became known as the poet of the Yishuv. In his political poetry, he clearly and bluntly took on the major issues facing first the Yishuv and later the new state. Some of his poetry, censured by the British, became lyrics for songs about the struggle for a state. In his later years, Alterman took up the cause of the Greater Israel movement. There was another side to his poetry—more lyrical and filled with images. It was this side of his poetry that helped to further advance modern Hebrew verse, providing as it did rich imagery and variations in verse structures. One theme in this poetry was the struggle between a more pristine natural world and the mechanized modern world, a theme that even came through in his love poetry.

Uri Zvi Greenberg (1896–1981), son of a distinguished Hasidic family, received a traditional religious education in his hometown of Lvov (western Ukraine). He was radicalized when he witnessed the 1918 pogroms there. He moved to Palestine in 1924. His early poetry in Hebrew was influenced by Walt Whitman. After the 1929 riots in Palestine, however, his poetry became more politicized as he moved to the right and joined the Irgun. He was in Poland as its representative at the start of World War II but managed to escape; his family died in the Holocaust. Greenberg embraced a Jewish identity that stressed being different and distant from all other peoples. He was messianic in his belief that Zionism would bring about the redemption of the Jewish people, and he used his poetry to express that vision.

After statehood, in the mid-1950s, a new generation of poets emerged, foremost among whom were Yehuda Amichai (1924–2000), Natan Zach (1930–), and David Avidan (1934–1995). Amichai and Zach both came to Palestine as children; Zach was native born. This was a generation that was more comfortable with Hebrew as their mother tongue. As a group, they shifted the main poetic influences on Hebrew poetry from eastern Europe to England and the United States. They wrote in understatements, drawing their poetic themes from ordinary parts of everyday life, using colloquial speech patterns.

Amichai was the major figure within this movement and is one of Israel's best-known modern poets. Born in Germany, he was raised speaking Hebrew and German. What set Amichai apart was his use of language; he was a master of wordplay. He coined new words, brought prose phrases into poetry, and incorporated both classical Hebrew and modern slang in his works. Amichai brought a unique blend of the individual and the social to his poetry. Although recognizing himself as part of the collective, he nevertheless maintained his right to view that collective through his own individual set of lenses. His production was legendary—more than 15 volumes in Hebrew, and as many translated into English.

Zach was another leader of the poetic revolution. His style is ironic and antiromantic; he avoids sentimental and symbolic expression in favor of a more open, experimental, and explicit language. Raw emotion, conveyed in as few words as possible, characterizes his works. Avidan introduced avant-garde poetry into the Hebrew canon. In 1968, he published *Personal Report on a LSD Trip*, followed by

My *Electronic Psychiatrist* in 1974. Several of his volumes have been translated into Arabic.

The generation of poets writing in Israel now live in a different world than the poets who preceded them. They do not have to struggle to create a space for poetry in the Hebrew language—that space has already been established for them, which has left them free to play with different poetic forms and structures, language, tone, and images. As a relatively new language, Hebrew lacks the linguistic richness of other tongues. One word in Hebrew may mean different things depending on its context and use. The modern generation of poets can play with that ambiguity in shaping their verse. Two exemplars here include Aharon Shabtai (1939–) and Meir Wieselthier (1941–). Shabtai, one of Israel's most powerful and provocative writers, has written more than 15 volumes of poetry. Wieselthier, known for his strong political poetry, is affiliated with the Tel Aviv school of poetry.

Modern Israel has had its great women poets as well. The earliest, known simply as Rahel (1890–1931; born Rahel Bluwstein) wrote beautiful, lyrical poetry that continues to capture the hearts of current readers. Rahel led a hard life as a kibbutz pioneer in Israel. She contracted tuberculosis while in Russia during the late 1910s. While her poetry captures the beauty of the countryside, it also focuses on her personal struggles, at times reflecting a sad, wistful tone. Her grave beside Lake Kinneret is a popular pilgrimage site for tourists and Israelis alike. Lea Goldberg (1911–1970) came to Palestine in 1935, having already earned a doctoral degree in Europe. Her poems are reflections of western European traditions—ordered rhyming and expressionism. She wrote about wanting love and light as well as about the wounds of love.

Dalia Ravikovitch (1936–) and Yona Wallach (1944–1985) were both native-born poets of the generation after statehood. Each lost her father at a young age. Ravikovitch was sent to be raised on a kibbutz, while Wallach grew up in the community that her father helped found. Ravikovitch's early poems are romantic fantasies, filled with kings, magic, witchcraft, and fairy tales. Her later work is marked by satire and sarcasm with free-flowing language that becomes almost colloquial. Wallach was active in the "Tel Aviv poets" circle that emerged around two literary journals in the 1960s. Her work combines diverse elements to create a nervous energy in her poems, with their fast pace and provocative sexuality. Rock and roll, Jungian psychology, and street slang are all rolled together in her lines. The work of a new generation of women poets has been collected and translated into English by Miriyam Glazer.[11]

Mizrahi poets prior to immigrating to Israel took a very active part in the cultural life of their countries of origin, writing in Arabic and achieving prominent positions among the literati of the Arab world. Immigration to Israel was a devastating experience for many of these writers as they experienced discrimination and a devaluation of their cultural heritage and their own contributions to that heritage. Their voice in Israel was not really awakened until the Mizrahi revolution of the 1970s, when younger Mizrahi Israeli poets began to publish. One of the first of these new voices was Erez Biton (1942–), who was born in Algeria and arrived in Israel with his family in 1948. At the age of 10, Biton lost his sight and left hand when a grenade he found in fields near his home exploded. He worked as a social worker and psychologist in development towns for seven years. He is one of the major figures in the Mizrahi consciousness movement in Israel that recognizes the similarities between treatment of Mizrahim and Palestinians by Israeli elites. He began publishing poetry in the late 1970s and has brought out three volumes in Hebrew. He currently edits the literary journal *Apirion*. In his poem "Fallen Soldier in the Middle East: A Father (Jewish or Arab) Mourning the Death of His Son," the narrator wishes his son were like an olive tree ripe with age or a palm tree rooted in place, ending with the simple wish that he be there.

Ronny Someck (1951–), born in Iraq, is another important early voice. He has worked with street gangs as a counselor and teaches literature and writing. He started publishing his poetry in 1968, with his first volume released in 1976. He has published eight volumes in Hebrew and one in English; his poems have been translated into 22 different languages. In his poems, he brings to life the bustling Mizrahi neighborhoods of south Tel Aviv, the odors and sounds. His poetry is distinguished by staccato rhythms, quick cuts, and unsettling transitions. Biton and Someck have been joined by an even younger generation of Mizrahi poets who are transforming the Israeli canon: Sami Shalom Chetrit and the female poets Bracha Serri, Tikva Levy, and Shelley Elkayam.

Palestinian poets have faced major difficulties in making their voices heard within Israel. The works of only a few major Israeli Palestinian poets, such as Mahmoud Darwish and Samih al Qasim, have been translated into Hebrew. Palestinian writers did not just face difficulties finding an audience for their work. Many of them were imprisoned, lost their jobs, or were driven into exile abroad because of what they were writing. However, the Israeli government could not silence their voices, and a new generation of poets is now able to write in a freer atmosphere.

Palestinian poets write about the loss of Palestine, about their love for Palestine, about the experience of being uprooted and homeless, and about their resistance to the current state of affairs. Poets writing in the period immediately after the 1948 war wrote out of desolation, expressing feelings of hopelessness and inscribing memories of their lost homeland. Poets born after 1948, who grew up in Israel, found themselves writing in restricted circumstances. Intellectual leaders were gone, their movements were restricted by the military government, and they were cut off from the rest of the Arab world. Nurtured on smuggled books and oral recitations, they re-created a new and vibrant culture of poetry within Israel.

The best-known Israeli Palestinian poet is Mahmud Darwish (1941–), born in al-Birweh, a village destroyed in 1948. At the age of seven, Darwish fled with his family to Lebanon after witnessing massacres in his village. After living there a year, his family infiltrated back to Israel and settled in another village. He grew up an "internal" refugee in Israel, which had a profound effect on his life. He started writing poetry while in elementary school. After completing high school, he moved to Haifa to work as a journalist, and there he joined the Communist Party and became active in politics. Jailed and placed under house arrest, he left for the Soviet Union in 1971, never to return to Israel.[12] He published his first collection in 1960 (*Wingless Birds*), but it was his 1964 volume *Olive Trees* that established his reputation as "poet of the Palestinian resistance." Two well-known Darwish poems are "Identity Card" (1964) and "State of Siege" (2002). In 2000, an uproar erupted when Education Minister Yossi Sarid added Darwish's poetry to the Israeli public school curriculum.

Another well-known Israeli Palestinian poet is Samih al-Qasim (1939–), a Druze who grew up in Ramah and Nazareth in the Galilee. Al-Qasim lost his job as a school teacher and was confined to prison or placed under house arrest because of his public criticism of the Israeli government's policies of discrimination against its Palestinian citizens. His poetry has been censored by Israeli authorities. In 2001, he was prevented by order of the Israeli government from traveling to Lebanon to meet with the Lebanese president. From 1986 to 1988, he and Mahmoud Darwish published their "letters between the two halves of an orange." In 1995, al-Qasim translated a selection of the poetry of Ronny Someck, an Iraqi Jewish poet, into Arabic in the volume *Jasmine*. Al-Qasim has published numerous volumes of poetry.

Taha Muhammad Ali (1931–), began his poetry career late in life (1983). He is self-taught, having made his living from running a souvenir store in Nazareth. Like Darwish, he too is an internal refugee, born in Saffuriya (now Tsippori). His poetry draws on his childhood in the village and on everyday experience, weaving classical and colloquial Arabic together. He has published three collections in Arabic and one in English. His poem *Fooling the Killers* (1988) is a good example of his work.

Nidaa Khoury (1959–) was born in the Galilee village of Fassouta. She has published seven volumes of poetry in Arabic, one of which, *The Barefoot River* (1990), was also published in Hebrew. Other Israeli Palestinian poets include Tawfiq Zayyad (1932–), Salim Jubran (1941–), Nazih Khayr (1946–), Yusuf Hamdan (1942–), Ahmad Husayn (1939–), Rashid Husayn (1936–1977), Fouzi El-Asmar (1937–), and Na'im Araidi (1950–).

Drama

Unlike drama's development in other world cultures, Hebrew culture has no clear tradition upon which it could build. Ancient Israel never developed a theatrical tradition; any plays that were written owed a great deal to Greek drama. "Just as music and the visual arts were, for various reasons, not within their orbit, neither was the drama or theatre, until the foundation of Israel in 1948."[13] During the Renaissance, actors began to develop one-act plays based on biblical stories. There could be no full-scale theatrical productions, however, because women were not allowed on stage, and men could not substitute for them because Jewish law forbids men wearing women's garments.

After the Renaissance, Jewish theatrical traditions began to develop, but they always reflected the larger cultural context within which the Jewish community lived. The sixteenth-century work of Leone di Somi and the eighteenth-century works of Moshe Haim Luzzato both have Italian overtones. One of the better-known Jewish plays, *The Dybbuk* (1920; by S. Ansky [Shloyme-Zanvl Rappoport]) was drawn from Hasidic folklore. Yiddish theater developed in eastern Europe in the 1860s and spread from there to every country that had received Jewish immigrants. As a theatrical tradition, it represented an offshoot of European traditions, especially the influences of Polish and German expressionism.[14] Yiddish theater thrived until after World War II. Between the Nazi destruction of eastern European Jewry and the dying out of Yiddish as a living language, Yiddish theaters began to shut down, although a few have managed to survive into the twenty-first century.

Modern Israeli culture developed as the antithesis of Jewish culture as it existed in the Diaspora. The new pioneers wanted nothing to do with the Yiddish culture and instead worked to reinvigorate Hebrew as a modern language and to develop a Hebrew literary tradition. They needed Hebrew drama, which meant they needed Hebrew playwrights. The birth of the new nation would require the birth of a new literary tradition.

Plays and Playwrights

Once the new state existed, drama was brought into the state-building efforts. The theater was to be used to educate the masses of new immigrants, to make them proper Zionists. Drama was not just an art form but an instrument by which to build a society.[15] To fulfill this function, the theater turned to realism. Like other forms of literature, drama presented the mythological Israeli sabra hero as its focus. Yigal Mossinsohn (1917–1993) closely adhered to this mythology in his play *In the Wastes of the Negev* (1949), a collection of romantic clichés, stereotypes, and echoes of the biblical story of Isaac's sacrifice. Natan Shaham's (1925–) *They Will Arrive Tomorrow* (1950) traces the dilemma of an Israeli platoon that has captured a landmined hill but lost the map showing where the landmines are. The play focuses on the conflict between the two commanding officers, Jonah and Avi. Shaham in this play has begun to evaluate and question the sabra hero myth. Yoram Matmor (1925–) went even further and tried to deconstruct the myth in his work *An Ordinary Play* (1956). It is a play within a play—the actors are rehearsing a play about Israeli youth after the 1948 war. The main character, Danny Keresh, is an antihero. He never appears onstage, represented only by a plank. Matmor attacked the generation of the Palmach, the elite force of the prestate army—leading to a political furor over his play.

After 1967, Israeli drama moved from uncritically supporting the state and Zionism to a theater of critique and protest. A close examination of Zionism was to preoccupy political drama for three decades.[16] Israeli dramatists turned to the genre of satire, particularly cabaret (influenced by German playwright Bertolt Brecht). Israeli cabaret walked a fine line between critiquing certain aspects of

Israeli society (the army, ultra-Orthodoxy, and the notion of the social good) and remaining within the national, communal fold. Two major playwrights of this genre were Hanoch Levin (1943–1999) and Yehoshua Sobol (1939–).

Levin achieved infamy for his work *The Queen of the Bathtub* (1970). In it he attacks the Israeli self-congratulation after the 1967 war. He pokes fun at yuppies, calling them the people of "everything's okay," he pokes fun at the sabra myth, and he presents a scene in which two Israeli matrons torment an Arab waiter, excusing their racism because one is the mother of a soldier and the other a daughter of Holocaust survivors. Levin went on to write more than 50 plays before he died of cancer in 1999. Yehoshua Sobol's play *Joker* (1975) follows five reservists in a bunker during the 1973 war. The five men, each representing a different segment of Israeli society, reveal in their discussion the weariness with war, its banality, and their lack of heroism and moral failure when they send an inexperienced soldier to set up an ambush. Sobol has written more than 20 plays. One of his most controversial has been *Jerusalem Syndrome* (1987), in which the world comes to an end when a soldier executes a civilian. The first performance was interrupted by shouts and threats against the actors. Sobol resigned from the production in the aftermath of the controversy over its staging. Sobol left Israel two years later to resettle in London. Hillel Mittelpunkt (1949–), another writer in this genre, filled his cabarets with outcasts, criminals, madmen, the grotesque, and the absurd.

The work of Yitzhak Laor (1948–) represents the anti-occupation trend in Israeli drama. Laor won the Prime Minister's Prize for literature in 1990 but did not actually receive it because Prime Minister Shamir refused to sign the certificate. Laor's *Ephraim Returns to the Army* (1985) tells the story of a military governor who is investigating the killing of a Palestinian by an Israeli soldier. In the play, Laor raises the ethical question of how an oppressed people have come to be the oppressors. Other prominent Israeli playwrights include Nissim Aloni (1926–1998), Joseph Mundy (1935–1994), Shmuel Hasfari (1954–), and Motti Lerner (1949–). There are very few women Israeli playwrights, reflecting the general bias against women in the theater. Miriam Kainy (1942–) produced the first authentic Arab hero in Israeli drama in her work *The Return* (1973, 1981), which explores a friendship between the Israeli Palestinian Riyyad and Ruben, whose family lived in what had been Riyyad's family's house. She also wrote the monologue *Like a Bullet in the Head* (1983), which explores the crisis an Israeli academic faces when his wife leaves him for one of his Arab students. Lea Goldberg (1911–1970) dealt with the Holocaust in *The Lady of the Manor* (1955).

Theater Companies

In 1979, theatergoers in Israel represented 20 percent of the population (roughly eight times higher in Israel than in the United States at this time).[17] Theater in Israel is not confined to the major cities. There is a significant tradition of bringing theater to the people. The core of Israel's theatrical world is composed of the Habimah Theater, the Cameri Theater, and the Haifa Municipal

Theater. The largest and oldest of these is Habimah, Israel's official national theater. Founded in Russia in 1917, Habimah ("the Stage") was the first Hebrew-
language theatrical company. In 1926, after splitting during a U.S. tour, half the
troupe decided to settle in Palestine and continue performing there. The initial
founders of Habimah had the company perform plays with Jewish themes in order
to give the company an identity as a national Hebrew theater. Today Habimah is
known for performing both classic and contemporary dramatic works in transla-
tion, as well as some original Hebrew plays.

The Cameri Theater was founded in 1944 by Yosef Milo and other actors who
had left Habimah. The members of the Cameri wanted a revolution in Hebrew
theater. They favored newer acting techniques, more use of vernacular Hebrew,
slang, and ordinary speech, and promoting original Hebrew plays. The Cameri
presented the first performance of Moshe Shamir's play *He Walked in the Fields* to
critical acclaim. It has established a reputation as one of the more progressive of
Israel's theaters.

Haifa opened Israel's first municipal theater in 1961, with Yosef Milo as director. The Haifa theater affiliated itself both to the Histadrut to give performances
for workers and to the Department of Education in order to work in the schools.
More recently, the Haifa Municipal Theater has made the decision to discover
new works and to encourage its own native talent—Jewish Israeli and Palestinian
Israeli. Haifa presents a high percentage of original plays, which are often politically provocative.

In addition to these three, Israel boasts a wealth of other theatrical companies.
Among these are the Khan Theater in Jerusalem, the Jerusalem Municipal Theater, the Kibbutz Theater, the Beersheva Municipal Theater, Beit Leissin, the
Gesher Theater, Almydan Arabic Theater (Nazareth), Diwan El Lajun Theater
(Umm el-Fahm), and Bet Hagefen's Arab Theater (Haifa). The Gesher troupe
performs in both Hebrew and Russian. Theater is subsidized by the government
and local municipalities—up to 60 percent of operating costs. Such funding has
come with a price. For many years, theater companies were subject to censorship
of their productions by the Film and Theater Censorship Board, although no censorship of plays has occurred for years.

Two of the more unusual theater companies in Israel are based in the mixed
cities of Jaffa and Acre. The Acre Theater Center began in 1985, and the
Hebrew-Arabic Theater of Jaffa started in 1991. Both companies have both
Israeli Jewish and Israeli Palestinian actors. Each also works with material from
real life, incorporating the fantasy of the theater with reality such that audiences
often forget which is which. The Acre troupe, for example, put together a production, *Diwan* (Arabic for "sitting together"), in which the audience was actually taken from the theater into the homes of Israeli Palestinians living in Acre's
Old City. The Jaffa company developed an epic using transcripts from court martial cases of Israeli soldiers for brutality during the first intifada. With renewed
political tensions in the country between Israeli Jews and all Palestinians, both

theater companies are struggling to survive and to keep alive their message that dialogue is possible.

Theater Festivals

Two major theater festivals are held in Israel each year, the Israel Festival (May–June), held in Jerusalem, and the Fringe Theater Festival, held in Acre during the eight-day Sukkoth holiday in the fall. The Israel Festival presents theatrical, dance, and musical productions, usually focused on existing works (rather than new ones) and involving performances by well-known international artists. Forty to 50 different events are staged at different historical sites in Jerusalem during the three weeks of the festival, with the main venue being the Jerusalem Center for the Performing Arts.

The Fringe Theater Festival in Acre began in 1980, modeled after Edinburgh's famous Fringe Festival. It was the first major Israeli festival to be set in a small town rather than a major population center. The festival is scheduled every year to coincide with the Sukkoth holiday. Acre's seaport and scenic walled Old City, with its Crusader-period underground halls and vaults, have provided the settings for a new generation of Israeli theater production. Acre has become a staging area where new productions are tested before going on to play in larger cities or in international venues. Up to 30 productions take place every year during the eight days of the festival, with an audience of 200,000 visitors. The Acre festival serves as a proving ground for aspiring playwrights, producers, and actors.

In addition to these festivals, there is an Arab Monodrama Festival that stages six to eight single-actor plays at Beit Hagefen (Haifa), a four-day Teatronetto Festival (Haifa, Jerusalem, and Tel Aviv) devoted to solo drama performances, and the International Festival of Puppet Theater begun by the Train Theater in 1982.

MEDIA
Newspapers and Magazines

Israelis are voracious consumers of news, with an almost-compulsive need to remain up to the minute. On the daily English Web site for *Ha'Aretz* (http://www.haaretzdaily.com/), one of Israel's leading newspapers, one can click on the "Flash News" to get up-to-minute reporting (something not available on most U.S. news sites). Until the 1960s, newspapers were the primary source for Israelis to get their news, since the radio station broadcast news only two or three times a day. In 1999, the most recent year for which data is available, 79 percent of Israelis read a daily newspaper at least once a week, 62 percent read the paper every day of the week, and a further 48 percent read magazines or journals at least once a month. Reading rates are highest among the Israeli-born public, where 86 percent read a newspaper at least once a week and 58 percent read a magazine at least once a month. Among Israeli Palestinians, reading rates are slightly lower:

63 percent read newspapers at least once a week, and 34 percent read a magazine at least once a month. The level of bilingual reading, however, is highest among this population, with 19 percent reading papers in both Hebrew and another language (compared with rates of 13 percent for the Russian immigrants, 8 percent for all other immigrants, and 2 percent for the Israeli-born Jews).[18]

Newspapers began to appear in Palestine in 1863, with the publication of the Jerusalem Hebrew weekly *Halevanon,* edited by Yoel Moshe Salomon and Michael Cohen. Six months later, a second Hebrew paper connected to the Hasidic movement started publication, *Hahavatzelet,* edited by Rabbi Israel Bak, who also set up the first Hebrew printing press in Jerusalem. The two papers were bitter rivals, going so far as to inform on each other to the Turkish authorities, who eventually shut them both down. In 1885, *Hahavatzelet,* which had resumed publication, was joined by a new paper, *Hatzvi,* edited by Eliezer Ben-Yehuda, the father of modern Hebrew. Ben-Yehuda's paper was more news oriented and less focused on publishing opinion pieces. He also used it as a vehicle to encourage the development of Hebrew as a modern spoken language; thousands of new words appeared in his paper for the first time. In 1901, the Turkish authorities gave him permission to publish his own paper, *Hashkafa,* available twice a week starting in 1904.

Many different political groups soon began to publish papers. In 1907 and 1910, two papers supported by workers' groups started, listing among their contributors David Ben-Gurion, Yitzhak Ben-Zvi, A. D. Gordon, and many other

Man reading *Ha'Aretz* while floating in the Dead Sea. Photo by Moshe Milner. Courtesy of the Government Press Office, State of Israel.

leaders of the Zionist movement in Palestine. The first Palestinian journal, *al-Karmil*, founded in Haifa in 1908, opposed Jewish colonization. In January 1911, the Arabic paper *Filastin* began publication, addressing its readers as Palestinians and warning about the consequences of Zionist colonization.[19] The first daily paper in Palestine was another Ben-Yehuda product, *Ha'Or*, edited by his son, Itamar Ben Avi, who had been working in France as a journalist. Ben Avi brought with him European ideas about what a newspaper should look like, concepts that he proceeded to implement at *Ha'Or*, earning it the reputation of being a "tabloid." In 1944, another Palestinian paper began to appear, *al-Ittihad*, founded by activists of the Arab Workers' Congress and edited by Emil Touma. On the eve of the state's establishment, there was a flourishing and vibrant press in Palestine, mainly owned by political parties, in addition to the independent *Ha'Aretz* (a liberal-democratic paper begun in 1919) and *Yedi'ot Ahronot* (founded at the end of the 1930s as an evening paper).

From its rich beginnings, the press in Israel has followed the same pattern seen in other parts of the world. Today, three large private conglomerates dominate the media in Israel—the Schocken family, which owns *Ha'Aretz*; the Moses family, which owns *Yedi'ot Ahronot*; and the Nimrodi family, which owns *Ma'ariv*.[20] In addition, all three families own publishing companies and numerous local newspapers. The Moses and Nimrodi families also own magazines and music firms.

The largest paper is *Yedi'ot*, with a circulation of 400,000 on weekdays and more than 750,000 on Friday (the weekend paper). *Ma'Ariv* is second, with about 160,000 on weekdays and 260,000 on the weekend. *Ha'Aretz* has a much smaller circulation, 50,000 on weekdays and 60,000 on weekends, but its influence is greater because it is read by the Israeli intelligentsia (equivalent to the *New York Times* in the United States). *Yedi'ot* and *Ma'Ariv* have been locked in rivalry since 1948, when the chief editor and dozens of reporters of *Yedi'ot* left overnight to start *Ma'ariv*, Israel's first evening newspaper. The defections seriously weakened *Yedi'ot*, but the paper did not fold. Instead, it turned to a new audience, Israel's Mizrahi community. *Yedi'ot* was the first Israeli paper to include a daily sports section, as well as a special sports supplement on weekends. As events have shown, it was a brilliant decision that secured the paper's position as number one in circulation. The rivalry between the two papers has not died out. In the mid-1990s, the publisher of *Ma'ariv* was convicted of wiretapping the telephone lines of the editors of *Yedi'ot*.

Besides the Hebrew press, a number of papers are published in other languages, including Yiddish, German, Hungarian, Polish, and Romanian. Immigrants from the former Soviet Union can read four dailies and dozens of periodicals in Russian. Several hundred local papers appear all over the country on Fridays, catering to the news for their particular community. The religious community has several papers, some of which are still linked to political parties: *Hatzofeh* (National Religious Party), *Yom Le'Yom* (Shas), *Hamodia* (Agudat Israel), and *Yated Ne'eman* (Degel Hatorah).

The English-language *Jerusalem Post* is unique. Founded in 1932 as the *Palestine Post,* its early audience consisted of British officials, educated Palestinians, and other English speakers throughout the Middle East and overseas. After statehood, the paper became the *Jerusalem Post* and took a leftist, pro–Labor Party line. In 1989, it was purchased by Canadian Conrad Black for his Hollinger media group. The editors and 28 members of the editorial staff resigned shortly thereafter. The new editors have made the paper a voice of Israel's right wing, the exact opposite of what it had been for years. Circulation is small, 25,000 on weekdays and 50,000 on weekends, but the paper has greater influence because it is read by diplomats and foreign journalists based in Israel.

There is also a vibrant Palestinian press in Israel. *Al-Ittihad,* published daily in Haifa, is read all over the country. It has a circulation of 12,000 during the week, with 16,000 on Fridays and Sundays. *Al-Sinnara,* a weekly publication founded in 1983 by a group of journalists, has a circulation of 35,000. *Ma'ariv* has ventured into the Arabic market with *Al-Ahali,* begun in 2002 and published three times a week. *Kull Al-Arab* is one of the most popular Palestinian papers, with 36,000 copies printed weekly. This paper, which features news and reporting almost exclusively about Israeli Palestinians, is run by noted Palestinian poet Samih al-Qasim. *Fasl Al-Maqal,* begun in 1996 and published on Fridays, is the "Arabic Ha'Aretz," with a circulation of 17,000 in Israel and another 5,000 copies in the territories. Other Palestinian Israeli papers include *Al-Akhbar* (25,000 copies), *Panorama, Hadith Al-Nas, Al-Sabbar, Al-Mithaq* (6,000 copies), and *Al-Ein* (25,000 copies).[21]

There are hundreds of magazines and weekly or monthly periodicals published in the country on a variety of topics such as nature, tourism, computers, and sports or geared to specific audiences such as women, young people, or children. A popular woman's magazine is *La'Isha,* published by the Moses family. The Nimrodi group publishes a woman's magazine and two weekly magazines for young people and children. *Bamahane,* first published in 1948, is the Israel Defense Forces weekly, which is also read by many civilians.

Unlike the United States, the Israeli government does not protect freedom of the press or speech as a fundamental civil right. The British instituted a regulation, the Press Ordinance of 1933, that required all news organizations to register with the interior ministry. Newspapers that endangered public order could have their licenses revoked. The new Israeli government did not abolish this law. Under the State Security Ordinance, an emergency regulation in place since Israel's founding, a military censorship board was set up with the authority to suppress news content deemed to threaten state security. The press, in effect, made a "voluntary" agreement with the army and government to submit its reporting on topics identified by the censor as sensitive for review prior to publication. If the censor rejected a piece, it would not appear in print.

During the 1950s, censorship was invoked frequently to silence reporting on both political and security scandals. When the government of Egypt arrested young Jews for committing acts of sabotage, Israeli papers wrote that there was no foundation to the charges even though editors knew the young men had been recruited by the Mossad, Israel's equivalent to the U.S. Central Intelligence Agency. The ensuing outrage of many journalists led the government to create a new institution: the Daily Newspapers Editors Committee. This committee, which still exists, hears briefings from senior government and military officials on matters they may not publish without securing permission. The intent of this committee was to promote the idea that if the editors knew about such things, they would agree to keep silent in the interests of national security. Calls for the abolition of this committee have increased.

Not every publication agreed with censorship. The weekly *Ha'olam Hazeh*, purchased in 1950 by journalists Uri Avneri and Shalom Cohen, fought against the prevailing government line. They uncovered and reported on government corruption and political and sexual scandals, and they regularly attacked politicians. Cohen espoused the idea that Israel must try to integrate itself into the surrounding Arab world, not a popular idea at this point in time. The path it blazed was later taken up by other newspapers. One prominent case of press freedom occurred in the mid-1980s, when the censor ordered *Hadashot*, a new, vibrant evening paper, recently started by the Schocken family (Ha'Aretz), to challenge Yedi'ot, closed for four days after it published a photograph showing an Arab terrorist being led away by security men, even though other papers had reported that the man died at the scene of his wounds. In 1989, the High Court of Justice further limited the censor's powers. They ruled that censorship could occur only when publication of the item in question would harm public safety. A new three-person committee, composed of a member of the public (who serves as the chairman), an army representative, and a press representative, was established for appealing the censor's rulings. The decisions of this committee are binding; it has in many cases overruled the decision of the censor.

Radio and Television

The British government established the first radio station in Palestine, the Palestine Broadcasting Service (operating as the "Voice of Jerusalem"). It came on the air for the first time on March 30, 1936. The British intended it to serve both the Jewish and the Arab populations, as well as British government officials. During the mandate, the station operated as part of the mandatory government, reflecting the official line on topics of the day. In addition to the official British station, a number of clandestine Jewish stations broadcast in Hebrew, including Haganah Radio, Voice of Fighting Zion (Irgun), and Fighters for the Freedom of Israel (Stern Gang).[22] For the Arabic citizens of Palestine, Radio Sharq al-Adna (secretly operated by the British) provided broadcast services until the end of the Mandate, when the station closed and moved to Cyprus where it continued operating until 1956.

The Palestine Broadcasting Service became the Voice of Israel (Kol Yisrael) after 1948. A second radio station, IDF Radio (Galei Tzahal), started in 1950, to serve the military. Both stations were government controlled, with no competition. In 1965, Kol Yisrael, now broadcasting on a second wavelength, became the Israel Broadcasting Authority. The IBA, headed by an executive committee (government appointed for a three-year term) and a director-general (appointed for a five-year term), is responsible for providing broadcasting from diverse perspectives. It is financed by radio advertising, public service announcements, and an annual fee paid by consumers.

Kol Yisrael and Galei Tzahal have a monopoly on radio news. At first, Kol Yisrael presented two or three news programs a day, but after the 1973 war, they began to broadcast up to 20 newscasts a day. Galei Tzahal was the first to interrupt regular programs with reports of breaking news. Today Kol Yisrael operates eight networks with diverse programming. Reshet Alef (first network) offers a discussion format on cultural and general events as well as children's programs. Reshet Bet (second network) covers news and current events. Reshet Gimmel (third network) is light music, Kol Hamusica offers classical music, Kol Haderech mixes traffic reports with music, and Reka, broadcasting in Russian and Amharic, is targeted at new immigrants. Kol Zion Lagola serves the overseas Jewish population, and Kol Yisrael in Arabic targets Israeli Palestinians and Arab listeners elsewhere. Galei Tzahal, which broadcasts around the clock, features two channels, one for news and talk shows and a second for music and traffic reports.

The government established the Second Television and Broadcasting Authority in 1993 to handle a second television channel as well as regional radio stations. The authority is a public body that selects licensees by tender and authorizes and supervises them. Licenses are granted for a four- to six-year period. These stations are self-supporting, with funding raised by advertising. The Second Authority set up 16 regional radio stations. Two of the stations are intended for specific audiences: Radio 2000 for the Palestinians of northern Israel, and Kol Hay in central Israel for religious Jewish listeners.

One impetus for increasing the number of radio stations may have been the proliferation of radio stations operating without a license ("pirate" stations). One of the first and best known was the Voice of Peace, started by Israeli peace activist Abie Nathan in 1973. Nathan broadcasted music and peace-oriented programs throughout the region from a ship anchored three miles off Israel's shore (and thus in international waters). Broadcasts began in 1973 and ceased in October 1993 when Nathan, facing mounting debt and the prospect of further competition from the new regional stations, shut the station down and sank the boat. Nathan's station had forced a broadcasting revolution in Israel due to its popularity with young people. Kol Yisrael added Reshet Gimmel, its first pop music station, to compete with Voice of Peace. In July 2003, a joint Israeli-Palestinian venture was announced to put Voice of Peace back on the airwaves. It will be based in East Jerusalem and broadcast in Hebrew, Arabic, and English; as of March 2004, the station has yet to begin broadcasting. It has changed its name to Sounds of Peace. The partners in this venture, Givat Haviva Jewish-Arab Center for Peace and the Palestinian English-language newspaper *Jerusalem Times*, have received financial backing for the venture from the European Union and the Japanese government. Other stations have followed Nathan's lead. Although they are illegal, the authorities have tended to let them be. One exception to this hands-off policy was the case brought against directors and broadcasters of Arutz-7, the off-shore right-wing broadcasting station. The station closed down after its directors and staff members were convicted in October 2003 of running a pirate radio station. Some are amateur, others provide ethnic music or religious programs, and some are commercial, funded by advertisements.

Television entered Israel quite late, largely because Prime Minister David Ben Gurion and other intellectuals were afraid it would have a negative impact on Israeli youth. Israel got educational television in 1965, two years before more standard entertainment was made available. The Rothschild Foundation funded the development of educational television (ETV) until it was turned over to the Ministry of Education and Culture, which continues to supervise it. Today ETV provides enrichment programs and current events broadcasts in addition to its educational programming. Its news program, *A New Evening (Erev Hadash)*, is highly rated. It broadcasts on Channels 1 and 2, as well as on cable television.

In 1967, regular television began. Part of what spurred its introduction was the government's realization of television's tremendous propaganda value. Thirty thousand Israelis already owned television sets and were watching broadcasts from Arab countries. Within eight months after the decision was made in 1967 to establish television, the first broadcast showed the military parade of Independence Day 1968. Israeli television (ITV) became part of the Israel Broadcasting Authority and thus another government monopoly. Channel 1, its only channel until the early 1990s, broadcasts news, original productions, children's programs, and entertainment programs and films. Palestinian viewers could watch an hour and a half of each evening's broadcasts in Arabic. The *Mabat* television news program with Haim Yavin, Israel's equivalent of Walter Cronkite, was watched every evening by 75 percent of the population. Walking through neighborhoods when it was broadcast could be eerie, as the same station echoed from almost every home. Another popular program was *Moked,* a political interview program. Such politically focused programs have remained popular, as Channel 1's *Popolitika,* a current talk show that features free-for-all arguing among leading politicians, demonstrates.

Channel 2, added in 1994, is split between three licensees, each broadcasting two days a week, with Saturday broadcasts done by rotation. This channel provides much more entertainment than Channel 1, including films and some serials. It also has its own news division, shared by the licensees. Cable television began broadcasting in Israel in the late 1980s. By the end of 1998, more than 70 percent of Israeli households had subscribed to cable.[23] The country was divided into license areas, with one licensee per area and funding provided by user fees. Mergers within the industry have reduced cable options to three main companies; ongoing merger talks within these companies will probably mean a single cable operator in Israel by the end of 2004. Israel now has its own television serials—such as *Ramat-Aviv Gimmel* (a cross between *Beverly Hills 90210/Melrose*

Place and *Dynasty/Dallas*), *Florentene*, which follows young people who live in Florentene, the new South Tel Aviv Bohemian district of ritzy lofts in a run-down industrial neighborhood, and *Lethal Money* (*Kesef Katlani*), a Mediterranean *Dynasty*—and no longer needs to rely on American imports.

Cinema

The cinema arrived in Palestine almost as soon as it existed; in 1896, Louis and Auguste Lumière shot footage in Palestine.[24] In 1902, Thomas Edison's cameraman was filming local scenes. Film exhibition began even before any movie theaters were built. Jerusalem's Europa Hotel screened *The Diary of the Dreyfus Trial* in 1900. Egyptian Jews opened the first movie theater, the Oracle, in 1908 in Jerusalem. Egypt was a major center of film production and distribution at this time, and theater owners would order Hebrew translations of international films from Cairo.

Filmmakers such as Moshe Rosenberg, Akiva Arye Weiss, Ya'acov Ben-Dov, Nathan Axelrod, and Baruch Agadati produced a variety of film products for their major clients, the Zionist organizations who were eager to bring representations of Palestine to Jews outside the country. Documentaries produced in Palestine were, in effect, Zionist propaganda films.[25] The first feature-length film of the Jewish Yishuv was the silent *Oded the Wanderer* by Nathan Axelrod, made in 1933. It tells the story of a native-born Palestinian Jew (sabra) who goes on a school outing and gets lost. He is brought back through the efforts of his father, teacher, and schoolmates, who must first release a tourist who has been kidnapped by Bedouins. The film contains a number of classical Zionist themes—the empty land waiting for people, the desolate land brought back to life by Jewish settlers, the image of the "new Jew"—a healthy, happy, and proud sabra—and the backwardness of the Bedouins and their longing to share in Western civilization as represented by Oded. The first Hebrew-speaking sound film was *Sabra*, produced by Alexander Ford, a Polish filmmaker. *Sabra* had many of the same Zionist messages in it, but it showed Palestinian Arabs defending their rights, which led some critics to claim the film was anti-Zionist.

Filmmaking after statehood can be divided into at least three distinct periods representing different film genres: the heroic-nationalist phase, the "bourekas" phase, and the personal cinema phase.[26] Between 1933 and 1948, filmmaking was dedicated to newsreels and propaganda films. Israeli films until the mid- to late 1960s focused on heroes—pioneering sabras, kibbutzniks, and soldiers—always with the Arab-Israeli conflict either as backdrop or as the main context. Many directors, producers, and technicians in the 1950s and 1960s were new immigrants. A classic film from this period was British filmmaker Thorold Dickinson's *Hill 24 Doesn't Answer*, a high-budget film ($400,000) made in 1955. The film won two honorable mentions at the Cannes Film Festival and was screened in Israel and abroad. Set during the 1948 war, it centers on four soldiers—an Irishman, a male American Jew, a male sabra, and a Sephardi woman—who must defend a strategic hill outside Jerusalem in order to guarantee Israeli access to the city. The four all die in battle but manage to preserve the hill for Israeli control because the Israeli flag in the woman's hand is seen as evidence by the United Nations observer that the four were claiming the hill. A scene in which an Arab businessman pushes the American Jew into a swimming pool plays to Israeli fears of being drowned in the sea by Arabs.[27] Another scene has the sabra rescuing a wounded "Egyptian" who turns out to be a German Nazi. The sabra wonders how many more of "them" are fighting with the Arabs against the Jews. (This theme appears in a number of other films as well.) Arabs in the film are reduced to symbols of violence and negativity contrasted with the positive heroism of the hill's defenders.

In *Sinaia* (1962, Ilan Eldad), a Bedouin woman hides an Israeli pilot from Egyptian soldiers. While the Egyptian soldiers torture her to get information, the Israeli soldiers rescue her. The helicopter taking her to safety crashes, and only her baby daughter survives. Here is the Arab woman rescued from her own primitive traditional culture by Israeli soldiers. This theme echoes with government propaganda about how Arab women were being freed from traditions by their new position as citizens in a democratic Israeli state. This film was released just before the Israeli government ended its military administration over Israel's Arab citizens.

The "bourekas" films (named after a popular Mizrahi pastry) were Israeli films that featured Mizrahi subjects as their main characters and that played on the rich/poor divide and class warfare in Israel. One of the best-known films of this genre is *Sallah Shabbati* (1964, Ephraim Kishon), which was nominated for an Academy Award. Sallah, a lazy, pleasant man, lives in the tent camps with his family. He finally gets housing by leading a demonstration to stay in the tent camp, which provokes the housing authorities to use the police to force him into permanent housing. The film, satirical from start to finish, pokes fun at the entire governmental bureaucracy, the political parties, and the Ashkenazi elite. Not all films about Mizrahim played to prevalent stereotypes. The films of Moshe Mizrahi show great sensitivity to women's roles in Mizrahi society in particular. His film *I Love You, Rosa* (1972) deals with the levirate marriage practice and one woman's demand to be set free, even though she has come to love the brother-in-law she must marry.

At about the same time, a different current was developing in Israeli films—one that focused on more personal productions and that would come into its own during the 1970s and 1980s. One film that displays this new sense of individuality was *Noa at Seventeen* (1981, Yitzhak Yeshurun). Set in 1951, the film follows Noa, who belongs to a Socialist-Zionist youth movement, as she questions authority and received wisdom. This was a time of tension in Israel, as socialists in Israel debated whether to follow centralized socialism or the social democracy found in the West. The film deals with the issue of the individual versus society. Another innovative film was *The Paratroopers* (1977, Yehuda Ne'eman), which has as its main character a man who volunteers for the elite paratroopers unit but who cannot bear the strain. He eventually breaks under the stress of peer pressure and a conflict with his commander and commits suicide. The film ends with the military suppressing an investigation into his death. This film exposed the myth of the heroic Israeli soldier, examining the tremendous social pressures that are put on young Israeli men to conform and do their military duty appropriately. *Yossi and Jagger* (2002), a film based on a true story directed by Eytan Fox (who also directs the television series *Florentene*), explores gay relationships in the Israeli army through its focus on two gay officers. One of the officers, Yossi, struggles to reconcile the reality of his relationship and sexual orientation with the ideal of the macho officer he is expected to be. This film overthrows entirely the image of the macho Israeli officer.

The Palestinian wave in Israeli cinema came after the Lebanon war, when films such as Uri Barabash's *Beyond the Walls* (1984), Nissim Dayan's *A Very Narrow Bridge* (1985), and Shimon Dotan's *The Smile of the Lamb* (1986) were produced. These films featured Israeli Palestinian actors and actresses, such as Muhammad Bakri, Yusuf Abu Varda, Makram Khoury, and Salwa Nakara-Haddad. The presence of these actors in the films often forced directors to reshape and radicalize certain scenes. Palestinian filmmakers have also been productive. Michel Khleifi has produced a number of films, including *Wedding in Galilee* (1987), *Canticle of the Stones* (1990), *Tale of the Three Jewels* (1995)(all feature films), and a documentary, *Forbidden Marriages in the Holy Land*(1995). Other productions include Ahmed Masri's *Airplane* (1980) and Elia Suleiman's *Chronicle of a Disappearance* (1996). More recently, actor Muhammad Bakri directed the film *Jenin, Jenin* (2002), which was banned by the Film and Theater Censorship Board. Israel's Supreme Court lifted the ban on the film on November 11, 2003, and it was screened on December 8 at the Tel Aviv Cinemateque.

NOTES

1. See Gershon Shaked, *Modern Hebrew Fiction* (Bloomington: Indiana University Press, 2000), for a useful overview of modern Hebrew literature.

2. Motti Regev, "To Have a Culture of Our Own: On Israeliness and Its Variants," *Ethnic and Racial Studies* 23, no. 2 (2000): 228.

3. Shaked, *Modern Hebrew Fiction*, 141–142.

4. Shaked, *Modern Hebrew Fiction*, 150.

5. Shaked, *Modern Hebrew Fiction*, 177.

6. Regev, "To Have a Culture of Our Own," 232.

7. Shaked, *Modern Hebrew Fiction*, 220.

8. Miri Kubovy, "*Inniut* and *Kooliut* Trends in Israeli Narrative Literature, 1995–1999," *Israel Studies* 5, no. 1 (2000): 244–265.

9. Ami Elad-Bouskila, "Arabic and/or Hebrew: The Languages of Arab Writers in Israel," in *Israeli and Palestinian Identities in History and Literature*, ed. Kamal Abdel-Malek and David C. Jacobson (New York: St. Martin's Press, 1999), 141.

10. Abdelwahab M. Elmessiri, *The Palestinian Wedding: A Bilingual Anthology of Contemporary Palestinian Resistance Poetry* (Washington, D.C.: Three Continents Press, 1982), 5.

11. Miriyam Glazer, *Dreaming the Actual: Contemporary Fiction and Poetry by Israeli Women Writers* (Albany: State University of New York Press, 2000).

12. Darwish returned to the Palestinian self-rule area in the territories in 1995 but was not allowed into Israel.

13. Glenda Abramson, *Modern Hebrew Drama* (New York: St. Martin's Press, 1979), 14.

14. Abramson, *Modern Hebrew Drama*, 205.

15. Glenda Abramson, *Drama and Ideology in Modern Israel* (Cambridge, England: Cambridge University Press, 1998), 15.

16. Abramson, *Drama and Ideology*, 36.

17. Abramson, *Modern Hebrew Drama*, 31.

18. Israel Central Bureau of Statistics, "Reading Habits of Persons Aged 14 and Over, by Various Characteristics," Table 9.7, *Statistical Abstract of Israel 2002*. http://www.cbs.gov.il/shnaton53/st09_07x.pdf.

19. The Cairo journal *al-Manar* warned in 1898, in reaction to the First Zionist Congress, that Zionism would take possession of Palestine, a charge they reiterated in January 1902. See Walid Khalidi, *Before Their Diaspora: A Photographic History of the Palestinians 1876–1948* (Washington, D.C.: Institute for Palestine Studies, 1984), 37–38.

20. *Ha'Artez* can be read in English at http://www.haaretzdaily.com/. *Ma'Ariv*'s English Web site is at http://www.maarivenglish.com/.

21. See http://www.arabhra.org/wrap/wraphome.htm for the English-language *Weekly Review of the Arabic Press*.

22. Douglas A. Boyd, "Hebrew-Language Clandestine Radio Broadcasting During the British Palestine Mandate," *Journal of Radio Studies* 8, no. 1 (1999): 101-115.

23. The cable services offer their subscribers approximately 40 channels, including British Sky News; CNN International; MTV; German SAT1, 3SAT, and RTL; BBC Asia; channels from Turkey, Russia, and Spain; Arab channels from neighboring countries; Eurosport; National Geographic; the French TV5; and Israeli stations. Israelis also receive the Christian Broadcasting Network (CBN) through the Middle East Network, located in southern Lebanon. The cable services also provide five special channels: movies, sports, children, family, and nature/documentary.

24. Ella Shohat, *Israeli Cinema: East/West and the Politics of Representation* (Austin: University of Texas Press, 1987).

25. Shohat, *Israeli Cinema*, 18.

26. Shohat, *Israeli Cinema*, 57–236.

27. Shohat, *Israeli Cinema*, 62.

4

Art and Architecture/Housing

FINE ARTS

A number of different issues color the production of art and architecture in Israel. Within Jewish culture, artistic traditions are recent developments compared with the longer history of crafts production and development. In Israel, artists are helping to create Israeli national identity, but on what is that identity based? What is native, and what is invented or borrowed from other native traditions? Is Israeli art Eastern art, Western art, or a blending of the two? What role do Jewish religious traditions and Jewish history play in the art or architecture that Israeli artists create? What place is there for Palestinian culture in Israeli art? Artists help to consolidate a national character and help people see themselves as connected in a nation-state while also providing important cultural criticism of and for their particular society. This is the political dimension of art making, and Israeli artists have chosen different paths to resolve this paradox, some of them moving back and forth between the two roles over the course of their careers.

Within Judaism, prohibitions against creating graven images or idols[1] produced a general anti-iconic attitude—no representational art was allowed, even if the piece was not intended for worship purposes. This orientation was not absolute, however. The walls of the third-century A.D. synagogue at Doura-Europus in Syria are covered with murals depicting biblical scenes, including human figures. Later synagogues in Europe were often decorated with animal figures. Given the general avoidance of representational art, however, Jewish craftsmen and artists turned to producing beautiful ritual objects, such as Kiddush cups, candelabra (the menorah), spice boxes for the ceremony at the end of Shabbat (havdalah), containers for the parchment scrolls (mezuzah) that were nailed to the right side of a doorway to mark the home as a Jewish home, and decorative elements for the

Torah scrolls (crowns, mantles, and breastplates). There were few great Jewish painters prior to the emancipation of European Jews in the eighteenth century. Best known for his painting of Jewish domestic life, the German Moritz Oppenheim (1799–1882) was one of the first Jewish painters to attain fame. Once that barrier was broken, however, Jewish artists left their mark. Israeli Jewish art is thus a modern phenomenon and not the successor of any grand Jewish tradition of painting.

Although the Quran says nothing specifically either for or against representational art, sometime in the middle of the eighth century, a prohibition against representing living things is recorded in Islam as well. The justification for the ban was that any representation of a living thing would be an act of competition with God, who alone can create life. Observance of the ban varied from region to region and through time; it was never completely followed. The ban probably reflects Muslim contact with Christian communities of the time and a fear that creating figural art would lead to worshiping idols. Instead, Islamic artists developed calligraphy—decorative, stylized writing—and geometric forms into high art. Islamic art itself reflects the many different cultures that were absorbed into the Muslim empires.

Christianity had no such ban on representational art. In the nineteenth and early twentieth centuries in Palestine, Christian Arabs practiced the craft of icon painting, passing it on from father to son. Among the leading painters were Jiryes and Tawfiq Jawhariyyeh and the brothers Ishaq and Andoni Ni'meh, Mina and Andoni Abu Shaqra, and Ishaq and Wadi' Sahhar.[2] One of those painters, Nicola Sayigh (d. 1930) from Jerusalem, became the leading pioneer of studio painting when he turned from icons to secular painting and produced a still-life series of peeled prickly pear cactus. Sayigh set the stage for the development of a Palestinian studio art tradition, at about the same time that Jewish artists were also exploring their craft in Palestine.

Painting in the Prestate Period

One can date the beginnings of Jewish Israeli art to a particular point in time. In 1906, Boris Schatz (1866–1932) arrived in Jerusalem to establish Bezalel, a Zionist art academy, with the goal of reviving Jewish art in the Holy Land. Prior to Schatz's arrival, the art produced in Palestine by Jewish artists was for religious purposes only and followed the dominant iconic tradition already present in Christian art of the period or drew from Middle Eastern art forms. The lithograph *The Site of the Temple* (1837) by Rabbi Yehosef Schwartz (1804–1865) became one of the principal representative images of sites in the Holy Land. Paintings by Moshe Shah Mizrachi (1860s-1930s) on glass or paper bear striking resemblance to traditional Persian miniatures.

Born in Latvia, Schatz dropped out of religious school to study in Vilna and Warsaw, after which he spent six years in Paris studying sculpture with Mark Antokolsky, before being invited by the Bulgarian king to establish an art academy and museum to promote Bulgarian art. While in Bulgaria, he became a Zionist and traveled to the 1903 Basel Zionist Congress to promote his vision of an art academy in Jerusalem. Schatz intended Bezalel to provide a trade and livelihood for Jewish Jerusalemites, to develop a home industry that would benefit remote villages, and to promote an original Jewish art style using local and Jewish motifs. He was guided in his endeavor by the Arts and Crafts ideas of William Morris in England and similar trends in Germany and eastern Europe. Morris and the Arts and Crafts movement advocated design based on simple forms, true to materials, and drawn from nature. There was also a moral and social dimension to the movement because Morris believed arts and crafts could change people's lives. Major Zionist leaders did not share Schatz's vision of Bezalel as an art academy. To them, it was a "rug factory" valued only for the money received from the sale of its crafts.[3] Schatz did not let this perception of his enterprise shape its future. By 1911, Bezalel had 32 active departments (silvermaking, woodwork, copper crafting, lace, ceramics, and enamel among others). Schatz sought to develop an Israeli folklore style, basing it on Arab culture and Muslim art. He studied Bedouins as models for what biblical Israelites looked, sounded, and acted like. It was common for Jewish immigrants to adopt the habits and dress of the Palestinians, develop a fondness for archaeology, and replace their Diaspora names with biblical or Canaanite names.

Bezalel's teachers were mature artists who had already developed their own styles of painting in their countries of origin. Their work in Jerusalem was a process of fitting the new Eastern setting into an already developed Western framework. Ephraim Lilien (1874–1925) worked in the German Jugend Stil (Art Nouveau) decorative illustration tradition. Present in Palestine only six months, he still left an imprint on several students who went on to become teachers at the academy. Shmuel Hirshenberg (1865–1908), who painted in an eastern European academic realist style, left a profound effect on the school, where he taught only a year before dying of a stomach disorder. His melancholic scenes of Diaspora life influenced students for years to come. Abel Pann (1883–1963) joined the school in 1920 after World War I and taught there until 1924. He produced pastel biblical paintings filled with background light and lithographs in a tragic mood of scenes drawn from East European Jewry and the Bible.

Schatz had a fierce attachment to academic art styles and a strong opposition to modern art. He kept the academy focused on producing semifolkloric, semiindustrialized objects. His opposition to modernism provoked a student rebellion during the 1920s. The end of World War I and the establishment of the British mandate in Palestine brought a number of new immigrants into the country, among them new artists with new ideas. As former Bezalel students returned to Israel from Europe, where they had been exposed to new schools of thought in art—Henri Rousseau and the "naive" approach, the "Fauvism" of Matisse and Dufy, and the expressionism of the Paris School—the center for artistic production in Palestine shifted from Jerusalem, the Holy City, to Tel Aviv, the secular city.

The Hebrew Artists' Association was founded in 1920 in Jerusalem and held its first exhibit in 1921 at the Tower of David in the Old City of Jerusalem. Bezalel artists dominated this exhibit and the one held in 1922. The year 1923, however, signaled the shift in power to Tel Aviv and its rebels. Bezalel's candidate was defeated that year as chairman of the Hebrew Artists' Association and the rebels held a prominent position in the "Tower of David" exhibition. There were no art galleries yet, so exhibits took place in homes, clubs, and public buildings. Increasingly, these activities came to be focused in Tel Aviv. Israel's Jewish art community was small, so artists, writers, and theater people all came together whenever there was an event. Tel Aviv's coffeehouses became the centers of this bohemian community. By 1929, the transition was complete; Bezalel was closed by the Jewish National Fund, which financed it.

The rebels looked to produce a locally grounded art that took its forms from the uniquely Palestinian conditions of light, color, and scenery. Their painting was concerned with three main themes: (1) the physical landscape (focusing on characteristics such as terraced hillsides, olive groves, or Arab buildings), (2) the human element (Arab and Jewish pioneer lifestyle), and (3) the biblical motif (search for identity and creating ties to landscape).[4] The conflict between Bezalel and the modernists was a conflict between the Jewishness of Bezalel and the Hebrew character of the rebels, between Diaspora culture and the new Hebrew culture developing in Israel.[5] Among the important artists of this period were Israel Paldi, Reuven Rubin, Nahum Gutman, Haim Gliksberg, Sionah Tager, Yosef Zaritsky, and Moshe Castel.

Yosef Zaritsky (1891–1985) emigrated from Russia in 1923 and quickly became one of the most prominent members of the local art community. By 1927, he had been elected chairman of the Artists' Association. He and his associates, Menachem Shemi (1898–1951) and Haim Gliksberg (1904–1970), were more inclined to expressionism—free, dynamic brush strokes and a rich color scale. They painted mostly landscapes, focusing on form and color and not their significance. Unlike earlier artists who used explicit markers (e.g., Arab and Asian elements) to link their art to its Israeli setting, Zaritsky and associates made the local link implicitly through their light and use of color and through the form of the hills and vegetation.

Reuven Rubin (1893–1974) returned to Israel from Romania in 1923. He was heavily influenced by the naive, primitive style of Henri Rousseau. His paintings depict Galilee villages, the budding city of Tel Aviv, Arabs on their donkeys, and Jewish pioneers at work. These same themes appear in the work of others among this group—as with Gutman's *Rest in the Field* (1926) and Shemi's *Fishermen* (1928). Picassoesque neoclassicism, Gaugin-like primitivism, Russian avant-garde art, and modernist trends swept through Israeli art. The Paris school of Jewish expressionism, especially the work of Chaim Soutine and his focus on color, had considerable influence on Israeli artists Moshe Castel (1909–1991), Menachem Shemi, and Arie Aroch (1908–1974). Israel Paldi (1892–1979) burned his earlier expressionist works while Rubin turned toward interiors and landscapes.

The Nazi rise to power in 1933 led to many Jewish intellectuals and artists leaving Germany and central Europe. The German immigration to Palestine brought great changes in the economic, scientific, musical, and industrial life of the country. Anna Ticho (1894–1980) and Leopold Krakauer (1890–1954), exponents of German expressionism, were joined by new immigrants Hermann Struck (1876–1944), Mordechai Ardon (1896–1992), and Jakob Steinhardt (1889–1968). Once again, the Israeli art world underwent upheaval as the new immigrants, with their own established styles, jockeyed for position in Israel's flourishing cultural circles. The German artists flocked to Jerusalem, to the salons of the Tichos and Krakauers. Steinhardt produced German expressionist wood-cuts, Aharon Kahana (1905–1967) was avant-garde, and Rudi Lehmann (1903–1977) sculpted while his wife Hedwig Grossman (1902–1995) worked in ceramics. Tel Aviv became the center of French influence, and Jerusalem that of German influence. The Israeli art world would remain divided for many decades.

One outstanding newcomer was Mordecai Ardon, who arrived in 1933. He had studied in the Bauhaus with Paul Klee, Wassily Kandinsky, and Lyonel Feininger. The German immigrants' association reopened Bezalel, which had been closed for six years, as New Bezalel under the direction of Yosef Budko (1880–1940). Ardon became a teacher at the school in 1935, and when Budko died in 1940, Ardon became director, where he remained until 1952. Between them, Budko and Ardon changed the character of New Bezalel. They stressed fundamental and systematic training in art professions, with an emphasis on skill and proficiency. Ardon's works combined symbolism, surrealism, and magic. Kabbalistic symbols, wheels, torn parchments, letters, hands, and watch numerals are all strewn across abstract landscapes.

Palestinian artistic traditions were also undergoing their own development. In 1933, Zulfa al-Sa'di (1905–1988), a student of Nicola Sayigh, held a solo exhibition at the Palestine Pavilion in the First Pan-Arab Fair in Jerusalem. Next to a series of iconic portraits representing historic and national heroes (Saladin, Sharif Hussein of Mecca, and Amir Faisal), she displayed a still life of prickly pears.[6]

In the 1940s, Marcel Janco (1895–1984) arrived in Israel. Janco was well known as one of the group that founded the Dada movement in Zurich in 1916. Upon arriving in Israel, he abandoned his abstract style of painting and turned instead to expressive canvases. A second major influence on art came from the work of the poet-philosopher Yonatan Ratosh (1909–1982). Ratosh called on the young intelligentsia to reject Judaism in favor of a purely local cultural awareness traced back to Canaanite culture. The Canaanite school appealed most to sculptors, although some artists, such as Zvi Gali (1924–1962), Aharon Kahana, and Moshe Tamir (1924–), turned to archaeological motifs in their works. The melancholy expressionism of Georges Rouault gained influence in Israeli art during World War II. During their period of isolation, Israeli artists concentrated on home in their painting. By the end of the war, they were ready for new sources of inspiration. Modernism—German and French expressionism, the naive art of

Rousseau, Fauvism, and cubism—were part of the past. Israeli artists began to make pilgrimages to Paris and to remain there for long periods of time.

Painting after Statehood

The 1948 declaration of Israel's statehood and the subsequent war left its mark on Israeli art. Pablo Picasso's *Guernica*, his powerful antiwar mural painted in 1937 in response to the Nazi bombing in April of that year of the Basque village of Guernica which destroyed 70 percent of the town, inspired Israeli variations. Marcel Janco's *Death of a Soldier* (1949), Aharon Kahana's *War and Peace* (1948), Zvi Gali's *Sovereignty* (1949), and Naphtali Bezem's *The Battle of Ramat Rachel* (1953) each echoed Picasso's masterpiece in its own way. Independence inspired a cultural revolution in Israeli literature and art. Gone was the Diasporic past; heralded instead were the new sabras, native-born sons and daughters of the land and their brash, plain-dealing, heroic culture. The new figure of the sabra figured in much of the art produced in 1948 and thereafter. Aharon Avni (1906–1951) painted soldiers' lives, as did Ludwig Blum (1891–1974). Moshe Tamir (1924–), wounded in the Jerusalem fighting, produced a fresco *Amnon Wounded*. Avigdor Arikha's (1929–) journey from the World War II labor camps in Romania to New Bezalel to the Jerusalem fighting and a severe injury led him to produce a series of paintings while sitting under bombardment in Jerusalem (e.g., his *Sleeping Soldier*). Sketching seemed to best fit the new sabra reality. Nahum Gutman (1898–1981), Shmuel Katz (1926–), Yossi Stern (1923–1991), and Arieh Navon (1909–1997) all produced fine sketches of the soldiers of 1948. One other theme that featured prominently in the art of 1948 was that of sacrifice. Abel Pann, Aharon Kahana, Mordecai Ardon, and Moshe Castel all produced works framed around the biblical tale of Abraham, Isaac, and the sacrifice required by God.

For Palestinian artists who were just beginning to move away from their more traditional iconic mediums, the 1948 war ended their movement right at its birth. Khalil Halaby (1889–1964) and Jamal Badran (1905–) both became refugees. Other artists, including Jamal Bayari from Jaffa and Ibrahim Hanna Ibrahim from al-Reyneh, were subjected to military government and status as unwanted citizens in the new state. Bayari died penniless in the late 1950s, and Ibrahim immigrated to the United States, where he died a few years after arriving.[7] The center for the development of Palestinian art passed to those artists living in exile, either in the West Bank or Gaza or in other Arab countries.

Independence brought a new development to Israeli art. The new state was invited to exhibit in the 1948 Venice Biennale, one of the premier international exhibitions for modern art. Yosef Zaritsky, who was president at the time of the Artists' Association, secretly assembled 33 works by 17 artists to send to the exhibit, bypassing the committee that had been established to choose the works. His actions produced outrage in the association, which voted to expel him. When Zaritsky left, 14 other artists, some of Israel's best, went with him. The 15 artists formed the New Horizons group, which developed an Israeli style that came to be known as "lyrical abstractionism."

Zaritsky and the other artists were reacting to the lowering of standards and democratization of the Artists' Association. The association had grown so large that it no longer had any real character. Its version of democracy meant that any member could exhibit in its events, so that exhibit quality had dropped at times to mediocre. New Horizons was influenced by trends then developing in French art, the lyrical abstract with its emphasis on *valeurs*, the idea of pure artistic values, stressing color, line, and the musicality of form. It was art as a system with its own internal formal laws.

The New Horizons group presented 12 exhibits between 1949 and 1963. Not all of its members painted in lyrical abstractionism. Janco's style was more figurative, and he left the group in 1953 to found Ein Hod artist's colony. Aharon Kahana tended to geometric abstractionism, Moshe Castel's work tended toward decorative painting in the style of Joan Miró, while Avshalom Okashi (1916–1980) took after Pierre Soulages. Picasso's influence can be seen in the works of Avraham Naton (1906–1959). Arie Aroch's (1908–1974) work is characterized by the spontaneity seen in children's drawings, in which the motor impulse is the primary constructive element. Yehezkel Streichman (1906–1993), who studied at Bezalel with Aroch, formed the Studia Art school in 1944 with Avigdor Stematsky (1908–1989). Streichman was very close to the French painter Georges Braque's artistic style, using deep layers of paint. Stematsky, also a Bezalel student, was influenced by Picasso. He worked in landscapes, which became progressively more abstract into the 1950s.

Studia produced a group of young artists who organized in opposition to New Horizons and its focus on making Israeli art into international art. The Group of Ten (including Eliyahu Gat [1919–1987], Elhanan Halpern [1914–1995], Moshe Propes [1922–1985], Zvi Tadmor [1923–], Claire Yaniv [1921–], and Ephraim Lifshitz 1909–]) argued for a figurative, native Israeli style, grounded in the local landscape and people. Most of these artists were born in the 1920s and were students of Aharon Avni. They left Avni at the end of World War II to join Studia with Stematsky and Streichman. Their patrons were leaders of the Artists' Association—Reuven Rubin and Haim Gliksberg. They began to exhibit in 1950 and held about 20 exhibitions during the 1950s. Eliyahu Gat is a good representative of the Group of Ten spirit. With Rachel Shavit (1929–), he formed a Climate group to encourage Israeli landscape painting. Gat moved from stylized landscapes to more informal abstract paintings to open landscape paintings, with brush strokes similar to the late work of Claude Monet and fiery color.

Through the 1950s, abstract art was alien to most of the Israeli public (and even many artists in Israel). Some artists (Ardon among them) attacked it as capitulating to the Paris school, a sort of art colonialism. Social conditions in Israel in the 1950s were grim. Mass immigration spawned immense tent cities to house people pouring in from North Africa and other parts of the Middle East.

Rationing was enforced as the fledgling economy struggled to function. Lack of jobs, a military government, and high-level corruption were all part of the Israeli social climate. A number of artists responded by adopting a social realist style. These artists gathered in the workers' city, Haifa, where they formed the Circle of Realist Painters in 1955. Artists working in this style included Naphtali Bezem (1924–), Avraham Ofek (1935–1990), Moshe Gat (1935–), Gershon Knispel (1932–), Dani Karavan (1930–), Dan Kedar (1929–), and Shimon Tzabar (1926–). Knispel traveled to Brazil to learn mural techniques and went on to cover the buildings of Haifa with murals. Gat sketched his mother and sister, as they sewed for a living, and workers in a shoe factory. Bezem responded to the deaths of the Arab villagers in Kafr Qasim in 1956 with *In the Courtyard of the Third Temple*, which features dead Arabs holding onto Israeli identity cards. Karavan was painting posters for left-wing rallies. This movement ended by 1960, as many of its members left the country to study overseas. Abstract art, as Ofek noted, "got the upper hand."[8]

By the beginning of the 1960s, abstract art had become the dominant trend in Israel. Yaacov Agam (1928–) was developing his kinetic art and making a name for himself in Paris. New Horizons continued to exhibit as a group until 1966. However, a new group, called 10 Plus, was founded in 1965 by 10 young artists born in the 1930s. Like New Horizons before them, this was not an ideological group, and their membership was not permanent. These artists were second-generation rebels who introduced freshness into the Israeli art scene. Only Raffi Lavie (1937–) participated in all 10 exhibitions. The exhibitions of 10 Plus confronted the artists with certain art problems to which they were invited to respond. Exhibition themes included miniatures, painting on textiles, social content (Pro and Con exhibition), Venus, and mattresses. These shows gave Israeli audiences their first glimpses of pop, kinetic, and environmental art.

The creations of the 1960s drew from different influences—the CoBrA group, with its wild and free style of painting;[9] American and French pop art, and influences from Spanish painters. Key figures of this new art were Raffi Lavie, Moshe Gershuni (1936–), Aviva Uri (1927–), Buky Schwartz (1932–), Uri Lifshitz (1936–), Igael Tumarkin (1933–), and Yoav Bar-El (1933–1977). Characteristic works of art of this period include Tumarkin's *Trouser Panic* (1962), Lavie's *Untitled* (1965), Uri's *Composition* (1969), and Gershuni's *Inner Tubes* (1969).

During the 1970s and 1980s, many Israeli artists turned to conceptual art (while just as many others continued developing their own styles). Art turned to exploring territory that was occupied, that was divided by borders, and that was wounded. Sculptor Yitzhak Danziger recruited a team of artists, ecologists and scientists to rehabilitate the remains of the Nesher quarry that disfigured Mount Carmel near Haifa. Jewish settlers in the now-occupied West Bank might discover earth peace sculptures erected opposite their homes. Artists met in the "Borders" exhibit at the boundary between Kibbutz Metzer and the Arab village of Misser, near the Green Line, to discuss and exchange earth excavated from pits. Gerry Marx created a performance piece in which he took photos of

Jerusalem, scattered them on the soil of a Golan settlement, and then shot at them with a rifle, "an American Jewish artist from Jerusalem shooting at a Jerusalem located in the Golan."[10]

From the 1980s onward, postmodernism made its presence felt in Israeli art. Susan Tumarkin Goodman's 1998 exhibit at the Jewish Museum in New York, *After Rabin: New Art from Israel,* aptly captured the turbulent, fractured state of Israeli society through a group of young artists whose work expresses intense personal concerns but is framed in a political and cultural context of struggle. These artists see themselves as presenting a subversive, marginal point of view in their critiques of Israeli society. Goodman presented the work of young artists such as the video of Aya (1967–)and Gal (1966–), *Prince of Persia* (1995), the black-and-white photos of Nir Hod (1970–), including *Israeli Soldier* (1998), and the oil painting of Nurit David (1952–), *Buba and Thistle* (1997), with works from more established artists such as Moshe Gershuni's (1936–) *After the Shiva* (1995), Igael Tumarkin's (1933–) *You Shall Not Kill* (1996), and Lea Nikel's (1918–) *Gesture for Rabin and for Peace* (1995). Tsibi Geva (1951–) painted names of Arab and Jewish cities in Israel, images such as the backgammon board, a widely popular game in this region, and a series on the *kaffiyeh* (Arab headdress). David Reeb (1952–) bases his paintings on newspaper photographs on the Israel-Arab conflict and works with product logos to create his general critique of society. Yossi Lemel (1957–) has produced a rich genre of political poster art on both Israeli and global themes.[11]

Left-wing art activism aside, the Israeli art world also marginalizes and disenfranchises both Mizrahi Jewish artists and Palestinian artists. In 1993, less than 20 percent of the students at Bezalel were Mizrahi, with most of those concentrated in jewelry, ceramics, and industrial design. The painting and sculpture areas accounted for only 5 to 10 percent of Mizrahi students.[12] At the Art Teachers Training College of Beit Berl, perhaps one-quarter of the students were Mizrahim in 1993.[13] The absence of Mizrahi artists continues into the museums and exhibitions that take place. In reviewing exhibit catalogs, Rueschemeyer found very few Mizrahi artists. The 1988 Tel Aviv Museum exhibit Fresh Paint, which featured 74 prominent artists, included only 6 or 7 Mizrahi artists.[14] The artists complain that Israeli galleries and museums are not interested in their art, and some end up leaving the country or selling and exhibiting their work overseas, where it is better received. Prominent Israeli Mizrahi artists include Zadok Ben-David (1949–, born in Yemen), who now lives and works in London; Pinchas Cohen Gan (1945–, born in Meknes, Morocco) who works in Jerusalem and New York; Benni Efrat (1936–, born in Beirut, Lebanon), who lives in Holland; Yosef Halevy (1923–, born in Yemen), who now lives in Holland; and Yehuda Porbuchrai (1949–, born in Iran) , who lived in New York from 1983 to 1986 but has returned to live in Tel Aviv.

As already noted, many of the most prominent Palestinian artists live and work in exile. There are, however, Israeli Palestinian artists who have achieved a measure of recognition. 'Asim Abu Shaqra (1961–1990), who died at 28, was widely seen as an outstanding talent. He studied at the Kalisher School in Tel Aviv. He is best known for his paintings of cactus—the sabra prickly pear, an important symbol for both Jewish Israelis (who took it as the symbol of the new Israel) and Palestinian Israelis (for whom it signifies patience and tenaciousness). He did not paint wild cacti but potted ones living on a Tel Aviv windowsill.

Asad 'Azi (1955–), a Druze from the village of Shefar 'Am, served in the Israeli army before studying art at Haifa and Tel Aviv Universities. In his paintings, 'Azi incorporates the rich folklore of his Druze heritage, blending high and low art. He works in mixed media—oils, textiles, wood carvings, and photocopied photographs. His *Identity Papers* series of 1988 combines his self-portrait with Byzantine icons and Islamic motifs. In his career, he has had 26 individual and 50 group exhibits, yet he continues to feel not quite at home in the village, and not quite at home in the Tel Aviv world of art.

Rana Bishara (1971–) grew up in Tarsheeha watching her father turn gold and silver into wonderful jewelry in his workshop. She studied fine arts and women's studies at Haifa University before moving to the United States to pursue graduate study in the fine arts. Bishara uses a conceptual and installation style that makes use of a variety of natural materials to convey her social and political messages. One series uses cactus as a medium for three-dimensional work. For some works, she may sew cactus leaves together to create images of other things, or she may combine cactus and ceramic or cactus and chocolate. Her most recent work, a series of photographic images silk-screened on glass in chocolate, was featured in "Made in Palestine" at the Art-Car Museum in Houston in 2003.

Sculpture

Avraham Melnikov (1892–1960) was producing sculpture that drew on the themes and motifs of the ancient Near East as early as 1922, when he exhibited an Assyrian-styled sphinx and reliefs. One of his best-known works is his stone lion to honor Joseph Trumpeldor and the seven defenders of the Tel-Hai community.[15] Zeev Ben Zvi (1904–1952) brought back cubism from his studies in Paris. A graduate of Bezalel, Zvi taught at New Bezalel in the 1930s. Batya Lishansky (1900–1992) introduced German expressionism in her statuettes.

In the 1930s, like the rest of Israeli art, sculpture was French influenced. Works from this period by Chana Orloff (1888–1968), Moshe Ziffer (1902–1989), and Aharon Priver (1902–1979) all demonstrate the realistic and neoclassical style of August Rodin and Aristide Maillol. The works in bronze display an expressive mood, tranquility, and balance. German sculptor Rudi Lehmann arrived in Haifa in 1933 and took a job in construction to earn a living. Lehmann had studied in Berlin, learning to combine expressionism with the formalism of Constantin Brancusi. He mainly sculpted animals in static poses.

Sculpture came into its full flower with the Canaanite movement of Yonatan Ratosh in the 1940s. Canaanite stone art provided rich inspiration for Israel's sculptors. Melnikov had already displayed an archaeological bent in his early work. The German artists who arrived in the 1930s also shared a keen interest in the ancient world and its symbols. It was Yitzhak Danziger (1916–1977), however, who would be the leader of the Canaanite sculpture movement. Danziger had met Melnikov while studying in London. His most important work was the statue *Nimrod*, the biblical hunter, that he created in 1939. Carved of Nubian sandstone, the statue is kneeling, with a bird of prey perched on its shoulder. The flat broad nose, low brow, and protruding eyes are similar to the stone monuments of Easter Island. It is a superbly primitive statue, full of raw energy and power. Another work from the same year, *Shabaziah*, combines the face of a Yemenite woman with the form of a Greek mask, again carved in Nubian sandstone.

Benjamin Tammuz (1919–1989) also was an important part of the Canaanite movement, having introduced Danziger to Ratosh. Tammuz created nude statues, *Temple Prostitute* (1941) and *Ashtoret* (1941), in the courtyard/studio that members of the group used in Tel Aviv. Yehiel Shemi (1922–2003) joined the circle in 1940 for a brief period. Many of Shemi's works from this period were destroyed in the 1948 war when Kibbutz Bet Ha'arava on the Dead Sea was captured by the Jordanians. *Head of a Hebrew Fighter* (1950) and *The Man of the Arava* (1956) are works made of local materials that exude great strength. Shoshana Heimann's (1923–) *Girl with Dove* (1946) also demonstrates this style, although she did not study with Danziger and Tammuz.

In the 1950s, Israeli sculptors turned to new materials, especially hammered and welded iron, for their art form. Their works were more abstract and on a more monumental scale. New Horizons sculpture drew from the earlier Canaanite traditions as adapted to the modern British use of welded iron and modern French and Spanish traditions. Elul Kosso (1920–1995) and Moshe Sternschuss (1903–1993) exhibited in the first New Horizons show. Kosso worked in wood in a primitivist style; Sternschuss chose an abstract bronze. Danziger joined New Horizons in 1955, after returning from London. He and Yehiel Shemi were pioneers in using iron in their works, exposing the inner structure in the British tradition. Dov Feigin (1907–) began to weld iron wires into motifs of birds and flying and to precisely cut out silhouettes of animals from sheet iron. In 1956, the Tel Aviv Museum held its first symposium on sculpture. In 1957, Mother's Park in Haifa was the site of an open-air exhibit of more than 50 iron sculptures.

During the 1960s, a major new figure returned to the ranks of Israel's sculptors, Igael Tumarkin (1933–). Tumarkin studied with Rudi Lehmann before moving to Berlin in the 1950s to work in Bertolt Brecht's theater in Berlin, then to Holland to work with the CoBrA group, and to France to work with the Spaniard Antoni Tapies. He settled in Israel in 1961. His art symbolically combines geometric elements with junk and casts of human limbs. Tumarkin continued to develop his art by exploring primitive cultures, adding to his repertoire new shapes and techniques from those studies. A classic work from this period is his *He Walked in the*

Fields (1967), depicting a soldier's torn and exposed body filled with rifle barrels, his trousers down, genitals exposed. Tumarkin created monuments, sculptures, and sculpture gardens across the Israeli landscape.

Another leading sculptor of the period was Pinhas Eshet (1935–), one of the members of 10 Plus. Eshet trained in Italy with Marino Marini. Beginning his career in Tel Aviv in the mid-1960s, Eshet worked in beaten and soldered copper. His theme for these works was the pregnant breast and belly, as seen in the 1968 piece *Pregnancy*. From copper, he moved to cast metal, reflective on the outside and painted on the inside. In the 1980s, he was casting heads and torsos using white porcelain imprinted with words, followed by monumental female figures leading a threatening dog in painted plaster and hammered iron.

Israel turned to memorializing its fallen—the Holocaust victims and soldiers who fell in war. Building these war memorials provided a boost for sculpture in the country. During the 1950s, such memorials had been spontaneous and anonymous. The monuments of the 1960s included several by Dani Karavan. His Negev Monument (1963–1968), a memorial to the Negev Brigade of 1948, was Israel's first environmental art. The concrete structure of tower, dome, tunnel, and trenches interacts with local conditions of wind and light to provide a stunning monument. Yehiel Shemi created *Sea Landscape* (1964–1967), a welded steel naval memorial at Achziv; and Buky Schwartz produced the *Pillar of Heroism* (1968) for Yad Vashem, the Holocaust Museum in Jerusalem. In their works, Tumarkin, Karavan, Schwartz, and Shemi drew on nature, symbols, and historical and current events as they searched to salvage what they could from the socialistic ideals of the prestate generation.[16]

The other major innovation in Israeli sculpture during the 1960s came from sculptors who had studied in London with Anthony Caro at St. Martin's School of Art. Included in this group are Buky Schwartz (1932–), Menashe Kadishman (1932–), Yehezkiel Yardeni (1931–), and Benni Efrat (1936–). Schwartz and Kadishman belonged to a group of young artists who were attempting to move minimalist sculpture out of the gallery and into open spaces. Kadishman stayed with the minimalist form as he changed the materials in which he worked—from figurative shapes cut from steel sheets to steel and glass sculptures that defied gravity, to painted and cut steel shapes hung in natural settings. Schwartz has worked in aluminum and stainless steel and in video and steel cutouts playing with optical illusion. Yardeni's first exhibit featured striped industrial fabrics, unframed, folded, and partially cut out to create a composition. He then moved to works in wood, mortar, and fabric with architectural and ecological themes. Efrat developed his concrete art mainly in the West. He played with illusion and reality in creating structures casting shadows that in reality were painted surfaces or a projector's light. He expanded his work into performance movies that he interacted with in real time, moving eventually to concentrating on the theme of ecological holocaust. His 2035 exhibit at Ramat Gan's Museum of Israeli Art filled the museum with olive trees and flocks of doves in iron cages to symbolically represent a future vision of nature confined.

Some of the most recent developments in Israeli sculpture have included the fused sculpture of Bianca Eshel-Gershuni (1932–), which combines soft and hard materials (feathers, fur, plastic, fiberglass), dolls, and photographs to create an autobiographical series on sex and death; the kinetic assemblies of Philip Rantzer (1956–), which use found objects, dolls, and other materials; and the tomblike structures of Jack Jano (1950–) built of wood and plaster. Zadok Ben-David produces mixed-media sculptures that verge on the absurd and allegorical, as in his *Evolution and Theory* (1997). The "Galilee" school of basalt sculpture that began in the 1980s includes the work of Dalia Meiri (1951–), Shaul Tully Baumann, and David Fine (1928–). Pieces include arrangements of basalt rocks in forms resembling those of past civilizations or Baumann's political sculpture where he imprints political texts on cactus leaves or basalt rocks.

Photography

Photography as an art form is a relatively recent development in Israel, but photographers have been documenting conditions in the country since Palestine became a tourist destination. Europeans discovered Palestine at the end of the nineteenth century, and amateurs and professionals alike documented their journeys there in photographs. By 1860, professional photographers such as Hippolyte Arnoux (in Port Said), G. Lekegian (in Cairo), the Bonfils family (Felix, Marie-Lydie, and son Adrien in Beirut), Pascal Sebah (in Istanbul), and Jean Sebah and Policarpe Joaillier (in Istanbul) had opened studios to meet the increasing demand in the tourist market for mementos of local sites. When the Suez Canal opened in 1869, the pace of travel to the region increased. By the 1890s, travelers were using snapshot cameras to document their journeys. The producers of these photographs came from a wide diversity of backgrounds: British royal engineers who took photographs in their surveys of Jerusalem (1864) and the Sinai (1868), ambassadors, district officers, journalists, and tourists.[17] Between 1898 and 1946, Eric Matson, a Swedish American photographer who lived in Jerusalem, documented life in the country. The Armenian photographer Garabed Krikorian opened the first photographic studio in Palestine in Jerusalem around 1885. He was soon joined by two more photographic studios in the city, that of Khalil Raad and of the American Colony group. Hana Safieh worked for the American Colony group and was apprenticed to and then collaborated with Eric Matson.[18]

The documentary function that photography played in Palestine from 1880 onward inhibited the development of photography as an art medium until the 1970s. The earliest Jewish Israeli photographers were immigrants, largely self-taught, who documented the building of the new state. Walter Zadek, who immigrated to Israel from Germany in 1933, founded the Association of Professional Photographers in Palestine in 1939. After the creation of the state, the dominant mode of photography was photojournalism. Tim Gidal, David Rubinger, Werner Braun, Boris Carmi, Zev Radovan, David Harris, and Micha Bar Am are some of the photojournalists who recorded the significant moments and people in the new nation's history.

In the 1970s, photography came into its own as an art form, as a number of Israeli artists began to experiment with photographs in their works. In 1971, Joshua Neustein (1940–) exhibited a series of photographs based on the interior-exterior principle for a conceptualist exhibit at the Israel Museum. The photographs followed a logical progression, from a photo of a section of wall on which hung a photo to a photo of the back of the photo to another of the back of the wall and beyond the wall to the museum's exterior. A 1974 Benni Efrat series featured photographs of eyes looking in all different directions, demonstrating fluctuating viewpoints when taken together. The 1979 *Visual Images* #8 of Yocheveld Weinfeld (1947–) combines painting assemblage, photography, and written messages to expose the personal intimate situations of family and femaleness.

By the 1990s, photography was strongly promoted at art schools in the country as teachers there (such as Michal Heiman, Simha Shirman, and Haim Lusky) sought to unite photography and art. Part of their inspiration was the drive to document events. In 1995, the Tel Aviv Museum featured an exhibit, "90/70/90," that presented current local photography from the perspective of its relationship to 1970s art photography. Shirman, son of Holocaust survivors, has recently been working on a series called *The Wanderings of the One Armed Rider,* in which he has photographed a number of people he has met, staging the photos with the same lighting and setup. The effect is that of an anthropological study or police photographs or the types of photographs produced in the Nazi death camps. Another recent work that demonstrates the best of current Israeli photography is *Embroideries of Generals, 1997,* created by Dafna Ichilov, Judith Guetta, and Galia Gur Zeev, who work together as the Limbus Group. Portraits of former chiefs of staff of the Israeli army are printed in monochrome on embroidery canvas. The piece challenges the traditional heroic masculine image of the male warrior by bringing it into the female world of home and craftwork.

Two major schools of photography are the Camera Obscura School of Art established in 1978 in Tel Aviv and Bezalel's Department of Photography. Major events for the display of photographic work include the photography biennale at Mishkan Le'Omanut in Kibbutz Ein Harod and the new Museum of Photography at Tel Hai in the northern Galilee.

Crafts and Design

Crafts such as ceramics, silver and gold working, weaving, calligraphy, glass making, and furniture design are also an active part of the Israeli art world. Prior to 1948, Palestine had a rich diversity of traditional crafts such as pottery, basketry, copperware, brassware, embroidery, mosaic work, tile making, and jewelry design and crafting. The Yemenite immigrants to the country brought with them their traditions of silver work, embroidery, and fabrics. Yemenite silver jewelry is known throughout the world for its intricate and distinctive filigree. Two generations later, the new immigrants from Ethiopia brought their craft traditions with them, providing a new source for design innovation. European crafts traditions were influential because they were taught at Bezalel to a new generation of craftspeople. Judaic themes and ritual objects make up a large segment of the craft market, but this is not the totality of Israeli design. Israeli craftspeople are artists who have established international reputations for their work, just like Israeli painters and sculptors.

Dan Reisinger is one of the top designers alive today. He has designed logos and branding systems for Israeli companies and organizations, including El Al, the Tel Aviv Stock Exchange, Bat Sheva Dance Company, and The Open Museum. He recently was included in the book *Masters of the 20th Century: ICOGRADA's Hall of Fame*, published by the international journal of visual communication, *Graphis*—the only Israeli included among this group of the top world designers. Amnon Israeli studied pottery under the "first lady of Israeli ceramics," Hedwig Grossman. His works combine the influence of nature with design motifs drawn from ancient and new models. He has taught at Bezalel, although today he works as a designer and teaches in his private studio.

Kakadu, founded and run by Aharon and Reut Shahar, produces furniture and other household objects in a unique style. Aharon Shahar studied carpentry, specializing in furniture production and design. Reut Shahar studied classical carpentry, jewelry design, and art at Bezalel Their creations express their belief that art should not be restricted to museums or galleries; instead, they create art that is functional and meant to be used as part of daily life.

The settlement of Clil, founded in 1979 in Western Galilee near Nahariya, is a community of artists and craftspeople. Crafts represented by the artists of Clil include pottery, glasswork, jewelry, basket weaving, and furniture making. Igael and Vered Mayer and Batia Gil Margalit design for Nahariya Glass, a company founded in 1967 by Igael Mayer's parents. Igael Mayer introduced new design techniques to the firm based on silk screen printing directly onto layers of glass. This method of fusing color into the glass allows them to produce stained-glass windows that do not degrade (as traditional lead-based windows do). Alon Gil runs his own ceramics studio, Jara, while Amir Poran makes gold and silver jewelry and watches through his company Poran Gaaton, started in 1989. Danny Segal works in local woods (oak, cedar, cypress, and pine) in his carpentry shop, Danny's Workshop, which makes furniture in which the wood "speaks."

Lakiya Negev Bedouin Weaving is a project set up in 1991 to provide Bedouin women with a livelihood based on their traditional weaving skills. The project produces rugs, wall hangings, pillows, and handbags using traditional colors (rust, black, olive green, dark blue, and natural, undyed wool) as well as special designer colors to appeal to the international market. Handspun wool from local sheep is dyed and hand loomed. Other traditional Palestinian crafts—olive wood carving, mother-of-pearl work, embroidery, copper and brass work, weaving, ceramics and tile work, and jewelry design—continue to be produced in Israel. The push for mass production for the tourist market has lessened the quality of products available in popular tourist markets, but Palestinians know where to go to find high-quality products and skilled craftspeople. Jerusalem Pottery and Palestinian Pottery in Jerusalem are two well-known Armenian pottery workshops that produce beautiful hand-painted ceramics. The founders of both workshops were brought to Jerusalem to maintain the mosaic facade of the Dome of the Rock.

Museums

Israel can boast more than 200 museums throughout the country that deal with archaeology and antiquities, history, arts, and crafts. The main national museum is the Israel Museum in Jerusalem, founded in 1965. This museum is actually a number of museums in one. It contains the collection of the Bezalel Museum of Fine Arts, Judaica, and Ethnography, as well as other ethnographic artifacts, numerous period art galleries, collections of art objects from other continents, the Shrine of the Book, housing the Dead Sea Scrolls, archaeological wings, a sculpture garden, East Jerusalem's Rockefeller Museum of archaeology, and the Ticho House art gallery and café. The Tel Aviv Museum of Art is actually older, founded in 1932; it houses a comprehensive collection of classical and contemporary art, especially Israeli art, as well as supervising the Helena Rubinstein Pavilion of Modern Art. Mishkan LeOmanut (Home of Art), established in 1934, was the first rural museum and the first kibbutz museum in the country. It houses Jewish painting, sculpture, and folk art from around the world. The Haifa Museum was built in 1949. Under its control, one can find the Museum of Ancient Art, featuring Israeli and Mediterranean archaeological finds, the Museum of Modern Art, the Museum of Prehistory, the National Maritime Museum, and the Tikotin Museum of Japanese Art. The L. A. Mayer Institute for Islamic Art (1974) in Jerusalem covers more than a thousand years of Islamic culture through its pottery, textiles, jewelry, and ceremonial objects. The Diaspora Museum (1978) is located on the campus of Tel Aviv University. It is a nonartifact museum, using audiovisual displays and other modern forms of technology to trace the history of Jewish communities in exile. Yad Vashem, located in Jerusalem, is dedicated to remembering the Holocaust through its historical museum, art gallery, and archive. Visitors can walk and ponder the Hall of Names, the Avenue of Righteous Gentiles, the central remembrance hall with names of the extermination camps on the floor, the Children's Memorial Pavilion, and the Valley of the Destroyed Communities.

ARCHITECTURE AND HOUSING

When one speaks about Israeli architecture, at one level, one could be referring to a multitude of different cultural styles and influences that developed over thousands of years since humans first settled there and began to construct permanent buildings. The ruins at Tel as-Sultan (Jericho) demonstrate that by 9000 B.C., hunters and gatherers were regularly visiting this location and leaving traces of their occupation. By 8000 B.C., a town, surrounded by a massive stone wall, existed at the site and was home to 2,000 to 3,000 inhabitants. Jericho's development as a city is an excellent microcosm for the history of architecture in Israel. Jericho was abandoned, only to be rebuilt time after time over the millennia as it came under Canaanite, Roman, Crusader, and Arab influence. The traces of all these architectural styles have been left for the archaeologists to find.

Architecture in the Prestate Period

Two basic periods characterize Israeli architecture: a prestate, Palestinian and Islamic period and the contemporary Israeli period. The prestate period can be further divided into consideration of the indigenous Palestinian architectural styles and styles introduced by the Jewish immigrants who began to settle in the country in the late nineteenth century. Two different types of buildings that served different functions best characterize Palestinian architecture: the mosque—the religious center—and the house, center of family life.

As the Muslim armies conquered new territories, they found impressive religious buildings constructed by these other societies. A need arose for a specifically Muslim place to congregate to pray and transact the political, social, and educational affairs of the community. In Mecca, prayer gatherings had either occurred at the Prophet's home or in a place outside the city walls (a *musalla*), an enclosed space surrounded by a wall. Muslims developed a new architectural structure to meet their needs for a flexible, centralized space, the hypostyle mosque. A hypostyle hall is an interior space whose roof rests on pillars or

View of Jerusalem. Photo by the author.

columns. With this style, large spaces can be constructed without the need for arches, and the building can be enlarged by simply adding more columns. From its earliest beginnings as a large square marked out by a ditch and a covered colonnade, the mosque evolved into its modern form of large enclosed open courtyard with water fountains for purification rites, tall tower (minaret) from which Muslims are called to prayer, an imposing, often domed, building that housed the niche (mihrab) marking the direction of Mecca, a pulpit (minbar), and an open floor area covered by carpets where the faithful could gather to pray. The walls and ceilings are usually decorated with fine mosaics or paintings that depict floral and other motifs from nature or abstract geometric and calligraphic designs. The changing Muslim dynasties who controlled Palestine each incorporated different architectural and decorative elements in their mosques.

The best representation of a distinctive Palestinian secular architecture is the Palestinian stone house built in rural and urban areas throughout the nineteenth and twentieth centuries.[19] Such homes were usually constructed communally through the labor of friends and family, each of whom might be skilled in a different area of the building process. Both men and women built these houses. To plaster a roof, men would mix soil with water and straw to make the basic plastering material; women would do the actual plastering work. Women also plastered interior walls every few years and built mud containers inside the house in which to store grain and beans. In every village, one man would be known as an expert mason and builder (al-banna).[20] When his fame stretched beyond his village, he became known as a master builder (mu'allim al-bina'). No such individuals exist in Western building traditions of architect and construction worker. Until the mid–twentieth century, these houses maintained a distinctive character with their straight lines in walls, doors, windows, and roofs. The thick gray stone walls (15 to 19 inches thick) served to keep the interiors cool in the summer and warm in the winter; inner ceilings were often vaulted to further emphasize warmth and privacy. These homes harmonized well with their natural settings.

Arabic architecture reflects the division of space into public, exterior areas and private, interior areas (al-dakhil). The stone houses were the interior domestic space, often family compounds, in which an extended family—a married couple, their married children, and their grandchildren—lived, worked, and played together. Because of the simple construction, new rooms could be added on as a son married and brought his wife into the extended family. The house was usually protected from the street by a walled courtyard, inside of which would be planted lemon trees, grape vines, and other plants to create a garden setting. The interior courtyard might also contain the family's well to provide water (in other cases, women carried water from the village well). Staircases on the outside of the house might lead from the courtyard to the roof of the house, a good place to gather and sleep in the hot days of summer so one could catch the breeze. In older homes, the oven (tabun) might be situated in the courtyard, a good arrangement for dispersing its heat in the summers.

Interior courtyards were protected spaces in which women could move about freely. Unlike American homes, there were no single-purpose rooms, with the exception of one room set aside to use as a guest salon, where the male members of the family could entertain visitors while the women remained in other more interior parts of the house. Bedding would be put down every evening for sleeping and removed during the day so that the same room could serve as a family room and eating space. Guest rooms were usually kept closed when not used for visitors and were more elaborately decorated, containing the household's better furniture, rugs, or cushions. A man who married more than one woman (a practice allowed in Islam) would provide separate rooms in the house for each wife and her children.

Every Palestinian Arab village prior to 1948 possessed a village guesthouse (*madafah*). If more than one family clan lived in a village or the village was large, each clan might have its own guesthouse. The *madafah* served multiple functions. It was the village law court, a coffeehouse, a reading room, a public meeting place, and a place for amusing oneself and for providing lodging for visitors.[21] Often no more than a large room whose roof was supported by arches resting on pillars, the room would be furnished with stone benches and low stools, the floor covered with mats on top of which were rugs and cushions. Decorated shelves and trays might be built into the walls. They were usually large spaces, suited for offering hospitality, in contrast with the more intimate and smaller rooms of the family home.

Palestinian towns and cities up to Ottoman times also reflected the division of space into exterior and interior. Many Muslim cities contain a maze of narrow, winding streets and blind alleys with no discernable order or markings to orient the visitor. People know how to find a particular house because they are familiar with that house from having gone there before. Family groups or other sectarian groups usually would gather together in a particular part of the town. Passersby were either of the area and so knew their way around or were immediately marked as strangers when they needed to ask directions of the locals. These residential quarters were usually separated from the more public parts of the town: the center of local power, often a walled fortress where the governor or other official lived; the main mosque, center of religious worship; and the market (suq) area. Within the suq, all the merchants or craftsmen working within a particular trade tended to concentrate together, so that one might have a street of jewelers or of rug dealers. The most prestigious businesses were those located closest to the principal mosque. The Old Cities of Acre and Jerusalem and parts of Jaffa give the modern visitor a taste of what the traditional city was like.

When the British assumed their mandate over Palestine in the 1920s, they brought with them Western ideas about land tenure and Western notions about how to build a city and what constituted proper architecture. Land tenure under Ottoman rule had involved granting use rights to property holders, as well as the recognition of village or tribal communal rights over land. While the Ottoman land reforms in the late nineteenth century had begun the process of converting

Eastern neighborhood of Acre shows the diversity of building styles typical of Israeli cities. Photo by the author.

land over to private property, the British hastened the transformation of land tenure ideas in Palestine through surveying and recording land ownership. They also brought with them new notions about city planning and how a city should be laid out.

Influential architects in this prestate period were Alex Berwald, Leopold Krakauer, and Richard Kaufman, all immigrants from Germany. Berwald came before World War I to design two major buildings in Haifa. He studied Islamic and Mediterranean architecture and attempted to blend these styles in creating buildings where the outer structure harmonized with the interior functions. He worked with Arab builders to learn their methods and created his own eclectic style. Berwald, who also taught architecture at the Technion, died in 1931.

Kaufman, who came to Israel as a young architect, was greatly influenced by the garden-city planning approach then popular in Great Britain. Garden cities were intended to be self-contained communities, surrounded by a greenbelt. The goal was to bring together the economic and cultural advantages of city and country life in the new community while discouraging sprawl and industrial concentration. Garden cities were planned to have large amounts of green space, with central civic and cultural institutions at the core of the city. Around this core would be parks, shopping, and residential areas, with industry confined to the outer edge. Tying it all together was a well-planned network of roads. Kaufman designed most of the villages and garden suburbs constructed in Israel between 1919 and 1929. He excelled at designs for the new collective settlements (the kibbutz and moshav) and at solving climatic problems in hot areas like the Dead Sea. Krakauer, who came to Palestine in 1924, was also celebrated for his kibbutz architecture. He researched in detail local conditions of climate, light, and building materials to create his structures.

The well-known architect Erich Mendelssohn was invited to Palestine in 1925 to construct the first electric power stations. Between 1934 and 1937, he designed and supervised the construction of commercial, public, and apartment buildings. His architecture was a compromise between traditional styles of building and the constructivist vision of the new schools of architecture developing in Europe.

A new school of architecture developed, represented by Arieh Sharon, Zeev Rechter, Dov Karmi, and Joseph Neufeld, among others. This group consisted of architects, both local and new immigrants arriving from Germany in the 1930s, who had studied in Europe and assimilated the architectural theory of Le Corbusier, Walter Adolph Gropius, Mies van der Rohe, and the Bauhaus. Bauhaus buildings were functionally simple, with irregular forms, flat roofs, glazed stairwells, pillars, and pergolas, made of steel and concrete. Sometimes the ground floor had columns or concrete trellises that adorned the building. Some buildings had massive, rounded corners; others had concrete teeth edging the stairwell. Tel Aviv was the first city in the world to be constructed almost entirely in the international style, and it still has the largest concentration of Bauhaus-style buildings (2,400 identified among the 4,000 that were designed) in the world.[22] The city came to be known as the "white city" because of its stuccoed constructions.

During the 1940s, construction was much more limited due to the political and military upheavals, first of World War II and then of the Zionist struggle against the British and the 1948 war. No new trends were introduced. Instead, architects refined elements that were already being used. More attention was given to balconies, which were enlarged and made more private so that they could be used as extra rooms. In rural and suburban areas, cottages with gabled roofs and red tile began to appear as the Swiss style began to replace the concrete boxes of the Bauhaus movement.

Architecture after Statehood

After statehood, there was an immediate shortage of housing in the country as immigrants from Europe and then North Africa streamed into the country. Between May 1948 and December 1951, the country's Jewish population doubled as 684,000 new immigrants entered the country.[23] New immigrants and veteran residents were first settled in the vacant homes of Palestinians made refugees by the war and the declaration of the Israeli state (which refused to allow them to return). As the immigrants continued to stream in, they were housed in vast temporary tent cities (ma'abarot) throughout the country. There was tremendous pressure on the government to provide housing, so prefabricated buildings that could be constructed cheaply and quickly became the fashion of the day. Rectangular concrete structures, four stories high with four to six apartments per floor, with a separate entrance and stairwell for each group of flats, became the norm. Average apartment size to begin with was 54 square meters (about 581 square feet); over the years, that figure has increased to 79 square meters or more (about 850 square feet).[24] A cluster of such buildings was provided with an area of small shops selling food, household goods, and sundries. Often large green spaces were left between rows of buildings to serve as a commons area where children could play and apartment dwellers could sit and visit. As the tent cities began to disappear, the pressure was lessened to construct quickly and cheaply. Israeli architects had continued to produce high-quality buildings during this time—often large-scale projects that were awarded by means of competition. The early pressure to construct quickly, however, has left its mark on many Israeli cities. They often contain a patchwork of buildings constructed in different styles and sizes depending on the era in which they were built. Acre, for example, has an intact Ottoman-period walled city, fine examples of Palestinian stone house construction on a gridded street layout that date to a mandate period, and a mish-mash of different concrete block buildings that vary according to the decade in which they were built. Cottages with red tile roofs— called the British cottages—can be found in one new neighborhood. In another, older part of town, the small original houses have been added to haphazardly over the years, resulting in a highly eclectic neighborhood appearance. In the northern part of town, residents can purchase stand-alone villas.

In the 1960s, Brazilian architecture provided new models for Israeli architects to copy. Brazilian architects had had to deal with the problems of sun control, ventilation, and concrete building materials, and their solutions provided new inspiration to the Israeli building trade. Buildings were raised on round stilts, with facades decorated with checkered patterns or brise-soleil (unbroken concrete awnings on the outside of buildings that shade the windows).

Considerable effort is placed now on town planning. Every city must have a master plan drawn up that guides its growth. One of the major problems for Palestinian villages in the Galilee has been the lack of such plans for their communities. This has inhibited growth in many Palestinian towns and promoted congestion and crowding as families were forced to continue to build on the same plots of land. Master plans are in the works for these communities, some of which are approaching city size in terms of population density.

There have been a number of high-profile building projects in the country that have allowed the skills of Israeli architects to shine. The reconstruction of the Jewish Quarter of the Old City of Jerusalem after 1967 provides examples of the work of a number of preeminent Israeli architects, such as Eliezer Frenkel, Yaacov and Ora Yaar, and Moshe Safdie. Frenkel and the Yaars were well known for their earlier restoration work on Old Jaffa. More recent projects include Moshe Safdie's Mamilla development just outside the Jaffa Gate of the Old City of Jerusalem, planned to include 280 apartments, retail shops, parking, a cinema, and three hotels. Another major construction project that he designed was the new community of Modi'in, midway between Jerusalem and Tel Aviv. Begun in 1996, the town now has a population of about 40,000 residents. Ada Karmi-Melamede and her brother Ram Karmi designed the new Supreme Court building in Jerusalem. The buildings of the complex are grouped around two walls expressing the north-south and east-west axes.[25] A recent controversy engulfing the architectural community in Israel has revolved around the role of architects in state politics. Young architects Rafi Segal and Eyal Weizman won a competition in 2001 to represent Israel at the 2002 World Congress of Architecture in Berlin. However, the Association of Israeli Architects canceled their entry when it was discovered they intended to present as their entry, "A Civilian Occupation: The Politics of Israeli Architecture," a piece that critiqued the complicity of Israeli architects in settlement construction.[26]

Architects and artists in Israel continue to struggle with their role in Israeli society. Will they uncritically reflect the desires of Israel's political elites and produce their vision of the Israeli nation, or will they choose the role of constructive cultural critic and hold a mirror up to Israeli society?

NOTES

1. Exodus 20:4 and Deuteronomy 4:15–19.

2. Kamal Boullata, "'Asim Abu Shaqra: The Artist's Eye and the Cactus Tree," *Journal of Palestine Studies* 30, no. 4 (2001): 71, 81 n. 9.

3. Gideon Ofrat, *100 Years of Art in Israel* (Boulder, Colo.: Westview Press, 1998).

4. Ran Shechori, *Art in Israel* (Tel Aviv: Sadan Publishing House, 1974), 12.

5. Ofrat, *100 Years of Art,* 50.

6. Boullata, "'Asim Abu Shaqra," 70.

7. Kamal Boullata, "Facing the Forest: Israeli and Palestinian Artists," *Third Text* 7 (1989): 81.

8. Ofrat, *100 Years of Art,* 191.

9. CoBrA artists used vibrant and unmixed colors to create paintings of spontaneity and imagination. They took inspiration from the totems and magic signs of indigenous peoples, as well as from Eastern calligraphy, prehistoric art, Western folk art, and children's art.

10. Ofrat, *100 Years of Art,* 306.

11. You can view his art at the following Web site: http://www.lemel.co.

12. Marilyn Rueschemeyer, "Ethnic Place and Artistic Creation: Dilemmas of Sephardic Artists in Israel," *Journal of Arts Management, Law, and Society* 22, no. 4 (1993): 347.

13. Bezalel and the Art Teachers Training College are in constant competition for the top spot among Israel's art schools. Where one attended school is an important asset for newly graduated students trying to break into the gallery circuit (Aviva Lori, "Brushed Off," *Ha'Aretz,* August 13, 2003).

14. Rueschemeyer, "Ethnic Place and Artistic Creation," 348.

15. Tel Hai was attacked in 1919 by Arab forces under the control of Emir Feisel. Other nearby Jewish settlements had been evacuated, but the settlers at Tel Hai refused to leave.

16. Susan Tumarkin Goodman, *Artists of Israel, 1920–1980* (Detroit: Wayne State University Press, 1981), 52.

17. Several collections of these historical photographs are available online. See the Middle East Photographic Archive, http://www.lib.uchicago.edu/e/su/mideast/Photo Archive.html; the E. W. Blatchford Collection, http://almashriq.hiof.no/ddc/projects/ jafet/blatchford/index.html; the Bonfils Collection, http://almashriq.hiof.no/general/700/ 770/779/historical/bonfils/bonfils.html; the Beirut Arab Image Foundation, http://www. fai.org.lb/english/fset-presentation.htm; and the National Photo Collection of Israel, http://www.gpo.gov.il/. Excellent historic photos of Palestinian life before 1948 can be found in Khalidi, *Before Their Diaspora*.

18. Further information can be found in Issam Nassar, "A Jerusalem Photographer: The Life and Work of Hanna Safieh," *Jerusalem Quarterly File* 7 (2000), 24–28, also available at http://www.jqf-jerusalem.org/2000/jqf7/nassar.html.

19. Susan Slyomovics, *The Object of Memory: Arab and Jew Narrate the Palestinian Village* (Philadelphia: University of Pennsylvania Press, 1998), provides discussions of traditional architecture and folklore (poetry) in an exploration of how the Palestinian village Ein Houd became the Israeli art colony Ein Hod.

20. Palestinian building skills continue to be employed in modern Israel. One of the biggest construction firms in the north of the country before it went bankrupt in 2003 was a Palestinian firm—Boulos. Jewish Israeli homeowners often use Palestinian craftsmen to do kitchen remodeling or build room additions.

21. Slyomovics, *Object of Memory*, 140.

22. Eric Silver, "Bauhaus on the Mediterranean," *World Press Review* 41, no. 11 (1994): 43; and Esther Sandberg and Oren Tatcher, "The White City Revisited," *Progressive Architecture* 75, no. 8 (1994): 33–34.

23. Helen Chapin Metz, ed., *Israel: A Country Study* (Washington, D.C.: U.S. Government, Secretary of the Army, 1990), 53.

24. Rebecca Torstrick, *The Limits of Coexistence: Identity Politics in Israel* (Ann Arbor: University of Michigan Press, 2000), 135.

25. Visit http://62.90.71.124/eng/siyur/index.html for a virtual tour of the Supreme Court building.

26. See Eyal Weizman, "The Politics of Verticality," *Open Democracy*, April 24, 2002, http://www.opendemocracy.net/debates/article.jsp?id=2&debateId=45&articleId=801.

cookies; coffee or sodas. Over the course of the visit, the food and drink will be replenished. If the visitor stays long enough, they may be invited for dinner.

Families typically eat three meals a day. The main meal of the day, usually a meat-based meal, is served between noon and two o'clock when children return from school (except on Fridays, when the evening meal is the main meal). Men and women may return home to eat with their families if their work allows, but it is far more common for working adults to eat at or near their place of business, especially since many large employers provide employee cafeterias with free or reduced-price meals. The lighter evening meal is usually served around seven or eight o'clock, once the heat of the day subsides. Eating the evening meal together remains important for many Israeli families. In other families, busy schedules mean family members eat at different times. Even for these families, however, the Friday evening and Saturday noon meals may be reserved for eating together.

Religion and Dietary Rules

Different religious traditions affect the types of foods eaten. Under Jewish dietary laws (known as *kashrut*), a number of provisions affect the types of foods one may eat and how dishes are prepared. Kosher refers, therefore, not to a particular type of cuisine but to the way that cuisine is prepared. Kashrut begins with what animals may be eaten. A land mammal has to have both cloven hooves and must chew its cud. Sheep, cattle, goats, and deer are permissible; camels, pigs, and hares are not. Water dwellers must have both scales and fins. All shellfish is forbidden, as are fish that scavenge (such as catfish). Acceptable fish include salmon, tuna, carp, and herring. Birds that are scavengers are forbidden, but it is permissible to eat chickens, geese, ducks, and turkeys. All winged insects, rodents, reptiles, and amphibians are forbidden. Not only are the flesh of these animals forbidden, but any products derived from them (milk, fat, eggs, or organs) are as well. Rennet, an enzyme used to harden cheese, is derived from forbidden animals. Therefore, many hard cheeses are considered nonkosher.

It is not enough, however, to observe the list of permitted and forbidden foods. Jews are forbidden to eat blood. The animals must be slaughtered by a licensed butcher (known as the *shochet*), who kills the animal by slitting its throat in one clean cut. Jews may not eat animals who die from natural causes or are diseased or flawed. Kosher slaughtering drains most of the blood from the carcass; the remaining blood is removed by broiling, soaking, or salting the meat. Finally, one is not allowed to mix meat and milk in the same meal, let alone the same dish. The prohibition against eating meat and milk together was extended to dairy and poultry by the rabbis who interpreted the rules as laid down in the Torah. They also decided not to permit people to cook meat and fish together or serve them on the same plate because they saw this as unhealthy. It is allowed to cook and eat fish and dairy together as well as eggs and dairy. The separation between meat and dairy extends even to the utensils used in preparing, cooking, and serving the food. Thus in a kosher household, people have two sets of dishes, silverware, pots and pans, cooking utensils, dish towels, and even separate dish pans for washing everything at the end of the meal. After eating meat for a meal, one must wait anywhere from three to six hours before eating dishes containing milk. Going from eating milk to meat, however, a person only needs to rinse his or her mouth and eat a neutral solid such as bread.

Muslims also have a set of dietary rules that restrict the foods they may eat (and so influence their cuisine). Foods are divided into lawful and permissible (*halaal*) or unlawful and impermissible (*haram*). Foods that are considered *haram* include all forms of alcohol or liquor (including foods containing alcohol), packaged foods containing animal gelatin, fats, or rennet (thus many cheeses or margarines are not permitted since they contain animal rennet, an enzyme), and all pork products. Muslims are not allowed to eat meat that has not been properly slaughtered according to Muslim laws. The animal must be killed quickly (throat slit), the blood must be drained, and the butcher must say the name of Allah (God) as he kills the animal. This is because Muslims are forbidden to eat meat that has been dedicated to another god (or person). Like Jews, they may not eat animals who have died naturally, nor may they eat animals who are carnivores or scavengers. *Halaal* and *haram* foods must be kept separated; if a *haram* food touches something that is *halaal*, it contaminates it.

Most forms of Christianity do not have rigorous dietary rules, so most Christians in Israel are free to eat whatever types of foods they want. Thus one can purchase pork or shellfish in Israel—they are permitted foods for Christians. Christian rules generally refer to certain periods of fasting (i.e., no meat on Fridays during Lent), although some sects do prohibit or look unfavorably on the use of alcohol.

Most of the Jewish Israeli population maintain some form of kashrut in their homes, and nearly 40 percent eat only kosher foods when in their workplaces or at restaurants.[2] So, while 70 percent of Israelis consider themselves to be "secular," these same individuals keep some kashrut, usually at home. It is common to find that a family will eat one main meal a day with meat, usually at lunch. Communal cafeterias at workplaces also serve a hearty, meat-based meal at lunch. The other meal then usually consists of milk-based products—cheeses, yogurts, creamy salads, or eggs. One reason kashrut has penetrated into secular households concerns the arrangements made between the Israeli state and Jewish religious authorities. Early on, Orthodox political parties gained control over various dimensions of public life (a state of affairs known as the status quo). Public institutions (e.g., military bases, hospitals, and prisons) must uphold the laws of kashrut when they serve meals. Most food produced, packaged, and sold in Israel is kosher and under rabbinic supervision. In addition, supermarkets and almost every hotel in the country, as well as a large number of eating establishments, maintain kashrut. Unlike in the United States, where Jews must work to preserve the rules, kashrut in Israel is so much an accepted part of life people do not have to even think about it to maintain it.

Ethnic Influences on Food

If what characterizes Israeli cuisine is the wide diversity of cooking styles one can find there, the most widespread influences out of that diversity would be cuisine from countries of the Middle East and the Mediterranean region, from North

Africa, and from central and eastern Europe.³ Foods of the Middle East and Mediterranean have made the greatest impact, largely because these cooking styles are based on the vegetables, spices, and other ingredients that are readily available in the region. Throughout the Middle East, the major staple grain is wheat, followed by rice. Rice, whole wheat, and cracked wheat are served boiled, steamed, or in pilaf (cooked in broth with vegetables, fruit, or meat). A popular rice dish mixes short lengths of vermicelli sautéed in butter into the rice before it is steamed. Rice may also be served mixed with lentils and sautéed onions, a dish known as *mujadarra*. Chickpeas and fava beans are additional sources of starch and protein. The most popular vegetable is eggplant, which may be roasted, fried, grilled, or pureed. Other important vegetables include tomatoes, peppers, both sweet and hot, and vegetable marrows (summer squashes), such as zucchini, as well as an assortment of wild greens. Lavish use of herbs, spices, and various members of the onion family, including garlic, characterizes Middle Eastern cookery. In addition to herbs and spices familiar to Westerners, Middle Eastern cooks use cardamom (*hayl*), cinnamon (*qurfa*), ginger (*zanjibil*), coriander (*kusbarah*), cumin (*kammun*), and mint (*nanah*) to flavor many dishes. Olive oil is the most important cooking oil, with sesame and corn oils used less often. Many Palestinian families own olive trees and produce oil from their trees, as well as preserving olives for eating later. Sesame paste (tahini) is an ingredient in many dishes or thinned with water or lemon juice to make a sauce. Pine nuts (*snowbar*) are roasted and mixed with rice and ground meat used to stuff vegetables. Thyme, ground and mixed with sumac, salt, and toasted sesame seeds, makes the delicious spice blend known as *zaatar*. A number of recipes use citrus fruit, especially oranges and lemons. Orange blossom water (*mazaher*), made from the essential oil of the orange blossom, is used in pastry and candy making as well as fruit salads and cold drinks, as is rosewater. Many Palestinian families grow lemon trees in the courtyards of their homes. Yogurt is widely used by itself, as a sauce, a soup, or thickened into cheese (*labaneh*). It may also be served as a beverage.

In the home of a Jewish family that immigrated to Israel from Iraq, Turkey, Iran, Syria, Lebanon, or Jordan, or in a Palestinian home, dinner might consist of a meze (appetizer selection) of traditional salads such as tabouleh (chopped parsley, tomato, and bulgur wheat spiced with lemon), hummus (ground chickpeas with tahini, lemon, and garlic), or baba ghanoush (grilled eggplants, tahini, olive oil, and lemon juice), served with pita bread and plates of olives, pickles, and white cheese (*labaneh*) and followed by a main dish of chicken and rice or meat. *Shwarma* (marinated lamb grilled on a vertical spit, thinly sliced for serving), *kibbe* (ground beef and bulgur wheat coating stuffed with minced lamb and pine nuts), and *kebab* or *shishlik* (skewered, marinated, and grilled lamb or beef) are all popular meat dishes. Among Middle Eastern influences, the cooking of Yemen holds a special place for its uniqueness. Yemeni dishes make use of strong flavors and special spice mixes such as *hawayij*—a blend of black pepper, caraway, cardamon, saffron, and turmeric; the fiery hot *zhug*—made by combining chiles, garlic, pepper, cumin, cardamom, cloves, coriander, and salt; and *hilbeh*—fenugreek seeds, *zhug*, and tomatoes. *Mellawach*, bread cooked flat like pancakes, is often spread with *zhug; kubaneh*, a bread made for Shabbat that is cooked all night in a tightly covered dish, is served with baked eggs, *zhug*, or sprinkled with sugar. One of the more exotic Yemeni dishes was roasted locusts sprinkled with saltwater, a kosher food that, in Yemen, helped the community survive during periods of drought and famine.[4]

Another unique ethnic style of cooking that is taking its place in Israeli national cuisine is Ethiopian. *Injera*, a spongy pancake-like bread, is used to dip into a variety of lamb, chicken, or beef *wats* (stews) or into vegetable dishes such as *gomen* (buttery greens cooked with onions and peppers) or *kik alecha* (yellow split peas with herbs and peppers). *Berbere*, a reddish paste, found in most Ethiopian kitchens and used in preparing many dishes, consists of hot red chili peppers, garlic, ginger, fenugreek, cardamom, cloves, allspice, nutmeg, white pepper, salt, and turmeric. Foods from Yemen and Ethiopia are often served in the traditional style, with diners at round copper tables seated on cushions. The bread and side dishes are piled on the table, and all diners partake from the same plate. The Druze adapted Middle Eastern cooking traditions. They often serve pomegranate seeds with salads and use the juice to prepare many sauces. They add orange blossom water to their coffee and grind sumac to a powder to use to flavor kebabs or to sprinkle on fish or salads. They even make their own special pita bread. Also popular are *kahk*, bracelet-shaped breads seasoned with cumin, coriander, sesame seeds, and sugar. *Sambusak* are half-moon shaped pastries filled with meat, cheese, or *tahinah* that are fried. Even the falafel one finds in Druze villages is different, flavored with cumin, coriander, cayenne pepper, onion, and garlic.

A second major influence in contemporary Israeli cuisine comes from the North African countries of Morocco, Algeria, and Tunisia. Among the most-renowned dishes of these countries are couscous, *tagine*, and *chakchouka*. Couscous is a form of pasta made from semolina wheat cooked by steaming. Couscous serves as the basis of (and gives its name to) a variety of stews that combine meat, vegetables, spices, and fruit. It is found in the cooking of all three countries, although Algerian versions usually include tomatoes; Moroccan versions rely on saffron; and Tunisian couscous is highly spiced. The dish is prepared in a special pot, known as the *couscousière*, which is a double boiler. The pasta is steamed in the top of the pot, while the stew is cooked in the bottom portion. The steam rising from the cooking meat and vegetables infuses the pasta with its flavor. Diners may season their couscous to their own taste by adding harissa, a crushed hot pepper sauce, to spice it up. *Tagines*, another form of stew found in North Africa, are cooked in special earthenware pots also called *tagines*. The pot portion is shallow and wide, while the cover, shaped like a pyramid, catches and concentrates all the steam rising from the dish. The pot, seasoned with olive oil, over time soaks in the spices used to cook the stews. *Tagines* often combine fruit (quince, prunes) or vegetables (carrot, turnips, potatoes, peppers, leeks, string beans, and fennel) with meat, usually lamb, although chicken and beef are also used. The stews are eaten with breads such as *khubz*, a traditional round, flat bread. Another popular dish, *chakchouka*, has made its way into Israeli households. In this dish, found throughout Israel, eggs are poached to near hardness over peeled tomatoes that have been sautéed together with onion, garlic, and a variety of herbs.

Finally, central and eastern Europe provide traditional Jewish cooking of the Yiddish kitchen. Dishes such as gefilte fish (fish balls made of finely minced fish, served in their own jelly and with horseradish accompaniment), *cholent* (a slowly simmered beef stew traditionally prepared for the Sabbath meal), kishke (a peppery blend of bread crumbs, chicken fat, and onions prepared sausage-like in beef casings), borscht (a soup made from beets and other vegetables), and *knaidlach* (egg and matzo meal–based dumplings) are standards of this cuisine. Other popular offerings include kreplach, dumplings filled with ground meat or cheese and boiled or fried; latkes, fried potato pancakes; and kugels, baked egg-and-noodle dishes that are served as main courses or sweetened with sugar, honey, and fruit as desserts. Bread comes in the form of the traditional braided egg bread (challah) that is blessed and served at Shabbat dinner on Friday evenings.

The typical Israeli breakfast owes its origins to kibbutz life. Kibbutz members needed a hearty meal to carry them through the day's work. A kibbutz breakfast buffet might consist of sliced fresh fruit (melon, oranges, apples, pears), sliced vegetables (cucumbers, tomatoes, peppers), olives, a variety of breads, yogurts, numerous cheeses or cheese spreads such as *labaneh,* eggs (hard-boiled, soft-boiled, scrambled, or poached), juice, and coffee. Sometimes the vegetable ingredients are chopped and mixed together in an endless variety of cold salads.

Just as there are a wealth of possible main dishes to be found on an Israeli table, so too with desserts. Fresh fruit is most favored in Middle Eastern cuisine, but sweets such as rice pudding (*ruz be haleeb*) flavored with rosewater or orange blossom water, baklava (phyllo pastry with nuts and a syrup coating), and *kinafi* (a form of cheesecake, made with stretchy cheese and served warm, usually purchased from a bakery) are quite popular. From North Africa, one might be served *muhallabia* (a honey cream pudding from Tunisia), stuffed dates (Moroccan), or spiced peaches (Algerian). Eastern European cooking is famous for its cakes and cookies: sponge, honey, or wonder cake, *rugelach* (jam-filled rolled cookies), *kichlach* (another type of cookie, often with poppy seeds), and blintzes (rolled pancakes) filled with jam or sweet cheese.

Israelis enjoy a wide variety of beverages. Visitors may be served either locally produced soft drinks (such as Tempo products) or the more global Coca-Cola products (which are also produced locally under license). Israelis are also great tea and coffee drinkers. Many people drink mint tea to quench their thirst during the summer months. Coffee is one beverage that crosses over all ethnic groups. If one wants the typical American percolated coffee, one asks for "filter" coffee. *Nes* refers to instant coffee (i.e., Nescafe, or the Israeli version, Elite) served with milk and sugar. *Botz* is finely ground coffee that is stirred into boiling water; the coffee is allowed to sit for a moment so that the grounds sink to the bottom, where it forms a sort of mud. In the summer, iced coffee (best made with real vanilla ice cream) can be a refreshing treat. The most well known coffee, however, is the Arabic coffee, the brewing of which is itself an art. The coffee is made in a special pot called an *ibrik*. After the pot is filled with water, powdered dark roast coffee is added on the top (as is sugar if making the sweetened form). The pot is placed on the heat and allowed to cook until the coffee begins to foam to the top. It is removed from the heat until the boiling ceases and the foam settles. The process of boiling until foaming and removing from the heat is repeated twice more. Some people serve it immediately in small cups, while others allow the grounds to settle to the bottom of the pot before serving.

Israel produces three brands of beer that hold their own with beers manufactured in Europe and the United States. Beer prices are quite low, comparable to the cost of mineral water or fruit juice in the supermarket. Popular foreign beers include Tuborg or Carlsberg (locally made under license by Coca-Cola), as well as imported beers. In Israel, the laws governing alcohol use by minors are quite weak. No laws control advertising, except to prohibit alcohol advertising in youth magazines, no laws regulate the importation of alcohol, and there is little enforcement of the law that prohibits the sale of alcohol to minors in pubs, clubs, or other public drinking places. Minors can purchase alcohol in supermarkets and grocery stores. Until 1998, when it was replaced by wine, beer was the most popular beverage with adolescents.[5] Israel has a number of wineries from the large, internationally known Golan Heights Winery (Yarden, Gamla, Golan, and Katzrin wines) and the Carmel-Mizrachi Winery to the boutique "micro"-wineries, such as Flam, Amphorae, and Ramat Arad. A wide variety of hard liquors and liqueurs (such as Sabra, a chocolate-Jaffa orange concoction) are also sold.

Traditional Israeli fast food is falafel (a deep-fried patty of ground chickpeas and spices) served in pita bread with a variety of salad items to spice it up, such as sweet or sour pickles, hot peppers, pickled turnips, hot sauces, lettuce, chopped tomato, and tahini sauce (sesame seed paste, lemon, and olive oil) to drizzle over the top. Falafel stands can be found everywhere and are a popular stop for locals looking for quick, inexpensive food. People can make an entire meal out of a falafel sandwich by piling the top with salad items and then refilling it several times, leaving the falafel to be eaten last. Some bakeries also serve special pita bread (*manquusheh*) that is coated with *zaatar* and olive oil. Another favorite fast food is *burékas* (pastry filled with cheese and spinach), which can be purchased from stalls in markets and at the bus stations. Israelis enjoy snacking on *garinim* (seeds)—sunflower seeds, pumpkin seeds, and watermelon seeds that are roasted and salted. In the major cities, American fast-food establishments such as McDonalds, Burger King, Kentucky Fried Chicken, Domino's Pizza, and Pizza Hut have sprung up. While some of these establishments keep kashrut at some of their locations, most now serve cheeseburgers or cheese and meat pizza, which has created an uproar among religious Jews and has given the religious political parties a new issue.

Special Holiday Foods

Each religion has foods traditional for its holiday. At Rosh Hashanah, the Jewish New Year, it is traditional to eat foods featuring honey—so that the new year will be sweet. People serve apples dipped in honey, honey cake, and a special round challah (egg bread) eaten dipped in honey. *Tzimmes* (a sweet stew that includes carrots, sweet potatoes, or prunes) is also commonly eaten. At Hanukkah, cooks serve dairy dishes and dishes like latkes, blintzes, or pastries that are fried in oil (because of the significance of oil to the holiday). *Sufganiyot*, jelly doughnuts, are a popular sweet treat for this holiday. At Purim, the favorite sweet is *hamentaschen* (literally, Haman's pockets). These triangular fruit-filled cookies are supposed to represent Haman's three-cornered hat. Cheese blintzes are the traditional meal for the festival of Shavu'ot, when dairy meals are eaten. At Tu B'Shevat, the New Year for trees, Israelis feast on dishes centered on fruits and nuts. One popular custom is to eat a new fruit that day. Yom Kippur, the Day of Atonement, involves a complete fast with no food or drink (even water) that lasts 25 hours; once the sun has set at the end of that day, families break the fast with multiple-course, festive meals featuring whatever foods are part of their tradition. For Sukkoth, a special shelter (called a sukkah) is prepared outside. It is in memory of the temporary huts that the Israelites lived in during their wandering in the desert. The family will eat its meals, and some people will even sleep in the sukkah during the seven days of the holiday. At Passover (Pesach), no leavened grain products can be eaten. The traditional Passover grain product (matzo) is unleavened and like a cracker in texture. Matzo can be ground into flour, crumbled and used as meal, in chunks as a noodle substitute, or in large 10-inch squares as bread. The family meal held the first night of this holiday is known as the *seder* ("order," because there is a specific set of rituals for the evening). During the meal, wine is blessed and drunk; a vegetable (usually parsley) is dipped in saltwater and eaten; matzo is blessed and eaten; bitter vegetables (usually horseradish) are blessed and eaten, and then eaten together with *haroset* (a mixture of apples, nuts, cinnamon, and wine) and matzo; a festive dinner is eaten that often features gefilte fish, matzo ball soup, and roast chicken or turkey or beef brisket. After the meal, a piece of matzo that had been set aside earlier is eaten as dessert, the *afikomen*. A special Moroccan holiday celebration that occurred at the close of Pesach, known as Mimouna, has become a holiday for all Israelis. People open their homes to family, friends, and neighbors. The table will be set with a white tablecloth and will hold the symbolic foods: milk or buttermilk, flour, eggs, honey, butter, fruits, nuts, yeast cakes, sweets, five dates, five coins, five beans, wine, and plain yeast. Stacks of *mufleita* (a uniquely Moroccan pancake that resembles a French crepe), eaten hot with butter and honey, and other intricate dairy dishes are also served.

The important Muslim holidays include Ramadan, the Id al-Fitr, and the Id al-Adha. During Ramadan, Muslims fast completely from food and water during the day. The evening meal that breaks the fast, called the *iftar*, is very festive. Observant Muslims may first eat a date to break their fast and then follow this with a meal of meze, soup, bread, meat, and fruit. Popular Ramadan dishes include *qatayef* (Ramadan pancakes), purchased from street vendors and brought home to be stuffed with sweetened white cheese, walnuts, and sugar, folded in half, deep fried, and sprinkled with rose water; a red lentil soup with cumin, coriander, and lemon juice; *ouzi* (a whole lamb stuffed with spiced rice, ground meat, and nuts); *fattoush*, a popular salad of lettuce, tomatoes, cucumbers, parsley, mint, toasted pita squares, lemon, and olive oil dressing; and *jallab*, a special drink made of a syrup of grape molasses, rose water, and sugar mixed with cold water and served with crushed ice and topped with raisin and pine nuts. *Souhoor*, the morning meal eaten before dawn and the start of a new fast day, usually consists of porridge, bread, and fruit. The Id al-Fitr, the three days of festivities at the end of Ramadan and the Id al-Adha, the commemoration of Abraham's sacrifice, are similarly celebrated with festive meals and many sweets.

Important Christian holidays include Christmas, Easter, St. Barbara's Day,[6] and Epiphany. For Easter, families may make leg of lamb or pork kebabs. Much time goes into preparing the traditional Easter cookie, *ma'amoul* (a walnut- or pistachio-filled cookie). The cookies, which are filled with date paste and crushed walnuts or pistachios, are shaped like the sponge the Roman soldiers filled with vinegar for Jesus to sip on while hanging on the cross or shaped like a crown of thorns. Women work together to prepare the dough, cut and stuff the cookies, and then shape them into the appropriate shape. A family might make 200 or 300 of these at a time. A popular treat for St. Barbara's Day (December 17 in the Orthodox calendar, December 4 for Protestants and Catholics) is *burbarah*, a pudding of boiled wheat, dried fruit, nuts, sugar, rose water, and pomegranate seeds. At Epiphany, women make *asaabee'a zeinab* (Zeinab's fingers), which are long deep-fried strips of flour rolled in sugar and scented with rose water. Christians also have their season of fasting and special foods to go along with it. During Lent, when Christians often abstain from eating meat, women prepare *mujaddara*, a rice and lentil mush, or *makhlouta* (a stew made from bulgur, rice, chickpeas, lentils, and black-eyed peas and spiced with allspice and cooked in a vegetable broth).

TRADITIONAL DRESS
Jewish Traditional Dress

The Torah makes no direct comment about clothing other than to forbid men wearing women's clothing, and women wearing men's garb, and the weaving of wool and linen together in fabric (*sha'atnez*). Sha'atnez served as a visual moral reminder to the Jews that they were to remain a people apart and not to mix or intermarry with non-Jews. Pagan priests wore mixed clothing and used it in their rites; the prohibition ensured that the Israelites would refrain from pagan practices. Male Israelites were instructed to put tassels (*tzitzit*) or twisted cords (*gedilim*) on the four corners of the wrap that covered them. The tassels reminded the wearer to remember and observe all the commandments of God. From this came the *arba kanfot*, a four-cornered garment with tassels at each corner worn by males. This garment is usually worn by pious men and boys under their outer clothing, but some Jews wear it as an outer garment or make sure the fringes are visible. The modern prayer shawl (*tallith*) used during religious services and prayer also incorporates tassels. The *tallith* is usually woven of wool or silk, in white with black or blue stripes at the ends; *tzitzit* hang from each of the four corners. Men were forbidden in the Torah to round the corner of their beards (once again, a practice that marked their uniqueness, their status as a chosen people), which led to the custom of growing sidelocks (*pe'ot*). In addition, the rabbis mandated that men and women should dress modestly (which prohibits them from wearing certain types of revealing clothing) and that married women should cover their hair. Such regulations do not prescribe a certain sort of "traditional" Jewish dress. In many countries, Jews dressed the same as the general population.

Ancient Israelite dress consisted of three basic garments: a long roll of cloth worn as an outer garment (*simlah*), a loin cloth (*ezor*), and a shirtlike garment with long or short sleeves that ranged between below knee to ankle length (*kethoneth*).[7] These garments were similar to those of neighboring peoples. Four elements distinguished male Jewish dress: (1) the tassels (*tzitzit*), (2) hair locks (*pe'ot*), (3) the prohibition against mixing wool and linen, and (4) small leather boxes (*tefillin*) containing passages from the Torah, worn on the forehead and left arm. Modern Orthodox or ultra-Orthodox Jewish men in Israel still use these elements in their daily dress, although the basic garments have been replaced by garments with roots in eastern European society of the eighteenth and nineteenth centuries.

The Mishnah (the oral laws) provides for head coverings for married women. Women meet this requirement in various ways—from wearing some sort of headdress to totally covering the hair. Religious Ashkenazic women either cut their natural hair short or shave it off completely and cover the head instead with a wig (*sheitel*) made of artificial or natural hair. It is considered a breach of modesty for a married woman to have uncovered hair in the presence of men other than her husband. Among conservative Jewish women, hats are popular for covering the hair. Jewish women living in Islamic countries adopted many different styles of headdress, from the Turkish/Palestinian *fotoz*, a turban that formed a half-moon shape, to the Yemeni *gargush*, a tight-fitting cap with wings that covered the neck and shoulders and fringe on the front to cover the forehead. Only later were men required to cover their heads, yet it is those head coverings, especially the skullcap (*kipah* or *yarmulke*) that have come to stand as a symbol of Jewish identity. The Shulhan Aruch (the code of law developed in 1565 by Joseph Karo) set down rigid rules requiring men to cover their heads at all times. This may have arisen from medieval rules that required Jews to wear distinctive hats when they appeared in public.[8] Male head coverings also varied from country to country— from the turban (*kaveze*) popular in Islamic countries to the fur hats (*shtreimel* or *spodik*) favored by Jews in eastern Europe.

Aside from these provisions, Jews dressed like non-Jews in the different regions of the world. This similarity of garb led some non-Jewish rulers to pass regulations to distinguish Jews from non-Jews by a symbol on their clothing or by a particular dress code provision. Early Muslim laws required Jews and Christians to dress differently. Jews had to wear turbans of black or yellow and tie their clothes with a rope not a belt. In medieval France, England, Germany, and Italy, Jews wore a badge (often yellow rings) or a special hat (high and conical, similar to a dunce cap or brimmed with a pointed top). The dress regulations had the effect of preventing Jewish residents from displaying wealth through their clothing. The regulations imposed by outside rulers had their reflections in regulations imposed within the community by the rabbis. They targeted women's dress, in particular, allowing very little jewelry and no embroidery.[9] Rabbis instituted a number of these regulations to protect the Jewish community—displays of Jewish wealth often provoked attacks from envy in the larger community (whose rulers encouraged them to vent their anger at poor living conditions on the Jews rather than the responsible rulers).

Distinctive Jewish costumes developed in some parts of the world, especially the Middle East and eastern Europe.[10] While to an outsider, these costumes appeared similar to local non-Jewish dress, native peoples knew what constituted "Jewish" dress. In Yemen, one could tell a Jewish woman by the embroidery on her dress and its color (black), her head covering, and special colors and trims on the woman's leggings. Men were distinguished by sidelocks and the hat they wore—a low, dark cap wrapped in a checkered cloth. Yemenite wedding apparel was truly unique. The bride wore an elaborate coat-dress of gold thread–brocaded fabric with leggings decorated with star motifs made of red and silk threads, an exclusively Jewish embroidery pattern. Her head covering was a high, towering pearl embroidered triangular piece framed by fresh flowers and branches of rue, believed to ward off the evil eye. She was lavishly bedecked with jewelry: ear hangings went from her head covering to her chest, which was buried under multiple necklaces of silver and coral beads, pearls, amulet cases, and silver bells. Both arms were covered with filigree bracelets, and her fingers might be loaded with up to 20 filigree rings. In Morocco, Jewish women's everyday dress was similar to that of Muslim women, although they were less veiled. It was ceremonial dress that set them apart from Muslim women. The *keswa el kbira* (great dress) derived from Spanish costume and was probably brought by Jews expelled from Spain. Made of velvet (green or red) and elaborately embroidered with gold thread, the dress consisted of a tight bodice, full skirt, a sash, and separate wide sleeves or a veil.

Western European Jews dressed like their non-Jewish compatriots, perhaps slightly more conservatively, with darker shades of clothing and less elaborate decoration. A distinctive Jewish costume developed in eastern Europe that continues to this day in Hasidic clothing. Men wore long black coats tied with a cloth belt and skullcaps (*yarmulke*) under fur hats (*spodik* or *shtreimel*). Long coats (*kaftan*) were popular male dress in much of Slavic eastern Europe, but Christian men wore brightly colored and elaborately embroidered *kaftans*, not the solid black Jewish men favored. Women's dress styles were similar to those of Christian women, although Jewish women wore an embroidered piece of cloth covering the front of their blouse and covered their hair with caps or other headdresses. In 1850, Czar Nicholas I forbade Jewish men to wear the long coats and sidelocks. While many Jews adopted the new regulations, the Hasidic community refused to accept it and fought it. They preserved a traditional Jewish costume and continue to preserve it to this day. This style of dress has become the emblem of Orthodox Jews, no matter where they live today. During the week, an Orthodox man's wardrobe consists of a wool suit with long tailored jacket in black, dark gray or dark blue, a white shirt, and a brimmed felt hat. On the Sabbath, the suit is black satin or silk, and he will wear his fur hat. Women are always dressed modestly. They never wear pants; dresses are long with sleeves covering their elbows; and they may not be flashy or attention drawing.

Palestinian, Druze, and Bedouin Traditional Dress

Palestinian traditional dress provided a wealth of information about identity, age, status, and residence, as well as personal taste.[11] Looking at an individual's clothing, one could tell if they were a city, village, or nomadic dweller; how wealthy the family was; their marital status; and in the case of women's clothing, even the region of the country or village where she lived. Items of clothing were typically made of natural fibers (silk, linen, cotton, or wool) from cloth locally manufactured or imported from other countries in the region (Egypt, Syria), Europe, and East Asia. Poorer villagers used locally produced cotton and wool. These fabrics were either left in their natural colors or were dyed using natural dyes (indigo, madder, cochineal, and other plant sources) or, later, synthetic dyes.

Typical male costume in the nineteenth and twentieth centuries consisted of a plain long shirt or tunic; some type of overcoat, long coat, jacket, or waistcoat; pants; a belt or sash; some form of footwear; and a head covering. The plain long shirt or tunic (*thob*) was made of white or indigo blue cotton or fine wool and covered the man's body at least to his knees. In the twentieth century, it was replaced by a long white shirt cut in European style (*qamis*). Men would hitch the *thob* up through a leather belt to form a pouch that served as a pocket to hold small possessions. Overcoats took a variety of forms: a sheepskin jacket with the wool turned inward, cloth coats with or without sheepskin linings, or a sleeveless cloak of wool (*'abayeh*) worn draped over the shoulders like a cape. The Druze wore a coat like an *'abayeh*, but it was tighter fitting and had short sleeves. City men wore another kind of coat over their long shirts—the *qumbaz*—adapted from a Turkish style. This coat made its way into the villages by the end of the nineteenth century, as city men adopted the European style of trousers and jackets. The *qumbaz* played an important role in the gift exchanges that took place at circumcision and marriage. It was customary in some villages for the young groom to give fine coats to the bride's maternal and paternal uncles. In many villages, the color of the *qumbaz* draped over the bride in her bridal procession signified which political faction she belonged to, Qays using red and Yaman using white. When a young woman married into the other political faction, she would wear her family's colors for the first part of the procession and then switch coats mid-way, signifying her passage into her husband's family's control. A variety of jack-ets and waistcoats, copied first from Turkish and later European fashions, became popular with urban men and then filtered down into village and nomadic society. During the British mandate (1922–1948), the European jacket became popular among all Palestinians and largely replaced the older overcoats and cloaks. A vil-lage man would thus wear three layers—the traditional *thob*, the Turkish-inspired *qumbaz*, and the European-style suit jacket, while a city man wore European-style trousers and jacket.[12]

About the same time that village men started wearing the *qumbaz*, they also adopted Turkish-style pants, the *sirwal*. These pants were tight fitting at the ankles and very wide at the drawstring waist. The overall look was thus baggy and loose-fitting upper pants with very form-fitting lower legs and ankles. At first, only wealthy villagers used these, but as contact with the British increased and men became more concerned with modesty, the use of these pants spread. During the mandate, the *sirwal* was replaced by European trousers among men of all ages and social classes. Today, a few older men continue to wear traditional garb: for Druze, long black robes and formal white turbans; for village men, the *qumbaz*; for Bedouin, the *thob* and *'abayeh*. Men either wore a leather belt with hooks for car-rying things or a sash of silk, cotton, or wool. Sashes displayed information about a man's wealth through their width and bulk (wider and bulkier meant wealthier in order to afford them). Footwear consisted of locally made shoes or sandals or bare feet. Shoes were always removed when one entered a house or the mosque because they were unclean.

Headgear clearly marked the major divisions in society. Until the 1930s, the type of head covering a man used indicated whether he lived in a town or village or was a nomad, his religious affiliation, and his wealth and political position.[13] Nomads wore the *keffiyeh*, a square head cloth, folded diagonally and draped over the head, with the two ends hanging on either side of the face and the third point hanging in the back. It was held in place by ropes of wool or camel hair (*'aqal*). Urban men wore the Turkish-style *tarbush istambuli*, a tall hat shaped like a over-turned round pot. Village men wore a skull cap under a felt cap under a smaller, rounder *tarbush* over which was wrapped a turban. A man's honor resided in his head (i.e., his reason and ability to control his emotions), so a man's headgear was an important visual symbol of his worth. Young boys signaled their passage into manhood by wearing *tarbush* and turban. The color of a man's turban also was important. Muslims wore green turbans (later, white), while Christians or Jews might wear red, black, or purple. During the time of the Arab Revolt (1936–1939), village and urban men adopted the *keffiyeh* and *'aqal* as an expres-sion of Palestinian nationalism; these items of headgear remain important mark-ers of Palestinian identity to this day.

Palestinian women's garments included baggy pants (*sirwal*), one or more under-dresses, an overdress (*thob* or *qumbaz*), a jacket, sashes or girdles, shoulder mantles, footwear, and head coverings. Exactly which garments constituted a woman's costume varied from region to region. Women in the Galilee used the *qumbaz,* while the *thob* was preferred by nomadic and seminomadic women. A woman's wedding trousseau included lavishly decorated clothing for weddings and other ceremonies, as well as plainer, simpler clothing for everyday wear. Many of the elaborately embroidered dresses sold to tourists in the Old City markets of Jerusalem are dresses for festive occasions. The women's garments, unlike men's, were embellished with patchwork of satin, velvet, or taffeta and elaborately embroidered. Women made and decorated their own garments, so their apparel was also a statement about their skills. A woman's choice of color, fabric, and pattern was a statement about her identity, a process not much different than Americans' use of clothing to express themselves. Younger women wore more vivid colors, and older women preferred darker, more muted shades, more in keeping with their position within society. The quality and quantity of the workmanship on a woman's garment was an indirect comment on the family's wealth. Women who had to work in the fields did not have as much time to create elaborately embroidered dresses. Some women earned a living by sewing for other, wealthier women.

The decoration on women's clothing tells a story all by itself. Palestinian women used appliqué, couching, satin stitch, and cross-stitch embroidery to decorate their clothing. Skirts, sleeves, and the bodices of dresses were often elaborately decorated—in some cases with inset panels of taffeta, satin, or velvet and elaborate embroidery. The dress panels would be embroidered as a woman had time and would be made into a garment once all the embroidery work was completed. When a dress wore out, it was common to recycle the embroidered pieces that were still in good shape into new garments. (A popular modern use for such pieces is to turn them into pillows or frame them for wall display.) Women used red, in various shades, as the primary color and mixed it with other colors such as blue, brown, purple, pink, yellow, green, or orange. Color schemes for dresses changed through time, as did the stitches used as new colors of floss became popular and as women were exposed to pattern books and magazines with European motifs. Each region of the country had its own traditions of design, although these changed with time as new materials and designs were incorporated. Thus grandmother, mother, and daughter might find themselves arguing over what constituted the regional style because that style was different for each of the generations. Traditional Palestinian designs were geometric and abstract—such as triangles, chevrons, squares, eight-pointed stars, and lozenges. While the designs themselves were abstract, they were named after common items found in the women's worlds—such as "palms" (*nakleh*), "cypress trees" (*saru*), "head of corn" (*'aranis*), and "moons" (*qamr*). European missionaries and educators introduced a more representational style of design that featured wreaths, urns, birds, and human figures.[14] Women around Bethlehem developed couching (shaping silver, gold, or silk cord into elaborate patterns that are tacked onto the garment with tiny stitches) as their distinctive style of embroidery. In fact, this work is known as "Bethlehem work" (*shughl talhami*). Brides often demanded garments made in this style as part of the trousseau that they received from their grooms.

Galilee women wore either a short-sleeved open-front coat or their own version of the *qumbaz*—with long, tight-fitting sleeves, a scooped neckline, and long side slits. The coats were made of a dyed cotton in shades of indigo blue, rusty red, or light brown, although women also made coats of satin (pink or red) and silk (black or purple). Under them, women wore a long-sleeved shirt, replaced in the late nineteenth century by a European-style, long-sleeved, waisted dress made of imported cottons. Beneath these, women wore ankle-length pants, either the *sirwal* pants or a newer type of pants with tight calves and frilled cuffs. Bedouin women in the Galilee wore a *thob*, a dress of black cotton (or more recently, satin or velvet) with long, tight sleeves and a long neck opening. Women in southern Palestine commonly wore a dress with a full skirt and long sleeves that were very wide at the wrist and came to a point. The points of the sleeves, which had to be tied behind the neck when the woman wanted to do any work, were a sign of wealth and leisure. Most dresses had round collars and chest slits, but some had V-necks or closed, scooped necklines. Colors of the dress varied by region, from white (Nablus and Tulkarm) to black (south of Ramla and Hebron Hills) to both (Ramallah and Jaffa and around Jerusalem). Women wore white cotton underdresses, but these were gradually replaced by the cotton print dresses popular in the north. Women also wore ankle-length underpants for greater modesty. Coats and dresses were worn with a girdle or sash over them. Even these items provided information about the wearer's identity, as different fabrics and ways of wearing the sash or girdle marked different regions of the country. Girdles were made from square pieces of fabric (cotton, silk, or satin) wrapped diagonally or long pieces of fabric, joined together and tied once or twice around the waist. Bedouin women used long, narrow sashes of handwoven wool, decorated with cowrie shells, glass beads, and tassels. Jackets, usually long-sleeved and short-waisted, were worn in some areas for warmth and decoration. Until the 1920s, only urban women wore shoes. Putting on shoes was a sign of upward mobility for village and nomadic women.

The final elements of Palestinian women's costume were headwear and jewelry. While urban women veiled outside their homes, village and nomadic women did not have to cover their faces. Women's head coverings consisted of a tight-fitting cap or bonnet with a scarf or veil tied or draped over it, sometimes secured by a headband. The headdresses that women wore for special occasions were usually heavily decorated with gold or silver coins. The women acquired the coins at marriage from their fathers. A woman owned her headdress and her jewelry and would add to each throughout her life as she could. These items represented her bank account; pieces might be sold to provide for family needs or traded in for more valuable pieces as family wealth increased. Because the coin headdresses and jewelry were worn on ceremonial occasions, they also served as a visible sign of the family's social status and wealth. Silver and gold jewelry in the form of necklaces with pendants, coins and large beads, heavy wrist bangles, or necklaces of glass beads, coral, amber, or mother of pearl were common. Pendants could be crucifixes (for Christians) or inscribed with Quranic verses in Arabic script (for Muslims). Blue beads and eye beads were very popular because they provided protection from the "evil eye."[15] Gold jewelry mass produced in Lebanon and Syria eventually replaced silver jewelry. Today, Israeli Palestinian women seek to acquire gold jewelry from their husbands and families as a way of securing their fortune. In Israel, women prefer gold to diamonds.

Modern Israeli Dress

In the Old City of Jerusalem today, among the press of tourists and Christian, Muslim, and Jewish residents dressed in typical Western fashion (everything from shorts and tank tops to blue jeans and T-shirts), one can still catch glimpses of traditional costumes. Older Bedouin or Palestinian women hawk their vegetables, squatting at the sides of the narrow alleys in their black *thobs*, embroidered in brilliant colors. They pull their white veils around them as people brush past. Sometimes women sell small pieces of embroidered dress panels to tourists or anyone who shows an interest. Striding up the lanes from the Jewish quarter, two Hasidic men might be seen in earnest conversation, waving their hands or curling their *pe'ot* as they vigorously debate the finer points of Torah. Wearing their long black coats, their heads crowned with fur hats, they look as though they have stepped out of an eighteenth-century painting. Further behind them, one might see another pair of men, also religious Jews deep in conversation, but they are dressed in modern black suits and wearing black fedoras. From the Armenian quarter, a monk dressed in his black cassock and tall hat strolls past. Coming from the Muslim quarter, two women hurry by, completely covered by their black veils (*abayeh*), their hands gloved and only their eyes visible.

Israelis have moved well beyond the early days of austerity and rationing when the norm was simple, practical garments of khaki, as epitomized by the cartoon character Srulik (Little Israel), who became Israel's national symbol. Modern Israel is home to a thriving high-fashion design industry. French and Italian fashions easily make their way across the Mediterranean and into the homes of Israeli customers. Famous Israeli designers of women's wear include Dorin Frankfurt, Kedem Sasson, Ronen Chen, Ginza, Reuma, Sigal Dekel, and Roni Rabl. Israeli swimwear has had an international reputation for years, due to the designs of Gottex, an early pioneer in the industry. Other designer swimwear lines include Diva, Pilpel, and Lagouf. Naot sandals have soared in popularity overseas, and many children are clothed in Sara's Prints sleepwear or underwear. Israeli women favor a style known as "sport-elegant"—something between American after-five dresses and leisure wear, outfits that can move easily from workplace to after-work social gatherings such as weddings or bar and bat mitzvahs.[16] Israeli designers emphasize comfort and make creative use of fabrics such as spandex, velveteen, and velour. Children's fashion is big business in Israel.[17] Manufacturer Pierre Galio designs garments for a wide variety of Israeli youth—from trendy Tel Avivans, who want clothes that are *gizit* (fashionable) and *coolit* (cool), to children from religiously observant families. Traditional Mizrahi tastes, Palestinian tastes,

Lingerie and other goods attract shoppers to a market stall outside the walls of Jerusalem's Old City. Photo by the author.

athletic tastes—there is a line of clothing for all different segments. Easy-care materials such as jacquard are popular, and Israelis have a fondness for chiffon. Even the flannel long johns and cotton jumpsuits of infant wear have given way to new fashions that feature undershirts, ribbed polos, playsuits with matching berets, jeans, and overalls in strong colors, as produced by manufacturers like Solog and Shilav.

Traditional costumes still make their appearances at festive occasions. Moroccan men and women don caftans to welcome visitors to their home at the Mimouna holiday. Yemenite brides may wear traditional Yemenite wedding gowns or Western-inspired white wedding gowns. Holidays such as the Ids may inspire Palestinians to wear traditional festive dress. Traditional costumes have been largely supplanted by Western-inspired clothing and the forces of globalization of culture. Traditional dress, however, remains important in Israel for expressing one's identity. Thus, for example, Ethiopian communities have retained their traditional garments and continue to manufacture items of clothing in Israel; the Orthodox community continues to dress in a style that sets them apart from other Jewish Israelis; and Palestinians display the *kheffiyeh* as a sign of support for Palestinian nationalism and Palestinian rights.

NOTES

1. Daniel Rogov, "Med-Rim Cuisine—Whatever It Is, It Is Not Israeli," Israeli Wine and Dining Web site. http://www.stratsplace.com/rogov/israel/med_rim.htm.

2. Daniel Elazar, "How Religious Are Israeli Jews?" 1996, Jerusalem Center for Public Affairs, Daniel Elazar On-Line Library, Israel: Religion and Society. http://www.jcpa.org/dje/articles2/howrelisr.htm.

3. Some useful resources to learn more about Israeli cooking are Claudia Rosen, *The Book of Jewish Food: An Odyssey from Samarkand to New York* (New York: Knopf, 1996); Joan Nathan, *The Foods of Israel Today* (New York: Knopf, 2001); and Sheilah Kaufman, *Sephardic Israeli Cuisine: A Mediterranean Mosaic* (New York: Hippocrene Books, 2002).

4. Reuben Ahroni, *Yemenite Jewry: Origins, Culture, and Literature* (Bloomington: Indiana University Press, 1986), 10–12.

5. Shoshana Weiss, "Marketing Beer in Israel," Institute of Alcohol Studies, *The Globe*, no. 2 (2001). http://www.ias.org.uk/publications/theglobe/01issue2/globe0102_p10.html.

6. Saint Barbara, daughter of the pagan Dioscurus, secretly converted to Christianity. When her father found out, he denounced her to the authorities. She was tortured and then executed in 306 A.D. by her father. He, in turn, was struck by lightning and reduced to ashes. Saint Barbara is the patron saint of firefighters, miners, and gunners.

7. This discussion is based on Alfred Rubens, *A History of Jewish Costume*, rev. and enl. ed. (London: Peter Owen, 1981).

8. Rubens, *History of Jewish Costume*, 11.

9. Rubens, *History of Jewish Costume*, 80–103.

10. The Israel Museum Web site (http://www.imj.org.il/eng/judaica/index.html) has pictures of traditional costumes, as does the one for the Diaspora Museum in Tel Aviv (http://www.bh.org.il/).

11. Two excellent studies of Palestinian costume are Shelagh Weir, *Palestinian Costume* (Austin: University of Texas Press, 1989); and Jehan S. Rajab, *Palestinian Costume* (London: Kegan Paul International, 1989). Both also provide valuable information about Palestinian embroidery designs.

12. Weir, *Palestinian Costume*, 54.

13. Weir, *Palestinian Costume*, 58.

14. Weir, *Palestinian Costume*, provides a comprehensive discussion of the elements of embroidery and garment construction, as well as photographs of the actual garments.

15. Many people believe certain people possess the ability to harm others by simply glancing at them. Babies are seen as particularly vulnerable and are often protected with amulets, blue beads, or glass beads decorated with an eye.

16. Barbara Sofer, "Label Droppings: New Names in Israeli Fashion," *Hadassah Magazine* 78, no. 8 (1997): 28–31.

17. Barbara Sofer, "Growing Up in Style," *Hadassah Magazine* 79, no. 9 (1998): 14–18.

6

Gender, Marriage, and Family

GENDER

Israel is often held up as an example of a society in which men and women are equal. The early days of men and women toiling together to build settlements, drain swamps, and cultivate fields, the images of smiling young women holding Uzis or women in uniform swarming over tanks, and the famous images of Golda Meir, prime minister from 1969 to 1974, all serve to bolster the claim that in Israel men and women are equal. By considering how gender is constructed in Israel, however, a very different picture emerges. Gender refers to the social and cultural characteristics that societies place on the biological fact of being born male or female. In a society with gender equality, one would expect the gender norms to be the same for men and women. Yet in Israel, "security, the army, and soldiering dominate the public sphere and are the bastions of male discourse. Family and familism are perceived as the pillars of Israeli communal and private lives and are the women's castle."[1] The difference in how men's and women's experiences are structured promotes gender inequality in Israeli society.

For both Jewish and Palestinian women, to be female is to be a mother and to be in the home. Married women who are childless in both societies face the threat of divorce and are devoid of social status. Women are expected by their families, communities, and the state to meet certain social expectations regarding procreation. Jewish women as mothers are charged with preserving the purity of the nation. There is a long history in Israel of women being called upon by state officials to serve as the mothers of the nation. David Ben Gurion turned women's fertility into a national priority in the early 1950s when he created a special state fund to give symbolic money rewards to "heroine mothers"—women who bore 10 or more children. Carrying the protection motif even further, Geula Cohen, a

Knesset (Israeli parliament) member from the Tehiya Party, had this to say: "[T]he Israeli woman is a wife and a mother in Israel, and therefore it is her nature to be a soldier, a wife of a soldier, a sister of a soldier. This is her reserve duty. She is continually in military service."[2]

Palestinian women are also viewed by their society and political leaders as the "mothers of the nation." Women are urged to contribute to the Palestinian cause by bearing many male children, who will grow to be fighters. The modern Palestinian woman is supposed to be a supermom—educated, employed, fertile, feminine, nurturing, a good cook, and producing "a solid new generation for the nation."[3]

The model for men is the Jewish male citizen-soldier, who serves three years of active duty and remains on reserve duty until he turns 55.[4] During the first 30 years of Israel's existence, the image of the Jewish warrior became the male model promoted at all levels of Israeli society.[5] The sabra, or native-born Israeli Jew, prickly on the outside, sweet on the inside, is a male image—tanned, strong, healthy looking, and with European features (often blond hair and blue eyes). Beginning in nursery school and continuing through high school, Israeli Jewish children fantasize about, anticipate, and prepare for their period of army service. The combat model is how Israeli Jewish men achieve and affirm their manhood.[6] They take behaviors such as control, risk seeking, or aspiring to tests (which have been "socialized" into their heads and bodies through military service) into a variety of contexts outside the military, such as business or leisure pursuits—where this control and risk seeking is seen as "desirable" or "successful" behavior. What is left out is how these behaviors play out in intimate relationships or in the family.

If Israeli Jewish men define their male identity through the army, Palestinian men define their identity as against the army. The humiliations they suffer, their inability to secure good stable work and provide for their families, the hostility directed at them by Israeli police, and their inability to control their own destinies and those of their children provide a markedly different context within which these men frame their masculinity. Within this context, family honor has taken on added importance. Men may respond to their lack of control over their own lives by reinforcing their control over women's lives.

That male and female gender identities have been constructed in these ways in Israel has had major consequences for Israeli women. Until the end of the 1970s, violence against women in Israel was not even on the public agenda. Between 1982 and 1991, feminist activists lobbied for changes in how rape was legally prosecuted in Israel. Sentences were increased, and new guidelines were established when rape involved a minor, led to serious physical harm or impregnation, or was combined with abuse. Rape centers were established, and the police were trained in how to proceed in such cases. Although the rape penalty has been increased to 16 years, judges continue to hand down light sentences. They justify the sentences by claiming that the convicted rapists are "normal" men who had family responsibilities, served their country in the army, or felt remorse for what they had done.[7]

From 1978 to 1998, women's participation in the labor force steadily climbed in Israel from 34.3 percent in 1978 to 46.3 percent 20 years later. In 2001, women accounted for 35 percent of full-time workers and 66 percent of part-time workers.[8] While more Israeli women are working, they are concentrated into occupations that are characterized by caregiving or service work. The main occupations for women in 1998 were as kindergarten or elementary teachers, secondary and postsecondary teachers, personal care workers, secretaries, domestic service, salespersons, bookkeepers, cashiers or bank clerks, nurses, or customer service. Men's main occupations included drivers, electricians, salespersons, welders, engineers, senior managers, general managers, wholesalers, and stock clerks. That year, a man made NIS 7,088 per month (roughly $1575 US), while a woman made NIS 4,352 ($967 US).[9] While some of the gap had to do with differences in hours worked (full-time versus part-time), women still earned less than men per hour worked, an inequality that existed across all educational levels.

The concentration of women into a few major occupational categories means that when Israel's economy experiences a downturn and government funding is cut for education and other social services, women will be disproportionately more affected than men because these branches employ more women. In addition, the concentration of women in only a few occupational categories tends to drive down wage rates within those categories because more women are competing for fewer slots. Women's preference for part-time work and the fact that they may drop out of employment periodically due to family considerations further weaken their ability to close the gap with men. When women have reduced earning power, they may be more likely to remain in difficult personal circumstances.

In Israel, there are very close ties between the political and military worlds, with ex-military officials often entering the government as politicians once they have left active duty in the armed services. Women cannot use the military as a springboard to politics because they do not reach the upper ranks of the IDF in any significant number. While Golda Meir's service as prime minister has often been used as evidence of women's equality in Israeli politics, the true picture is that women are poorly represented in national and local politics. A 1999 study of women's political participation conducted by the Adva Center found that Israel ranked below all regions of the world except South Asia in the percentage of women in the national parliament (Knesset).[10] Women have generally ranged between 7 and 9 percent of the Knesset's members over the years, although there are 17 women in the current Knesset (14 percent). This is still well below the rates of participation seen in western Europe and the Scandinavian countries, where women's participation reaches 37 percent. Only nine women (including three in the current government) have served as cabinet ministers in 16 different Israeli governments. In 1980, researchers estimated that while women constituted 40 to 50 percent of total party membership, they accounted for only 7.5 per-

Israeli women serve in the Armored Corps. Photo by
Nati Narnik. Courtesy of the Government Press Office,
State of Israel.

cent of the leadership positions.[11] Since 1978, when direct election of mayors
began, only four women have been successful at getting elected. On local councils, women are also in the minority.

In the 1999 party primary process, both Labor and Likud reserved spots on
their lists for female candidates. However, in the Likud's case, this accounted for
only four spots on the list (at 10, 20, 30, and 35), and the Likud women actually
placed higher in the internal elections. Labor's complicated system actually hurt
women candidates because voters assumed they would get one of the reserved
spots. Shinui reserved two slots for women in the top 10. Such quotas are not
nearly as comprehensive as the quota laws passed in Latin American countries or
Scandinavian countries, where 30 percent of slots must be reserved for women.
While their numbers have been low, Israeli women Knesset legislators have been
remarkably effective at getting legislation passed. The eight women in the Fourteenth Knesset were responsible for 40 percent of all legislation passed in the
three years it sat.[12] In 1992, the Committee for the Status of Women was estab-

lished as an ad hoc committee. It became a statutory (permanent) committee in 1996. The women in the Knesset have also been known to break party discipline in order to work together to pass legislation that would benefit women.

MARRIAGE

Marriage is highly valued and encouraged among all sectors of Israeli society. Through marriage, young men and women become full adults in their community. To not marry is to remain in an ambiguous state, not quite child but also not quite adult. Married couples produce the next generation of children who will keep alive the family's name. The legal age of marriage in Israel is 17 (although younger people may marry under certain circumstances). The average age at first marriage has increased among all Israelis in the period from 1952 to 2000. For men, the average age at marriage is 27.2 among Jews, 25.8 among Muslims, 28.9 among Christians, and 25.5 among Druze. For women, the average age at first marriage is lower, at 24.8 among Jews, 21.5 among Muslims, 23.8 among Christians, and 21 among Druze. The Jewish and Muslim communities had the highest rates of men and women aged 19 and younger getting married.

There is strong pressure across all religious faiths for people to marry a partner from their own faith, although Muslim men may marry Jewish or Christian women with no problem because Muslim religious affiliation passes through the father. Israeli marriage law bolsters the familial and social pressure. Israeli law prohibits child marriage and polygamy, but there is no civil, state-sanctioned marriage in Israel. Therefore if an Israeli Christian man and an Israeli Jewish woman wanted to marry, they must marry outside the country and then register their marriage with the civil authorities once they return. There is no legal way they can be married in Israel, unless one partner converts to the other's religion. By law, a rabbi, priest, or imam who performs a marriage ceremony for a person of another faith can be jailed for up to six months. There is equally strong pressure for young people to marry persons of similar ethnic and class background. About 25 percent of Israeli Jewish marriages are between an Ashkenazi and a Mizrahi partner and that percentage has remained fairly stable.

Marriage for Israeli Jews

Historically, marriages were arranged in Jewish society and were seen as contracts between two families rather than contracts between two individuals. The levirate, a practice by which a childless widow would marry one of her dead husband's brothers, provides evidence that the marriage bond was a bond involving families and not individuals. Even though the husband had died, his family still had the right to provide a new spouse for the woman so that she could have children for their family. Read in this light, the biblical substitution of Leah for Rachel when Jacob first married also takes on new meaning.[13]

In Orthodox communities in Israel, arranged marriages are still the norm. Often the services of a matchmaker (*shadchan*) are employed to find a suitable partner. The matchmaker is responsible for checking out the backgrounds of prospective spouses to ensure a good fit and a stable marriage. Outside of the Orthodox community, secular Israelis have adopted the Western view of marriage as a contract between two individuals, entered into because they love each other and have chosen each other. However, because marriage is a matter of personal status law, even secular Israelis must get married according to Orthodox religious law if they want to marry in Israel.

The two individuals who want to marry must be able to prove that they are both children of Jewish mothers. The Ministry of Religious Affairs maintains a list of Israeli citizens who are not Jewish according to Orthodox law and who may therefore not marry an Israeli who is considered Jewish under Orthodox law. The two individuals must also not fall into any other category that would forbid their marriage. They must not be considered to be bastard children (*mamzerim*). A male Kohen (of the priestly caste) may not marry a divorced woman. A childless widow must have been released from her obligation to marry her husband's brother. A divorced woman must have received her bill of divorce (*get*) from her husband. A woman whose husband has disappeared but is not known to be dead cannot remarry until his death can be proven. A nursing woman cannot marry until her child is weaned. Finally, a widow must wait at least three months before she remarries so that if she turns out to be pregnant, there will be no doubt about who the child's father is.[14] Even when both partners are Jewish, if they want a truly secular ceremony that does not involve the Orthodox authorities, they must marry outside the country and register the marriage civilly. Marrying within Israel in a private ceremony does not allow the marriage to be registered by the state, and none of the legal benefits of marriage (insurance, housing, education, etc.) can be claimed.

The actual wedding ceremony involves additional preparations. Prior to the wedding, the bride must immerse herself in the ritual bath (*mikveh*) to purify herself before the wedding. In Mizrahi communities, it is customary to hold a henna ceremony for the bride, which is attended by her female family members and friends. All present mark out designs on their hands with needles onto which henna (a reddish or yellowish powder) is rubbed to bring out the designs. The custom is intended to keep away evil spirits.

Weddings can take place on any day other than Shabbat, a festival, a day of public mourning, or during the period between Pesach and Shavu'ot. They can be performed anywhere. Most Israeli couples choose to hire wedding halls or hotel banquet rooms, a few others may use synagogues, and still others have weddings outdoors in garden settings. Wedding invitations are distributed by hand to family members and mailed to other guests. Guests are not expected to respond, so invitations may arrive as close as a week before the event. It is not uncommon for 300 or more guests to be invited to the wedding. A wedding is a major event in Israeli society, and families spend considerable sums of money on them.

In the typical lavish wedding, the bride's gown is rented and her hair and makeup are professionally done before the wedding. Most couples have a professional make a wedding video. Prior to the actual ceremony, couples in their wedding garb often pose in various key locations around town. The actual wedding and reception are then added to the video later to produce a professional film. On the wedding day, the families of the couple form a receiving line at the wedding location to greet guests and discreetly receive the envelopes containing checks that each guest passes over while going through the line. These envelopes, the Israeli wedding gift, are placed in a locked box usually provided by the banquet hall. Guests are expected to gift an amount that will at least cover the cost of their dinner. If they are close family or friends, their checks should be even more generous.

Once all the guests have arrived, the bridal couple makes their entrance. The bride will take a seat while the groom negotiates the financial conditions of the wedding (*tenaim*) and the signing of the marriage contract (*ketubah*) with the rabbi. The wedding contract details the husband's obligations (10) and rights (4) to his wife. He is obligated to provide her with food and shelter, to cohabit with her, to pay alimony in case of divorce, to pay medical expenses, ransom her, pay burial expenses, provide for her and her daughters upon his death, and bequeath his estate to the sons of the marriage. His rights concern her because he is acquiring her. Therefore, he has the right to the fruits of her labor, to property she discovers by chance, to property she already owns, and to be the sole benefactor of her estate.

The groom goes to the bride and covers her face (thus ensuring that, unlike Jacob in the Book of Genesis, he is not tricked into marrying the wrong woman) and is escorted, usually by his parents, to his place under the wedding canopy (*huppah*). The rabbi gives blessings and the bride is brought to the canopy, which she may encircle before joining the groom to his right. The rabbi blesses wine, and the couple drinks from the cup. The groom places an unadorned gold ring on the bride's finger while saying that she is now consecrated to him. Next, the *ketubah* is read aloud. The bride and groom then recite the seven blessings, at the end of which the couple drinks wine again and the groom steps on and breaks a glass. To complete the ceremony, the couple are secluded together to symbolically consummate the marriage. This ends the formal ceremony, and the gathered group then turns to eating, dancing, and generally making merry.

Marriage for Israeli Palestinians

Traditionally in Palestinian society, marriages were also arranged, by fathers (with advice from mothers), who decided whom their sons and daughters would wed. Within Muslim and Christian societies, marriage holds a high positive value, and people should marry during their lives. The entire family of the prospective groom might be pulled into the process of looking for suitable candidates and negotiating the terms of the marriage contract. More distant relatives might be called upon to visit the home of a possible candidate in order to check out both the young person in question and the person's family. As negotiations became more serious, more senior family members would be sent as delegates. Once the girl's hand has been formally requested in marriage, an engagement ceremony is held, during which the women of the two families come together to exchange gifts. Because Palestinian society is patrilineal, one favored marriage pattern was traditionally for a young man to marry one of the daughters of his father's brothers (i.e., his first cousin on his father's side), although the total number of these weddings is actually quite small. This marriage kept property in the family and provided the new bride with some security in her new home, since her in-laws were also her aunt and uncle.

Like Jewish Israelis, weddings are major events for Palestinian Israelis. In many ways, some of the outward forms of the wedding are shared across the whole society. A wedding is a status event, and considerable funds will be spent, if available, to make sure it is the most spectacular event possible. Professional videos, rented intricate bridal gowns, and elaborate hair styles and makeup are all part of a Palestinian wedding as well. It was common during the late 1980s for couples to have their wedding videos broadcast on local cable channels, where everyone in the community could view the event. Guests bring money as gifts, and weddings are celebrated with food and drink. The bride may be processed through the streets to her new groom's family home. What differs is the ceremonial tradition that unites the couple, since some Palestinians are Christian, others are Muslim, and still others are Druze.

Muslim marriage also requires a contract (*nikah*) between the bride's legal guardian, usually her father, and the groom. The contract stipulates that the woman is freely consenting to the marriage and it establishes the amount of money or property (*mahr*) that the husband must give to legally validate the marriage. The *mahr* may be paid at once or split into two payments, often a small one to be paid at the time the contract is signed and a larger one to be paid in case of divorce or death. The amount of the *mahr* often serves as an indication of the "worth" of the bride and her family, so negotiations can be serious. Among middle-class or elite families, it may represent a formality. The actual ceremony before the religious official is brief. The religious official asks the groom and bride three times if they concur to the marriage. Once they have replied "yes" three times, the ceremony is complete. The couple may then move on to the wedding hall for the official public celebration.

In another example, the Orthodox Christian wedding ceremony begins at the door of the church, when the priest invites the couple into the church for the betrothal ceremony. He blesses the rings and places them on their right hands. Their sponsor then exchanges the rings three times to symbolize the intertwining of their lives. They then move on to the wedding ceremony. The focal point of the wedding is the crowning. The crowns are joined by a ribbon that symbolizes their unity. The priest takes the crowns, blesses them, and crowns the couple king and queen of their home. The sponsor also exchanges the crowns three times. After more readings, the couple drinks wine from a common cup. The priest and the couple circle a table on which holy objects lay. The crowns are removed, and the priest reminds the couple that they are now bound together.

Divorce

Just as marriages are the domain of religious law in Israel, so too is divorce. When marriages end, the parties involved must go through the appropriate procedures or ceremony within their religious community to dissolve the marriage. Matters of child support, alimony, and child custody are also handled by the appropriate religious authority, although recent revisions in the law brought about by feminist activists have given the civil courts jurisdiction in matters of custody and maintenance if the case is filed there first. The overall divorce rate in Israel is low compared with other Western countries. Of the more than 885,000 couples who married in Israel between 1964 and 1999, over 19 percent were divorced by 1999.[15]

Within Judaism, a husband may begin the writing of a divorce decree (*get*) on the grounds of his wife's adultery, apostasy, immoral behavior, refusal of conjugal rights, inability to bear children, incurable disease, mental illness, refusal to cohabit, or in light of defects or diseases that were hidden from him before the marriage. A woman may not initiate the writing of a decree but must appeal to a rabbinical court, which has some power to compel her husband to divorce her.[16] Her grounds can include immoral behavior, habitual cruelty, incurable disease, sterility, refusal of conjugal rights, apostasy, refusal to support her, if he works in an occupation that makes him repulsive and prohibits them from living together, or if he has fled as a criminal.

The actual process of the divorce involves the writing of the *get*, which must be given to the wife by the husband—with both the giving and acceptance being by consent and free will. Regardless of whether both parties or only one sought the divorce, the *get* must be freely given and freely received for the divorce to be final. The wording must be exact as required by Jewish law, and both official names, nicknames, and their fathers' names must be accurately recorded. The date of the *get* and the place in which it was written must be recorded, to prevent mistaken identity and possible misuse of a *get*. Once the *get* is written and signed by witnesses, the husband places it into the outstretched palms of his wife's hands. She may be ordered to close her hands and raise her arms, still holding the *get*, or to put it under her armpit, or to walk toward the door or the judges to verify that the *get* is her property. Once the *get* is completed properly, the couple are divorced. After the divorce is final, the husband is no longer obliged to support his spouse, so there is no alimony. The obligation to maintain an estranged wife can often convince a husband to grant a *get*. On the other hand, some married women refuse the *get* so that their support payments will continue. While he is not obligated to support his ex-wife, the man is obliged to support his children, an obligation that is absolute.

Divorce proceedings favor men in Islam as well. A man may divorce his wife without cause (a *talaq* divorce) by saying the formula "I divorce thee" three times before witnesses. Once divorced in this way, the wife may receive only the payment of the *mahr* as stipulated in the marriage contract and maintenance for a period of time long enough to confirm that she is not pregnant (*'iddah*). Women may not divorce their husbands in this way. They have two possible avenues to gain a divorce, each of which exacts a price from the woman. Divorce through ransom (*khul'*) enables a woman to buy herself out of her marriage by paying off her husband, returning the *mahr*, or waiving her right to a delayed *mahr*. The other form (*tafriq*) involves petitioning the court for a divorce on grounds of male impotence or desertion. In terms of child custody, women are at a disadvantage since Muslim society is patrilineal. Children remain in the custody of their mother while they are young, but once they have passed the age of 7 to 10, they return to the father's custody. In many Muslim countries, women have been guaranteed further rights such as child-support payments or shared legal guardianship of minor children or required registration of *talaq* divorces. These changes, however, have been instituted through national civil family law codes rather than revision of the traditional Sharia codes. Israeli Muslim women do not have these protections. In November 2001, the Family Courts Law was amended to allow Muslim women to handle matters of maintenance and custody in civil courts rather than religious courts (a right Jewish women already enjoyed). This law may radically alter women's position after divorce as the civil courts grant custody based on the welfare of the child and are known to award more generous maintenance payments than the Muslim courts.

Members of some Protestant and Orthodox Christian churches in Israel can initiate divorce proceedings through their church. However, since the Catholic Church does not grant divorce, members of any of the Catholic-affiliated churches have no alternatives in Israel except to seek an annulment within the church's formal process. Orthodox churches have developed the principle of "economy" (*oikonomia*, meaning "flexibility"), by which divorce and subsequent remarriage are permitted. The divorce, negotiated individually through a priest, must be for grave reasons, such as abandonment, permanent insanity, adultery, forcing the spouse into prostitution, or endangering the life of the spouse. The church is thus officially certifying that a marriage has already failed in such circumstances, rather than formally dissolving it. A divorced Orthodox man or woman will only be allowed to remarry if they were the innocent party, and they must wait to remarry, usually at least a year. When they remarry, the liturgy for the wedding is a penitential one to remind them that this is occurring because of human weakness. A Catholic who is granted a annulment is free to remarry immediately. Under the revised Family Court Law, Christian women only gained the right to use civil courts for issues about maintenance during their marriage.

FAMILY

People everywhere in the world have developed systems of classification for determining which people are close or kin and which people are distant or strangers (what anthropologists term kinship systems). Once one has classified people, one knows how to treat them. For example, people have different obligations to and expectations from people they call kin than people who are nonkin. Kinship notions around the world are based on principles of descent, tracing the people to whom one belongs through the bonds created by birth and blood. Marriage adds an additional web of relationships.

In Israel, for both Palestinians and Jews, kinship is determined by the ties one inherits through one's father, known as patrilineal descent. A child is born into the family or tribe of his or her father and will inherit rights and obligations from only that side of his or her family or tribe. Judaism adds an additional layer to this because Jews inherit their Jewishness—their basic right to belong to the Jewish nation—from their mothers, through matrilineal descent. Within Palestinian society, the primacy given to the father's side of the family is reflected in the terms used to label different kin. An aunt (*'amma*) and uncle (*'amm*) on the father's side are called by different kinship terms than an aunt (*khala*) and uncle (*khal*) on the mother's side. These kinship terms mark out a set of social relationships so that children learn to treat their *'amm* or *'amma* with the respect due lineal kin, while more informal relations can be had with one's *khal* or *khala*.

Within Arab society, and thus within Palestinian society, people are perceived as nearly interchangeable representatives of their kin group. Thus anything that touches a kin also touches the individual. An insult to a kinsman is perceived as an insult to the entire patrilineal family. Similarly, if a member of the family does something shameful, it brings dishonor on the entire patrilineal family; if an individual earns glory or honor, it brings benefit to the entire family. Within Israeli Jewish society, the early Zionist stress on the group (the *kvutza*), as a substitute for the families often left behind, has given way to a more individualist orientation within society.

Family remains the major component of people's lives in both Palestinian and Jewish communities in Israel. University students go home to visit their families every chance they get rather than partying with their friends. Young adult Israelis live at home with their parents until they get married and establish their own homes. Less than 10 percent of young people aged 20 to 30 live alone.[17] In some cases, even once they are married, Israelis continue to live in their parents' house.

That said, there are as many different family forms in Israel as there are different groups of people. Some households are nuclear families with both parents working and sharing equally in the household responsibilities. Other households may live as extended families, with grandparents and other aunts, uncles, and cousins under the same roof and all contributing to the family's welfare. Those same extended families may later break up into nuclear family units due to tensions among household members or changes in the family's wealth. Households in which women or men live alone tend to be more common among Israelis 55 or older; women are more likely to live alone than men. Even so, it is less common for older people to live alone in Israel than it is in other developed countries.

The number of single-parent households in Israel has doubled from 4.5 percent in 1975 to 9.9 percent in 2001.[18] Part of this increase can be explained by the same trends producing single-parent families in the West: increases in divorce rates and births out of wedlock. A unique factor to Israel, however, was the arrival of a large number of single-parent families in the waves of immigration from Ethiopia and the former Soviet Union. In addition, there has been a change in the characteristics of these families. In the early 1970s, women were single parents because they were widows (58.5 percent); in the early twenty-first century, women are single parents because they are divorced (54.8 percent). Most of the single mothers in Israel in 2000 were Jewish women who were born in Israel or who immigrated before 1990. They accounted for 70.5 percent of such mothers. The majority of those who were divorced were Mizrahim; the majority of those widowed were Ashkenazim. Single parenthood is much rarer among Muslim women, only 2.8 percent of whom are single parents, mainly due to widowhood. For Christian and Druze women, the numbers are even smaller (.4 percent and .2 percent). In 2000, about 25 percent of Israeli single-parent households were living in poverty.

One major trend that can be seen in many families in Israel is that of male privilege and male control over the family, regardless of whether the family is Jewish or Palestinian. The head of the family is the man, and his word must not be challenged. Mothers are usually responsible for the care of the home and the children, but any major decisions about the children's lives will ultimately be made by the father, although he will consult with her. In Jewish families, male privilege is tied to the fact that men continue to do army service for years. Since men go off to war, women must do their part by supporting their fathers, brothers, sons, or husbands in these endeavors. When men come home from the army on leave, their mothers, sisters, or girlfriends are often expected to cater to their every need.

Ashkenazi families resemble the Western nuclear family. They are smaller and more democratic, and children are given a great deal of autonomy. Mizrahi and Palestinian families tend to follow patterns present in Arab families overall. Within the household, authority is determined by seniority and sex. Older males prevail over everyone else, then younger males, then older females, and then younger females. In theory, the father has absolute authority over all the activities of the members of the household. He decides what education his children will receive, what occupations his sons and daughters will enter, and whom his children will marry. Women are expected to be devoted wives and mothers, hard working and faithful, good cooks and housekeepers, and quiet obedient companions to their husbands. In practice, however, the wife often exerts considerable influence in the family given her control over the home and domestic life. That control is often exerted behind the scenes, in a nonovert manner, so that to the public view, it appears that the male controls the household. Mizrahi and Palestinian families tend to place a high value on male children and on larger households, although these patterns are changing.

In Palestinian families, the extended family of three generations still is found in many villages. This is partially due to the lack of available housing for forming nuclear families and not to any holding on to traditional forms. In urban areas, nuclear families are becoming more common. An individual's status in society is linked to his or her family's position in society and to his or her own position within the family. The family remains the primary focus of an individual's loyalty. In Israel after 1948, their families were all most Palestinians had to help them reconstruct their world. They have a protective attitude toward relatives, who are preferred as business partners because they are believed to be more reliable than nonrelated individuals. When a Palestinian family decides to build a house, it is other family members who will contribute their labor to make the house a reality. Families provide networks that can be activated for a number of different reasons—such as schooling, finding jobs, or dealing with government bureaucrats.

Israeli women, Jewish and Palestinian, often hold paid employment, but they still remain responsible for all the household duties as well. Israeli women are more likely to take positions that allow them to attend to their families first. Israeli working mothers do not report the same levels of stress about balancing work and household responsibilities as do working mothers in the United States. Employers are expected to understand that the woman's family duties will come first.

Family resonates deeply in Israeli lives for other reasons as well. For those Israelis who survived the Nazi Holocaust in Europe, establishing and raising a family was one way for them to cope with the trauma they had suffered. Such parents worked hard to make sure their children had everything they wanted. Their children often felt the need to excel in order to make their parents feel better or felt guilt at the fact that their parents had suffered in ways they never would. As this generation raises their own children, many of them are trying to come to terms with the legacy of the Holocaust in their lives so that their children can grow up without the burdens of guilt and parental expectations that they felt.

Palestinian parents too have their own burdens. Many Palestinians who lived through the events of 1948–1949 made a practice of not speaking of these times to their children in order to spare them. Life under military administration was demanding, and parents wanted to protect their children as best they could. It was better, many thought, not to talk of those times, to retreat into family and village life, and to remain detached from the outside world. The second generation of Palestinian Israelis therefore grew up knowing few details of what their parents had suffered. It is only with the third generation and recent changes in Israeli society that grandparents have begun to talk to their grandchildren about their history. This means that young Palestinians today have a far different sense of their identity than their parents did.

Finally, immigrant families face the same challenges as immigrants in many parts of the world. Parents who were raised in more traditional ways may find it hard to adapt to the new country, its values, and its behaviors. Often the children lead the way. Family remains important as an anchor in the strange new land, but family structure also begins to change as the children are socialized into new ways of acting and thinking.

NOTES

1. Hanna Herzog, "Homefront and Battlefront: The Status of Jewish and Palestinian Women in Israel," *Israel Studies* 3, no. 1 (1998): 61.

2. Quoted in Simona Sharoni, *Gender and the Israeli-Palestinian Conflict: The Politics of Women's Resistance* (Syracuse, N.Y.: Syracuse University Press, 1995), 44.

3. Rhoda Kanaaneh, *Birthing the Nation: Strategies of Palestinian Women in Israel* (Berkeley: University of California Press, 2002), 69.

4. See Eyal Ben-Ari, *Mastering Soldiers: Conflict, Emotions, and the Enemy in an Israeli Military Unit* (New York: Berghahn Books, 1998), 106–117, for a discussion of the links among military service, masculinity, and the consequences for civilian life.

5. Anita Shapira, *Land and Power: The Zionist Resort to Force, 1881–1948* (New York: Oxford University Press, 1992), 368.

6. Ben-Ari, *Mastering Soldiers*, 112.

7. Mimi Ajzenstadt and Odeda Steinberg, "Never Mind the Law: Legal Discourse and Rape Reform in Israel," *Affilia* 16, no. 3 (2001): 337–359.

8. Israel, Central Bureau of Statistics, "Population Aged 15 and Over, by Civilian Labor Force Characteristics and Sex," Table 12.1, *Statistical Abstract of Israel 2002*. http://www.cbs.gov.il/shnaton53/st12_01.pdf.

9. Israel, Central Bureau of Statistics, Prime Minister's Office, The Authority for the Advancement of the Status of Women, *Women and Men in Israel* (Jerusalem: Central Bureau of Statistics, July 2000), 12.

10. Shlomo Swirski and Yaron Yechezkel, *Women's Representation in the Legislature and the Executive in Israel and Worldwide* (Tel Aviv: Adva Center, February 1999).

11. Shevach Weiss and Yael Yishai, "Women's Representation in Israeli Political Elites," *Jewish Social Studies* 42 (1980): 171.

12. Naomi Chazan, "Politics and Women Go Together," *Jerusalem Post*, March 12, 1999.

13. In the Book of Genesis, Jacob, son of Isaac and Rebecca, brother of Esau, agrees to work for seven years to wed Rachel, only to be given her older sister Leah (whose face was covered by a veil). He had to work another seven years to earn Rachel as a bride.

14. Jacob Neusner, Alan J. Avery-Peck, and William Scott Green, eds., *The Encyclopedia of Judaism* (New York: Continuum, 1999), 803–804.

15. Israel, Central Bureau of Statistics, *Vital Statistics: Marriages and Divorces 1999*. http://www.cbs.gov.il/publications/vital99/vi1198-e.pdf.

16. The court's tools range from revocation of drivers licenses to prison terms for uncooperative parties. Since the man must freely give the *get*, however, in the end the court cannot compel a man to divorce his wife. Some men have served lengthy prison sentences rather than comply with the rabbinical courts.

17. Israel, Central Bureau of Statistics, Prime Minister's Office, The Authority for the Advancement of the Status of Women, *Women and Men in Israel*, 3.

18. Shlomo Swirski, Vered Kraus, Etty Konor-Attias, and Anat Herbst, Special Issue: "Solo Mothers in Israel," *Israel Equality Monitor* 12 (2003).

7
Social Customs and Lifestyles

LIFESTYLES
The Cycle of Time

In Western countries, the workweek begins on Monday and ends on Friday. Saturday and Sunday are usually days of rest, with Sunday being a religious day. Days begin in the middle of the night, at midnight, and run 24 hours until midnight is reached again and a new day begins. In Israel, as in Judaism, a day is calculated from sundown one day to sundown the next day. This means that holidays or religious days of rest actually cross over a two-day period. The workweek begins on Sunday and runs until midday on Friday. From sundown Friday to sundown Saturday is the Sabbath, the religious day of rest. Public transportation shuts down, and many businesses and shops are also closed. Thus the Israeli "weekend" only really runs from sundown Saturday to Sunday morning, when work and school begin once again. For Muslim Israelis, the day of rest is Friday, while Christians celebrate their day of rest on Sunday.

The Israeli calendar for holidays is based on the traditional lunar religious calendar used in Judaism. In such a calendar, each new month begins with the new moon. A 12-month lunar calendar loses 11 days every year, while a 13-month calendar gains 19 days every year. In the fourth century, Rabbi Hillel developed a fixed calendar of 12–13 months with standardized lengths of months that run over a 19-year cycle. At the end of every 19 years, the lunar and solar years realign. The first month of the year is Nissan, followed by Iyar, Sivan, Tammuz, Av, Elul, Tishri, Cheshvan, Kislev, Tevet, Shevat, and Adar. The months vary in length from 29 to 30 days. Adar II, a thirteenth month of 29 days, is added in years 3, 6, 8, 11, 14, 17, and 19. Israel also runs on the same solar calendar as most of the rest of the world.

Thus Israelis keep track of two different calendrical systems, but it is the lunar system that sets the dates for national and religious holidays.

Urban versus Rural

With 91 percent of Israel's population living in urban areas, Israel is an urban society. A number of Israel's cities blend quarters hundreds of years old with newer, more modern neighborhoods (e.g., Jerusalem, Safed, and Acre). Other communities begun as centers of agriculture have urbanized over the years as their population increased. Still other cities were built after statehood to house and provide employment opportunities for new immigrants streaming into the country (e.g., Carmiel, Kiryat Gat, and Dimona). City life in Israel looks much like it does anywhere else in the world. Most cities now have their shopping malls (or *canyonim*) and any number of American-style strip malls, home to McDonalds, Burger King, Kentucky Fried Chicken, Office Depot, and Ace Hardware. New buildings, shopping centers, and homes are going up all over the country. Pubs, dance clubs, a wide variety of ethnic restaurants, chic boutiques, movie theaters, convenience stores, and fast-food stands selling pizza, burgers, falafel, and ice cream can all be found in most urban areas. One still finds open-air markets selling fruits and vegetables and other inexpensive consumer goods (plastics, housewares, clothing). Small businesses continue to flourish, not yet driven out of business by mega-competitors. Most cities feature a public square that may be a favorite spot for local teens to gather on a Saturday night to talk, listen to boom boxes, and mingle.

The other 9 percent of Israelis live a more rural lifestyle, where farming still plays a role in their lives. About 1.2 percent of Israeli Palestinians live in villages of varying sizes classified as rural by the Israeli government. In such communities, land and housing is privately owned, and farmers work independently of each other. Another 1.8 percent of Israelis live on kibbutzim (discussed in the next section). Moshavim, another form of agricultural settlement in which each family owns its own house and land but joins together cooperatively to market and purchase needed large equipment, account for another 3 percent of the population. The new community settlements (*yishuv kehilati*) account for the remaining 3 percent. In these communities, residents' family lives are separate, and they work outside the community. Unlike other towns in Israel, instead of a municipal government the residents of *yishuv kehilati* voluntarily and collectively handle the affairs of the community. Even rural areas in Israel, however, are not far away from cities. During the late 1990s, it was common for Palestinian women from villages in the Galilee to travel to Nazareth or Jenin (and more occasionally, to Tel Aviv) to spend the day shopping and drinking coffee in the trendy cafes.

Kibbutz Life

Kibbutzim are a uniquely Israeli institution. About 80 percent of the kibbutzim were established prior to 1948. They were based on a socialist ideology of equal-

ity and communal sharing among all members. All members of the kibbutz contributed their labor to the collective enterprise; each member then drew from the
kibbutz what he or she needed to survive. Major stress was placed on membership
in the collective. Members rotated through the different jobs, and all work on the
kibbutz was done by members, and members only. In the early days, many kibbutzim used communal child-rearing strategies. Children spent most of their time
together with an assigned caregiver rather than in a nuclear family unit. Parents
would see their children at meals and after work was completed in the evening.
The children then slept together in the nursery. During the prestate period, the
kibbutzim played major roles in the areas of agricultural development, settlement, and defense, representing the ideological heart of the pioneer movement
in Israel. Kibbutz society contributed greater percentages of their children to elite
army units than did other population sectors in Israeli society. As pioneers and
socialists, kibbutz members were seen as an Israeli elite.

Today, more than 100,000 Israelis still live in 268 kibbutzim scattered across
Israel. They range in size from fewer than 100 members to 1,000 members. The
average tends to be several hundred. During the 1960s, living standards rose
faster on the kibbutzim than they did in Israel as a whole. Communal child-care
facilities are a thing of the past. However, kibbutzim still maintain communal
dining, sports, and educational and recreational facilities. In the early 1970s, the
kibbutzim began to shift away from agriculture and toward industry in order to
remain profitable. The triple-digit inflation and high interest rates of the 1980s
spelled ruin for many kibbutz factories that had taken out loans to develop industry. Rather than allowing their communities to crash with them, the government
and banks bailed out the kibbutzim, but the kibbutzim were forced to sell off agricultural land, cut operating costs, and restructure the benefits given to members.
Today, the kibbutzim still farm and run some industry, but a larger proportion of
their members are employed as white-collar professionals, and the kibbutzim
themselves have entered the service economy, providing laundries, restaurants,
and child-care centers, and opening their grounds to tourists and other forms of
recreation. Factories must employ nonkibbutz labor, as only 38 percent of kibbutz
members choose to work on the kibbutz.[1] Considerable tension has arisen with
nonmember employees in kibbutz factories over the wage rates and benefit structures they receive compared with members. With all of these economic changes,
many kibbutzim have moved away from their communal ethos to a more family
and individualized orientation. For many Israelis, particularly those struggling to
make ends meet, the kibbutzim still represent an Israeli elite—stable, economi-
cally sound communities with high standards of living.

Leisure Activities

The early years of statehood were times of austerity. People did not have the
money to go out to dinner or to discos or bars, take vacations, or entertain lavishly. Instead, they stayed home and entertained themselves by visiting with fam-

ily and friends or going to the occasional movie. Games and songs were a popular evening's entertainment. On the radio, one could listen to the station Kol Yisrael (Voice of Israel). When they tired of being at home, Israelis would take to the streets to stroll along avenues, such as Dizengoff in Tel Aviv. Cars were luxuries, so leisure involved activities that could be reached by walking, taxi, or bus. School children benefited from school trips that took them to different parts of Israel in order to teach them geography and love of the land (*ahavat ha'aretz*).

Today, Israel is increasingly a car-based society as prices have dropped and more people can afford to own a car. One of the most popular weekend diversions remains going out to open-air cafes to see and be seen. Discos, bars, dance clubs, and restaurants offer nightlife that goes on into the early hours of the morning. During the 1990s, Israel experienced its own boom of materialism and consumerism as tariffs were lifted on some Western goods. Cable television brings more than 50 channels to Israeli homes. In addition to the Israel Broadcasting Authority's channels, residents in different parts of the country can pick up broadcasts from other nearby countries—Egypt, Jordan, and Lebanon. In addition to popular foreign films, a thriving Israeli film industry keeps movie attendance steady by releasing one new movie a month. Israelis are also avid book readers, buying 11 million books in 1996.

Hundreds of thousands of Israelis participate in sports such as soccer, basketball, tennis, running, swimming and diving, table tennis, tenpin bowling, and beach-ball games. Thousands of runners take part in regular annual marathons in Tel Aviv, Jerusalem, the Dead Sea, and the Sea of Galilee while tens of thousands of other participants compete in shorter "fun runs." Nature hikes are especially popular, with the Society for the Protection of Nature offering a number of different treks all over the country. Fifteen thousand walkers every year join in the Jerusalem March, a hike up to the capital.

Overseas vacations are now well within the reach of most Israeli families. Popular tourist destinations include North America, western Europe, Egypt and the Sinai since the signing of the peace treaty, eastern Europe (especially Prague, Warsaw, and Budapest), Turkey, and Greece. More adventurous young people, just released from army service, choose to explore more exotic locations and backpack their way through South America, Thailand, India, China, or Kenya. Internal tourism has picked up as many Israelis vacation at home, going to the Dead Sea or to bed and breakfasts at moshavim in the Galilee. Horseback riding, water parks, and theme parks have made their appearance as the kibbutzim and moshavim try to capture internal tourist dollars.

Sports

Sporting traditions did not play a major role in the development of Jewish culture in the Diaspora. King Herod encouraged boxing, archery, and racing events, but for many centuries there was little interest in engaging in sports in Jewish communities. Attitudes began to change during the nineteenth century, as German and Austro-Hungarian Jews took part in Germany's Gymnastic Movement and other organized sports. Attitudes shifted in eastern Europe at about the same time, as community leaders encouraged young people to physically train their bodies so they could defend their communities from mob attacks. Gymnastics, bodybuilding and other competitive sports were encouraged.

The movement spread from eastern Europe to other areas. Soon there were Jewish gymnastics clubs in Constantinople, Bulgaria, and Berlin. Rising anti-Semitism furthered the development of the Jewish clubs, as Jewish members were forced out of German clubs. The clubs formed a loose association that eventually became the Maccabi World Union at the Twelfth Zionist Congress in 1927. The very name *Maccabi* signaled the ideal of a fighter and an autonomous Jewish state, harking back as it did to the Maccabee brothers who restored the Hasmonean kingdom in Judah during the Hellenic period. Maccabi clubs spread all over the world, and their athletes were among the elite competing in international games and at the Olympics.

The Israeli Maccabi movement started in Jerusalem in 1912, at first connected to the General Zionist movement (later part of Likud). Very quickly, however, they depoliticized. In 1923, the Histadrut labor federation started its Hapoel (the worker) association to bring sports to the masses (rather than training elite athletes). The right-wing Revisionist movement created its sporting organization, Betar, in 1924. Not to be outdone, the religious Hapoel Hamizrachi started the Elitzur Association, in 1939. In 1953, the Academic Sports Association (ASA) was created.

Until the 1980s, sports and politics were intertwined in Israel (except for Maccabi). Given their labor connections, Hapoel clubs prospered; by 1970, they had 300 branches and 85,000 members. By comparison, Maccabi had 75 branches and 18,000 members, Betar had 74 branches and 5,000 members, and Elitzur had 8 branches and 10,000 members. Since the 1980s, sports teams have been sold off to private owners and the political connections severed, although old associations die hard. Politics has affected one further arena. Isolated by the surrounding Arab countries from participating in the appropriate geographical regional leagues, Israel has instead become part of the European sports community.

The two most popular spectator sports in Israel are soccer (Israeli football) and basketball. Israel started participating in international competition in soccer shortly after the state's founding, but soccer was played in Palestine long before this.[2] Since 1990 and the emigration from the former Soviet Union, Israel's sports teams have seen their level of performance rise as talented Russian players have joined Israeli teams. Soccer is king in Israel. The Israeli national team qualified for the World Cup Finals in 1970 in Mexico but lost in the first round. Hapoel Tel Aviv brought home honors by reaching the quarter finals of the Union of European Football Associations (UEFA) Cup in 2002, beating favored teams Chelsea and Parma. Israeli Palestinians have played an integral role in soccer. Rifat Turk

(Hapoel Tel Aviv) and Zahi Armeli (Maccabi Haifa) have both won championship medals and played for the national Israeli team in the 1980s. Hapoel Taibe became the first Arab-owned club to compete in Israel's top soccer division in the 1996–1997 season. The women's national soccer team has won several international matches. It was ranked seventy-first in the world as of August 2003.

A basketball league was formed in Israel in 1954, although clubs had been playing the game since the mid-1930s. Maccabi Elite Tel Aviv won that first championship game and has dominated the league ever since, winning the title 43 times (with a winning streak of 23 times between 1970 and 1992). The team has also won the national cup 33 times. Maccabi was the first team to enter the European Cup for Champions in 1958, and they have won the cup three times, in 1977, 1981, and 2001. There are currently 12 teams in Israel's Premier League, representing clubs from all over the country. Women's basketball is flourishing, with major matches pulling in several thousand fans. The teams Elitzur Ramla and Elitzur Holon often play for the championship title, but in 1998–1999, A. S. Ramat HaSharon won for the first time ever. This team also reached the final of the European Roncetti Cup before losing to Spain.

In 1932, the Maccabi clubs worldwide came together in Tel Aviv in Palestine for the first Maccabiah Games, the international Jewish Olympics. Five hundred athletes from 23 countries participated, with an additional 1,500 local gymnasts taking part in the opening events. In 1935, with games again held in Palestine, 1,700 athletes participated. Maccabi clubs in Germany were forced to close after 1933 due to Hitler's rise to power. In 1935, many of the athletes who came to participate in the games remained in Palestine as political refugees from Nazi power. A third competition scheduled for 1938 was canceled because of British fears of

Two aspiring soccer players. Photo by the author.

another wave of asylum seekers. The Arab Revolt was still in progress, while in Europe, war loomed on the horizon.

The Maccabiah Games resumed in 1950, with only 800 participants since a number of athletes had died in the Holocaust. The organizers of the event decided at this point to open the games to all Jewish competitors, regardless of whether they belonged to a Maccabi club. Ever since the fourth game in 1957, the Maccabiah has been held every four years (the next one will be in 2005). The sixteenth games, held in 2001, drew more than 3,000 athletes from 41 countries to compete in 44 different events. The events include track and field, swimming, water polo, fencing, boxing, wrestling, soccer, basketball, tennis, table tennis, volleyball, and karate.

Israel has been a regular participant in the Olympic Games since 1952. One of the more sober moments for Israeli athletes came at the 1972 Munich games, when 11 Israeli athletes were seized as hostages by 8 members of a Palestinian guerrilla group known as the Black September Organization. Two athletes were killed immediately; the remaining nine died in a shoot-out between the terrorists and West German police. Israel has won four Olympic medals: at the 1992 Barcelona games, when Yael Arad won silver in women's judo and Oren Smadja won bronze in men's judo; at the 1996 Atlanta games, when Gal Friedman won a bronze in windsurfing; and at the 2000 Sydney games, when Michael Kalganov won a bronze in kayaking.

Social Relations

Israelis pride themselves on their informality. Soldiers in the army are not required to address their officers formally. Little attention is paid to appearance or bearing. Students in schools show the same informality with their teachers. Israelis see themselves as direct, honest speakers (*dugri* talk), as spontaneous and warm, creative, and able to take the initiative. They are willing to take risks (have *chutzpah*) and are self-confident. Their informality can be experienced by Westerners as rudeness or lack of tact. Life in Israel resembles a pressure cooker at times, and Israelis have learned how to cope with high levels of tension. To many Westerners, Israel can be too intense.

The friendship group (*chevreh*) is an important aspect of social relations in Israel. Israelis are not as mobile as Americans. They grow up, go to school, and return after the army or college to live in the same communities near the people they have always known. Friendships under these circumstances can grow to be very deep, with strong feelings of loyalty and mutual responsibility. Friends are expected to help each other with business, love, or family problems. Israelis, therefore, do not make friends quickly, and when they do, they have high expectations of what their friends will do for them.

Generosity and hospitality are valued highly in Palestinian Israeli society as well as in Mizrahi Jewish society. Patterns of hospitality and gift giving among Israelis of European origin are more similar to American patterns, where it may be reserved for only close friends. In Middle Eastern societies, hospitality and gift giving mark the host as a particular type of person. One's treatment of guests and the gifts one gives at various occasions are scrutinized and assessed in order to determine how worthy that person is. This can place tremendous pressure on people to maintain certain standards of expenditures for these purposes. Guests may be received daily and must be served coffee, soda, juice, cake, cookies, nuts, or fruit. Some younger people would like to adopt a more modern lifestyle, one with greater privacy, but are caught up in the hospitality spiral by the expectations of the people around them. When visiting in someone's home, it is common for a guest to also bring gifts of special foods, candy, or flowers.

Most Israelis tend to live in homogenous communities. Thus, little in the way of intergroup social relations can develop in these settings. There are seven Israeli cities that are considered to be "mixed" Palestinian-Jewish locations: Jerusalem, Tel Aviv-Jaffa, Ma'alot-Tarshiha, Ramla, Lod, Acre, and Upper Nazareth. It is within these communities that the possibility exists for friendship across ethnic boundaries. Such friendships do occur. People meet at work or get to know one another as neighbors. It is difficult, however, to sustain these relationships when national tensions spark between the Israeli government and the Palestinian Authority. A number of groups in Israel are seeking to foster dialogue and relationships across ethnic lines. Some notable examples include the community of Neve Shalom/Wahat as-Salaam—a mixed Palestinian-Jewish community—and groups such as Ta'ayush or Bet Hagefen in Haifa.

NATIONAL PERSPECTIVES
National Holidays

Israel celebrates three major national holidays—Holocaust Remembrance Day (Yom Ha'Shoah), Memorial Day (Yom Ha'Zicaron), and Independence Day (Yom Ha'Atzmaut)—and one minor day, Jerusalem Reunification Day. Of these national holidays, only the major ones are public holidays.[3] The dates for these according to the Hebrew calendar are Holocaust Remembrance Day, the 27th of Nissan; Memorial Day, the 4th of Iyar; Independence Day, the 5th of Iyar; and Jerusalem Reunification Day, the 28th of Iyar.

On Yom Ha'Shoah, Israelis remember the 6 million Jews who perished in Europe during Nazi rule there. In 1951, the Knesset chose this day for remembrance because it was the first day of the Warsaw Ghetto Uprising. This was followed by passage of the Holocaust Day law in 1959. On this day, places of entertainment are closed by law, and radio and television stations broadcast somber music and stories of survivors. The official opening ceremony occurs at 8:00 P.M. on Holocaust Eve and is broadcast live on television and radio. Holocaust survivors open the memorial service by lighting a torch in memory of those who died. At 10:00 A.M. the morning of Holocaust day, a siren sounds for two minutes throughout Israel. Everyone stops whatever they are doing—drivers stop

Girl in costume for Purim celebrations in Jerusalem. Photo by Nati Harnik. Courtesy of the Government Press Office, State of Israel.

and exit their vehicles, workers stop working, children stop playing, people stop talking, and all stand silently at attention. During the day, since 1989, the Knesset with the assistance of Yad Vashem performs the ceremony "Everyone Has a Name," during which the names of all of the Holocaust victims are read aloud.

Yom Ha'Zicaron is the day officially set aside to remember Israeli soldiers who died while on active duty for their country. Again, all places of entertainment are closed during this holiday. At 8:00 P.M. on the eve, a siren pierces the evening air for two minutes all over the country. Official national ceremonies begin as soon as the siren ends, initiated by the president and the army's chief of staff at the Western Wall in Jerusalem. Local ceremonies may involve solemn processions to the town hall, silence for the siren, laying wreaths at monuments, and reading the names of the fallen. Prayers and memorial speeches of sympathy for the families' losses by local officials follow. At 11 A.M. the next day, the siren again sounds for two minutes, and all activity ceases as people stand at attention. Memorial ceremonies are held at the 42 military cemeteries throughout the country. The day concludes with a torch lighting ceremony at 8 P.M. at Mount Herzl in Jerusalem.

Israelis move from the somber tone and sorrow of Memorial Day immediately into the celebratory, festive mood of Independence Day, Yom Ha'Atzmaut, which can be a somewhat jarring experience for the first-time visitor. On Independence Eve, residents of cities and towns gather for public celebrations sponsored by their municipal government. Gone is the serious tone of the previous evening's events. These celebrations may include humorous skits and rousing speeches about Independence Day, musical performances by popular entertainers, and carnivals with rides and games. Independence Day was instituted as a public holiday in 1949. On Independence Day, many Israelis head to the countryside for picnics, a day at the beach, nature hikes, and visiting with friends and family. Grilling out is popular. Army bases are open to the public with air shows and naval displays. The Israel Prizes for distinction in artistic, literary, or scientific enterprise are also presented on this day.

On May 12, 1968, the government chose the 28th of Iyar to celebrate the reunification of Jerusalem. From 1948 until 1967, Jerusalem was a divided city; Israel controlled West Jerusalem, while Jordan controlled East Jerusalem and the Old City. In 1967, when Israel conquered East Jerusalem, the Israeli government immediately moved to annex it to Israel to reunite the city. Palestinians who live in East Jerusalem are not Israeli citizens but carry special passes that mark them as residents of East Jerusalem. Jerusalem Reunification Day became an optional national holiday in 1998 when the Knesset passed the Jerusalem Day Law. On the eve of Jerusalem Reunification Day, Israelis march through the city to the Western Wall, for festive prayer services. The main ceremony, a memorial to the soldiers who fell in the battle for the city, takes place at Ammunition Hill, where some of the heaviest fighting occurred in 1967. Members of the Temple Mount Faithful, an Israeli Jewish group that seeks to rebuild the Temple, also march from Ammunition Hill through East Jerusalem to the Old City and the Western Wall.

Israel's national holidays are problematic for their Palestinian citizens. Israeli Palestinians, who learn about the Holocaust in school, draw comparisons between Nazi treatment of Jews and Israeli treatment of Palestinians in the Occupied Territories. While they can empathize with the pain of Israeli Jewish families who have lost sons in battle, those fallen soldiers may have been responsible for the deaths of Palestinians. What Israeli Jews celebrate with joy as the day their independent state was formed for Palestinians represents a day of defeat, as more than 750,000 Palestinians were left refugees and stateless when the war ended. Jerusalem Day celebrates yet another Palestinian defeat.

Palestinians have developed their own "national" holidays. Land Day (Yom al-Ard) began on March 30, 1976, when Palestinians went on strike to protest Israeli government seizures of Arab land in the Galilee to build Jewish settlements. Six Israeli Palestinians were killed by Israeli security forces that day. Land Day continues to be observed in Palestinian communities throughout the country with gatherings, parades, speeches, and strikes to protest the state's discrimination against its Palestinian citizens. More recently, Palestinians have begun to celebrate their own holiday in response to Israeli Independence Day. Catastrophe Day (Yom al-Nakbah) is May 15, the date of Israel's founding.[4] Residents observe a minute's silence at noon to remember the catastrophe. Cultural and educational events for children, memorial ceremonies, and demonstrations also mark this day. Israel's state symbols all draw in one way or another on the heritage of Judaism. With Israel's national identity rooted in Jewish traditions and symbols, non-Jewish citizens feel like there is no room for them. They want the symbols of Israeli national identity to be symbols to which all Israelis can relate.

Family celebrating the Mimouna holiday with a picnic. Photo by Amos Ben Gershom. Courtesy of the Government Press Office, State of Israel.

Celebrations unique to different Jewish ethnic groups have also attained the status of unofficial "national" holidays. One of the best-known celebrations is the Mimouna, unique to Moroccan Jewry. It is a festival that celebrates the values of friendship and togetherness. Festivities begin at nightfall as Passover ends. All dress in their finest clothing, and it is common to see men and women dressed in traditional Moroccan caftans, elaborately embroidered in gold and silver threads. Festive tables are set, and people spend the evening eating, visiting home after home, singing, and exchanging greetings and blessings. On the next day, people carry the celebrations into the parks with a day of picnicking. This day of picnics has come to be celebrated by most Israelis—Jewish and Palestinian—as everyone heads to local public parks for a day of grilling and eating, music, and visiting. Politicians have recognized the day's value and spend the day spreading "greetings" from gathering to gathering.

Other festivals include the Sahraneh of Kurdish Jewry, after Sukkoth, which was the national holiday of the Jews in Kurdistan, and the Sigd holiday of the Ethiopian Jewish community, on the 29th of Cheshvan. At Sahraneh, Israeli Kurds pitch their tents in Jerusalem's Soccer Park (Gan Soccer) for an evening of prayer, grilling and eating, dancing, and singing to traditional Kurdish music. Here too local politicians have learned to make their rounds. Sigd is a pilgrimage festival that commemorates the giving of the Ten Commandments and the law and the desire of Ethiopian Jews to return to Zion, Jerusalem. In Ethiopia, it was celebrated by a half-day fast and a pilgrimage to the top of the nearest mountain. Religious leaders would offer prayers on the mountain top, and then the community would descend and hold a festive meal. In Israel, Ethiopians from all over the country gather in Jerusalem at the Western Wall or at the Sherover Promenade, which overlooks the Old City, to hold their prayers of thanksgiving at their return.

The Role of the Army in Israeli Life

Diaspora Jews were generally not fighters. For that reason, when the new state was formed, it needed to create a new image of the Israeli fighter. At the same time, there was a great deal of concern that this fighter not be a bully. This led to the development of two important elements in Israel's army. First, it is a citizen soldiery, where all Israelis are expected to serve their country (with some exceptions). Second, the army adopted a principle called purity of arms (*tohar neshek*); one's weapon should be used as a last resort, and one should never blindly obey a manifestly unethical command. The excuses of Nazi soldiers, that they were simply following orders, echoed through Israel's budding military, and its leaders were determined never to hear their soldiers make similar statements.

Military service in Israel is mandatory for all male and female citizens and resident aliens. Young people are conscripted right out of high school at the age of 18. Males serve a period of three years, while females enlist for 20 months. It is rare for an exemption to be given to a male because military service is such an important socializing element in a young man's life. Women are often not called, and exemptions are more freely given to them. Students at the Orthodox religious schools (yeshivas) do not serve in the military. Christian and Muslim Palestinians are also exempt from service. Although they can volunteer, they are usually not accepted. More recently, the government has been allowing Christian Palestinians and Bedouins to volunteer, a signal that they may eventually begin to conscript the young men of these two communities. Druze and Circassion males have been drafted to serve since the beginning of the state. Until quite recently, there has been no exemption from service on grounds of conscientious objection because there was no conscientious objection movement in Israel. A conscientious objection movement has been growing in Israel, however, and more and more young men are going to jail rather than serve.

Young men try when inducted to make it into one of the elite volunteer units: the paratroopers, air force pilots, the submarine service, naval commandos, and certain army reconnaissance units. Recruits compete to get into two regular combat units that have achieved a measure of fame: the Golani Infantry Brigade and the Armored Corps. Women serve in the Women's Army Corps (*Chen* in Hebrew, which also means "charm"). They work as file clerks, secretaries, nurses, social workers, course instructors, flight controllers, radio operators, and drivers. Women have not been involved in direct combat since the 1948 war. While in the service, young men learn to bond with their unit, a bond that will stay with them for the rest of their lives. Once they have left active duty, Israeli men remain subject to a period of reserve duty every year (*miluim*) until they turn 54.

Women remain on reserve until the age of 34 if childless, but few women are actually called. Reserve duty may bring parts of the unit back together again for anywhere from 30 to 60 days each year.

Completing military service is an important rite of passage in Israeli life. In fact, it is so important that the army employs social workers to work with delinquent youth or youth who lack an adequate education in order to make sure they complete their term of military service. It is common for an employer to ask to see one's discharge papers. Often times, if one has no papers, one loses the job. In addition, a number of social welfare benefits have been established by the government for which military service is one of the criterion. Serving in the military has come to be seen as an important marker of citizenship. Thus, young people from those communities that do not perform military service experience discrimination in hiring, housing, and other social welfare programs.

NOTES

1. See Jon Fidler, "Kibbutz: What, Why, When , Where?" Focus on Israel, Israel Ministry of Foreign Affairs Web site, November 2002. http://www.mfa.gov.il/mfa/go.asp?MFAH0gal0.

2. Khalidi, *Before Their Diaspora*, 70, contains a photo dating from the early twentieth century of a soccer match in the Palestinian quarter outside the Old City of Jerusalem.

3. The other public holidays are religious in nature: the first and last days of Passover, Shavu'ot, Rosh Hashanah, Yom Kippur, Sukkoth, and Simchat Torah.

4. For more information about the Yom al-Nakbah, see Khalil Sakakini Cultural Center. http://www.alnakba.org/. The center, located in Ramallah, promotes Palestinian arts and culture through exhibits, talks, films, children's activities, theater, and lectures.

8

Music and Dance

Modern Israeli classical and popular music and dance draw their inspiration from a wide variety of sources, including Jewish religious traditions, Arabic and Middle Eastern elements, the folk traditions of hundreds of different countries where Jewish communities lived, and modern Western and Middle Eastern musical and dance traditions. Music and dance were important components of the nation-building process, as the new Israeli state sought to develop its own unique national identity and as communities within that state sought to maintain their own distinctive ethnic identities (especially the Palestinian and Middle Eastern communities). Israel can be seen as a bridge between East and West. In their musical and dance compositions, Israeli artists worked to develop their vision of that bridge and the new blended culture it could lead to. It is a process that still continues to this day.

MUSIC

Judaism holds music in high regard as it forms an important piece of the religious ritual structure. Services at the Temple were accompanied by instruments such as the lyre, drum, cymbals, and wind instruments, as well as by singing. Religious singing remained part of Jewish ritual after the destruction of the Temple and encompassed a number of different musical modes: synagogue prayer chants, *niggunim* (songs without words), Hassidic prayer and folk-song melodies, and Nusach—the musical calendar of public prayer.

In Islam, there are differing attitudes to the production of music. Purists are opposed to any musical expression at all because they believe that music may lead good Muslims to sin. Other religious authorities permit singing the Quran and call to prayer, but not musical instruments. Still other scholars and musicians see no difference between secular and religious music and permit both. For the mystical elements within Islam, such as the Sufis, music is not only permissible, but it is seen as a vehicle that allows ritual participants to reach unity with Allah.

The early immigrants to Israel brought their music with them and kept it alive in the new land. In Palestine, they found an already-vibrant Palestinian musical tradition. The new immigrants sang while working in the fields or building settlements and roads; they sang at celebrations, at schools, and to their children. Palestinian natives also sang and played music at celebrations and village events. As Jewish communities grew in size, their residents wanted public performances of music like those they had experienced in Europe. To meet the demand, talented community members gathered together to present musical evenings. By the 1920s, Palestine was home to a vibrant musical culture of institutes, town concerts, choirs, and instrumental groups.

Classical Music

Shulamith Ruppin established the first school of music in Tel Aviv in 1910. By the early 1920s, there were two schools in Tel Aviv, one in Jerusalem and one in Haifa. The first symphony orchestra was founded in 1923, followed by the creation of an Institute for New Music in 1927 and a Philharmonic Society in 1933. By the 1930s, music lovers could enjoy a chamber opera, chamber orchestra, choir, musical society, or a string quartet. In 1925, the country's choirs gathered in the Jezreel Valley, an event that stimulated choral singing and composition. The theater companies also commissioned new, specifically Jewish music for their productions.

Music in Israel developed further due to events in Europe. In 1933, as Hitler assumed power in Germany, the great conductor Bruno Walter, back from a successful U.S. appearance, was forced to cancel concerts due to threats they would be disrupted because he was Jewish. This was the start of the Nazi campaign to eliminate Jewish influence from German cultural life. By 1939, more than 1,500 musicians, composers, and other musical professionals had lost their jobs and could no longer produce music in Germany. Silenced in Germany, musicians fled the country, immigrating to Israel and the United States. The musical heritages of both countries were enriched immensely by the flood out of Germany.

The year 1936 was pivotal. The British opened the radio station Palestine Broadcasting Service with programming in English, Hebrew, and Arabic in April. In December, the Italian conductor Arturo Toscanini conducted the first performance of the newly formed Palestine Orchestra (which became the Israel Philharmonic Orchestra in 1948). Bronislaw Huberman recruited world-class musicians from Germany, Poland, Russia, and other European countries. Joining the orchestra eventually saved them from the Holocaust visited on the Jewish community of Europe. The symphony served to draw other musicians to the country, and musical life in Palestine took off.

The Palestine Broadcasting Service (which became Kol Ysrael [the Voice of Israel] in 1948) had its own modest chamber music group and produced solos as well. Eventually it developed a small-scale orchestra of its own—today known as the Jerusalem Symphony Orchestra. The radio station became the greatest consumer of music in the country. Its trilingual structures meant it was broadcasting both European and Eastern music. Its broadcasts provided encouragement for local composers and gave them a forum to be heard.

Orchestras and Ensembles

From that auspicious start, classical music flourished in Israel. Today Israel boasts a wealth of orchestras and ensembles that stretch across the country. Besides the Israel Philharmonic and the Jerusalem Symphony, these include the Israel Chamber Orchestra, the Beersheva Sinfonietta, orchestras in Haifa, Netanya, Holon, Ramat Gan, and Rishon Letzion, the Israel Kibbutz Orchestra; chamber music ensembles such as the Jerusalem Quartet, the Yuval Trio, the Jerusalem Camerata, the Kashtaniot Camerata of Ramat Hasharon, the Aviv Quartet, the Jerusalem Trio, the Carmel Quartet, and the Ariel Quartet; and choral groups such as Jerusalem's Liturgica, the Tel Aviv Chamber Choir, Rinat (the Israel National Choir), Shahar Choir, and Yoav Choir. The Soviet immigration in the early 1990s of more than 1 million people brought new life into classical music in Israel. Large numbers of professional musicians, including instrumental and vocal performers of high caliber, as well as music teachers came to Israel.

Today, young Israelis begin musical training by attending one of more than 30 conservatories or taking private lessons with any of hundreds of available teachers. They continue their studies at a degree-granting music academy in Jerusalem or Tel Aviv. Frequent master classes with visiting international guest artists are available throughout the country. Music appreciation programs such as Keynote (Mafteach) and Classickid seek to foster an appreciation of classical music in a new generation of Israeli children. Keynote introduces its young listeners to both classical Arabic music and modern Israeli classical music, two forms of music less popular with adult listeners.

Festivals

Music lovers can attend a series of music festivals held in different venues around the country. The Zimriya, held every three years in August, had its fiftieth anniversary in 2002 as an international choral music event. The Israel Festival, held in Jerusalem every May and June, features a program of music, dance, and theater highlighting Israeli and international talent. The Ein Gev Festival in April, Abu Ghosh Festival in May, June, and October, Kol Hamusika Chamber Music Days at Kibbutz Kfar Blum in July and August, the Bernstein Oratorio and Song Competition in September, the Bernstein Composing Competition in October, the International Guitar Festival in November, and Liturgica in

December and January mean that a classical music lover could attend nonstop national and international music events in Israel throughout the year.

Composers

Five musicians/composers represent the founding fathers of modern Israeli music due to their influence on subsequent generations of Israeli musicians.[1] They are Paul Ben-Haim (1897–1984), Oedoen Partos (1907–1977), Josef Tal (1910–), Alexander Uria Boscovich (1907–1964), and Mordecai Seter (1916–1994).

Ben-Haim moved to Palestine in 1933 from Germany, where he had established himself as a pianist and conductor. Shortly after arriving in Israel, he met the singer and folklore collector Braha Zefira and began to work closely with her. Through her, he was exposed to Near Eastern folk music and came to incorporate it into his own compositions. Ben-Haim saw Israel as a bridge between East and West and felt Israeli composers could contribute much to synthesizing the musical traditions of the two regions.[2] Ben-Haim produced works for solo instruments, chamber music, songs, choral works, liturgical music, piano compositions, and symphonic pieces. His orchestral work *The Sweet Psalmist of Israel* (1953) has been performed throughout the world. In this piece, solo instruments lead the orchestra in each of three movements. The piece refers to King David and uses harpsichord and harp with the orchestra. Ben-Haim was awarded the Israel Prize for his work in 1957.

Oedoen Partos, a Hungarian violinist and composer, immigrated to Tel Aviv in 1938. From 1938 to 1956, he was solo violinist for the Philharmonic Orchestra; in 1951, he became director of the Tel Aviv Music Academy. His early work displays the emotion and vividness of the Hungarian Bartók-Kodály school. Partos, too, was introduced to Middle Eastern melodies by Braha Zefira, who commissioned him to write instrumental backgrounds for her songs. In 1951, Partos wrote his first pure symphonic work, *Ein Gev*, for which he was awarded the Israel Prize in 1954. The work was inspired by the scenery and spirit of Kibbutz Ein Gev, where an annual music festival was held every spring. His quintet *Māqamāt* (1958), for flute and strings in three movements, represents an important piece in which he tries to synthesize Eastern and Western musical elements and techniques.

Josef Tal came to Israel from Berlin in 1934. He worked with musical theater and opera. *Saul at En Dor* (1955), his first operatic work, was an immediate success. He followed this with *Amnon and Tamar* (1958), *Ashmeda'i* (1970), *Massada 967* (1972), and *The Experiment* (1975). His strongest opera, musically and dramatically, is *Josef* (1995) written especially for the New Israel Opera's first season in their new opera house in Tel Aviv. Tal was also the first Israeli composer to use taped material in his compositions, and in 1961, he founded the first studio for electronic music. Among his electronic compositions are *Exodus II* (1958) Concertos no. 4, 5, and 6 (1962–1970), and Concerto for Harpsichord and Electronic Tape (1964).

Alexander Boscovich (born in Transylvania [Romania], immigrated in 1938), worked mainly with eastern European Jewish music before coming to Palestine. Like the others, he struggled to bring Eastern and Western music together in his works. Boscovitch stopped composing in the late 1940s and did not resume creating music until the 1960s. He struggled with depression and spent those years mainly teaching and studying. Mordecai Seter, who emigrated from Russia in 1927 and studied composition in Paris from 1932 to 1937, wrote some of the most interesting work by an Israeli composer. Seter combined traditional Hebrew liturgical elements with modal counterpoint in his composition *Cantata for the Sabbat* (1940) and his *Motets* (1951). He also composed a number of works for the ballet and modern dance, such as *Midnight Vigil* (1961) for Inbal and *Judith* (1962) and *Part Real-Part Dream* (1965) for Martha Graham.

Karel Salomon (1897–1974) exerted a major influence on Israeli music as music director of the Palestine Broadcasting System/Kol Yisrael from 1936 to 1958, when he became head of Kol Yisrael's transcription service. Salomon arrived in Israel in 1933 from Germany with his reputation already established as a conductor, singer, and composer. In Israel, he demonstrated his versatility as he turned his hand to writing songs, chamber music, and orchestral works to meet the musical needs of the developing community. Over the course of his career, Salomon wrote symphonies such as *Nights of Canaan* (1949) and *Israeli Youth Symphony* (1950), which became a favorite of youth and amateur orchestras; cantatas, including *Kibbutz HaGaluyoth* (Ingathering of the Exiles, 1952), *Le-Ma'an Yerushalayim* (On Behalf of Jerusalem, 1958), and *Chaye'i Adam* (Life of a Man, 1967), based on biblical texts; and even an opera, *Nedarim* (Vows, 1955), based on events in the life of the great poet Yehuda HaLevy. Menachem Avidom (1908–1995) helped to build the Israeli piano repertoire with his piano compositions, such as *First Pieces for Miriam, Little Ballet for Daniela*, and *Yemenite Wedding Suite*, some of which are especially suited for young pianists.

The middle generation of Israeli composers consists of individuals for whom creating Israeli music was less problematic. Some had immigrated to the country at a young age and so had absorbed a different ethos than composers who moved to Israel as mature adults. The most successful composers of this generation included Abel Ehrlich (1915–), Jacob Gilboa (1920–), Ben-Zion Orgad (1926–), and Zvi Avni (1927–). Ehrlich, trained in Yugoslavia, came to Palestine in 1939. One of his most original compositions that demonstrates the character of his work is *Bashrav* (1953), a piece for unaccompanied violin (which he later adapted for violin and string choir and then symphony). The piece is in rondo form, where a basic theme is repeated and undergoes variation with each repetition. Ehrlich used the principles of the Arabic *māqām* in his melodic line and also used the quarter and three-quarter notes common to the Eastern scale. Overall, he composed more than 400 vocal and instrument works.

Gilboa, who came to Israel from Vienna in 1938, began serious composition studies in Israel with Yosef Tal and Paul Ben-Haim. In 1965, he was exposed to the musical avant-garde in Cologne and brought those experiences back to Israel and into his compositions. He first attracted international attention with his *Twelve Jerusalem Chagall Windows* (1966), miniatures for high mezzo-soprano solo, five female voices, and a baroque ensemble employed in a modern fashion. The piece interprets in sound his impressions on viewing Chagall's windows at Hadassah Hospital. Gilboa pre-records the playing of instruments and then uses the tapes during live performance at various points, running at double speed. *Fourteen Epigrams for Oscar Wilde* (1973), *From the Dead Sea Scrolls* (1972), and *Red Sea Impressions* (1976) are among the works that employ this technique. Gilboa also screens slides of paintings to accompany his musical performances.

Ben-Zion Orgad, who came to Israel in 1933 from Germany at the age of seven, is the first Israeli composer to grow up with Hebrew as his main language. This allowed him to use Hebrew prose and poetry differently than composers who mastered Hebrew later in their lives. In his works, he plays with Hebrew, using it to create melodic lines. It is these works that best express his personal style. In *The Old Decrees* (1971), he created an oratorio using five documented witness stories about Crusader cruelties against Jews in 1096. Many of his orchestral compositions use strange combinations of instruments and instrumental structures; *Taksim* for harp solo (1962) is an early example of this technique.

Zvi Avni, who immigrated to Tel Aviv in 1933 from Germany, is the most lyrical of the Israeli composers of this generation. Avni also used texts in compositions but he was not as drawn to their melodic qualities as Orgad. In the 1970s, he became involved in electronic music and established a special department in this area at the Jerusalem Rubin Academy. Avni was a prolific composer and produced both vocal and instrumental works. His *Desert Scenes* premiered in 1992, conducted by Zubin Mehta. In it, Avni tried to capture his encounters with the desert, the wide spaces, silence, echoes, and inner voices the desert evokes in its viewers.

Noam Sheriff (1935–) and Ami Ma'ayani (1936–) are two Israeli-born composers who achieved an international reputation quickly—facilitated by study periods in Europe or the United States. Sheriff's *Festival Prelude,* first conducted by Leonard Bernstein in 1957, has been performed all over the world. The piece uses a psalm intonation in the opening and closing parts of the prelude, with folkloric tunes in the sprightly middle section. Sheriff went on to write chamber music and songs, as well as pieces for solo instruments. Many of his later works use elements of Hebrew liturgical music as well as Near Eastern tones and instrumental combinations. The climax of his career was his *Pasion Sefardi* (1992), composed for the Israel Philharmonic's commemorative concert in Toledo, Spain for the five hundredth anniversary of the Jewish expulsion. The work consists of eight movements for soprano, mezzo-soprano, two tenors, bass, choir, and orchestra. Ma'ayani first gained prominence in Israel for his compositions for harp, which won the Engel Prize in Tel Aviv in 1963. He gained broader recognition when his *Mismorim,* a work for solo voice and chamber orchestra based on the Psalms, was performed at Lincoln Center in 1965 and received high praise from both critics and audience. Ma'ayani composed *Hebrew Requiem* in 1977 for an international competition on the Holocaust and the national rebirth held in honor of the thirtieth anniversary of Israeli statehood. The piece, written for contralto solo, mixed choir, and symphony orchestra, won first prize. The piece interweaves the Latin text of the Requiem mass with poems of Yitzhak Orpaz, an Israeli noted for his surrealist, experimental style.

Two renowned female composers, known especially outside Israel, are Shulamit Ran (1947–) and Betty Olivero (1954–). Both were born in Tel Aviv. Ran studied under Paul Ben-Haim and continued her musical education in New York, studying composition and piano. She has written numerous works for piano, harpsichord, and chamber music with piano, as well as a song cycle. Stylistically, she is characterized by a blend of modernist and post-Romantic traits that produce a direct effect on both players and audience. In 1991, she received the coveted Pulitzer Prize for a symphony she composed for the Philadelphia Orchestra. Olivero studied piano and composition at the Rubin Academy and Yale University. She has written for voice and orchestra, and double bass and chamber orchestra. One of her better-known pieces is *Tenuot* (Movements, 1990), which juxtaposes small chamber groups and a full orchestra. Individual elements of music are placed at various points in acoustic space and are linked by melodic fragments that come and go in such a way as to lend movement to the overall symphonic structure.

Habib Hassan Touma (born in Nazareth, [1934–1998]) studied at the Haifa Conservatory until entering composition studies at the Israel Conservatory in Tel Aviv. He went on to earn a doctorate in musicology in Berlin, where he taught for many years. His motivation in studying Western music was to begin a renaissance in Arabic music. Touma did not like the way popular musicians were incorporating Western musical elements into Middle Eastern music. He sought to create a merged music, using Eastern modalities that would challenge and appeal to Western-trained performers and audiences. His works have tended to use flute, piano, and oboe. *Oriental Rhapsody* (1957), an early work for two flutes and drum, uses original melodies derived from more classic Arabic melodies but with Western concepts of texture and form.

Touma is not the only Israeli composer seeking to blend music. Two younger composers, Moroccan-born Avraham Amzallag (1941–) and Israeli-born Tsippi Fleischer (1946–) both work to create compositions that unite Arabic and Jewish elements. Amzallag, who studied flute, has composed a number of pieces that adapt traditional Middle Eastern melodies, rhythms, and structures to Western instruments. His compositions include *Taqsim* for flute (1968), *Dulab* for oboe, *Dulab* for flute (1979), and *Mizmor* for oboe and strings (1979). Fleischer goes even further than Amzallag as she sets Arab poems to music and uses traditional Arab instruments in her compositions. She has composed a song cycle *Girl, Butterfly, Girl* (1977) for voice and chamber orchestra, *The Gown of Night* (1987), a collage of Bedouin children's voices for magnetic tape, and *War* (1988) for clarinet and saxophone with a variety of percussive elements.

As the 1950s ended, the Israel Association of Composers had only 50 members. Today it has 200, at least 20 of whom are recent immigrants. For publishing music, the Institute for Israeli Music, Israeli Music Publishers, and the Israeli Music Centre serve the needs of Israeli composers. Almost 3,000 works have already been published, and there is a thriving music recording industry.

Opera

Opera debuted in Israel in 1922, when the Hebrew Opera performed Gounod's *Faust* in Tel Aviv completely staged to a piano accompaniment. In 1923, the famous Russian conductor Mordechai Golinkin arrived in Palestine. Golinkin wanted to create opera in the Holy Land and set about realizing his vision immediately upon arrival. He founded the Palestine Opera, which opened with Verdi's *La Traviata* in Hebrew on July 28, 1923. Golinkin lacked a proper stage, but he had soloists (experienced new immigrants), a choir (members of the Kadima amateur choir), and an orchestra (students from the Shulamith Conservatory). He produced six operas in his first season, all favorably received. However, Golinkin could not find financial backing for his venture and, unable to pay his singers, closed down the Hebrew Opera in 1927. In 1941, the Palestine Folk Opera opened. While it had better financial support to start, it too could not achieve lasting financial security. At the time of its closing in 1946, the company had staged 17 operas and ballet performances.

Edis de Phillipe, an American soprano, took up the cause of opera in Israel. She and her husband headed a new company, the Israel National Opera (INO), founded in 1947. They premiered Massenet's *Thais* on April 15, 1948. They staged more than 1,000 performances between 1947 and 1958 throughout the country with a temporary home at Habimah Theater in Tel Aviv. De Phillipe brought in international guest artists because there were not enough trained Israeli singers to keep the company going. Placido Domingo performed with the INO for more than two years in the early 1960s. Again, however, there was no money to invest in opera, and the company limped along until finally closing in 1982.

As the INO closed, a nonprofit association began operation to create and promote operatic activity in Israel. The group concentrated on training workshops, led by American professionals, for singers, designers, directors, and production teams. In 1985, it was ready to mount its first production, Purcell's *Dido and Aeneas,* with the Cameri Theater and the Israel Chamber Orchestra. In 1994, the company found a home for itself at the Tel Aviv Performing Arts Center. Since 1989, a number of Russian immigrant artists have found employment with the company in Israel, boosting the ranks of available singers and reducing their dependence on foreign guest artists. Until 2000, the company staged 10 to 11 productions a year and launched an international opera festival at Caesarea in May and June. It generated 50 percent or more of the income it needed itself, something unprecedented in the world of opera. Recent government budget cuts to cultural institutions have forced the company to make cutbacks.

Klezmer Music

Klezmer is a Yiddish word that combines two Hebrew words: *kle,* which means "instrument," and *zemer,* which means "song." It refers to eastern European Jewish dance musicians and to those modern musicians who play in that tradition. What sets klezmer music apart from other eastern European music is the wailing, laughing and soblike catches that ornament the tune. Hasidim employ klezmer musicians at their gatherings to liven them up. In a typical klezmer group, the melodic line is carried by the cornet, clarinet, and violin, while traditional brass instruments (valve trombone and alto horn) and piano provide the underlying rhythm. Klezmer music remains popular among the Hasidic community in Israel, where a unique northern Galilee–Mount Meron tradition has developed. Among younger musicians, the advent of the tape recorder has meant that they can tape performances previously heard only once or twice a year and study them on their own time. A cassette-tape industry has developed among the younger musicians to release their own productions locally.

Popular Music

Folk Music: Land of Israel Songs (Shirei eretz Israel)

Folk music calls to mind tunes that are sung communally, that everyone knows, and to which no composer's or lyricist's name is attached. They are the songs a culture has always sung. In Israel, folk culture had to be created because there was no such thing as "Israeli" folk culture. The genre of *shirei eretz Israel* (land of Israel) refers to songs composed between 1920 and 1960. Immigrant composers and lyricists began to produce songs that reflected their experiences of building the new Israeli state. These are the nationalist songs that extol love of land, agricultural life, and even political events such as war. Musically, the songs draw inspiration for their melodies from the homelands of their composers, from lyrical Russian ballads to the pounding rhythms of Balkan circle dances. Into these largely eastern European melodies, composers added Middle Eastern musical elements, drawn from the native Palestinian dances, the *debkes.*[3] Prominent composers included David Zehavi, Mordechai Zeira, and Alexander (Sasha) Argov, with lyrics contributed by noted poets such as Yaakov Orland, Alexander Pen, and Natan Alterman. Some songs feature text from the Bible or from Hebrew prayers.

Naomi Shemer is one of the most popular singers of this music. Her song "Jerusalem of Gold," composed in 1967 for the Israel Song Festival right before the Six Day War, became a classic. It was named the most popular song of Israel's first 50 years in a 1998 survey carried out by radio, television, and newspapers.

These songs were not intended for studio recording. Printed into pamphlets, they were distributed to music teachers in elementary schools, youth group and kibbutz music directors, and others so they could teach and use the songs for group gatherings. The state-controlled radio system broadcast them prominently. Special army entertainment units also conserved and introduced new songs in this acoustic style. Choreographers created Israeli folk dances for some of the songs, further reinforcing their "folk" character. From these origins came Israel's tradition of communal public sing-alongs (*shira ba'tzibur*), which are making a comeback. Since 2001, Israelis have been attending sing-alongs in clubs and private homes in a nostalgic attempt to return to a more glorious past when there was hope for peace and a good Israel.

Israeli Rock

A 1964 proposal to bring the Beatles to Israel failed because a government committee was not willing to give scarce foreign currency to the promoter to bring in a band they saw as having low cultural value and being a bad influence on young people. The Beatles never played Israel, but Israelis were nonetheless exposed to the Beatles. They also listened to music from France, Italy, and Greece that was as popular as Anglo-American pop-rock. An Israeli rock culture materialized around 1970 as a form of rebellion against the earlier *shirei eretz Israel* tradition.[4] The 1967 war victory set off a wave of celebratory, nationalist songs. Musicians turned to rock's electrified music and protest lyrics as they sought to be part of a larger international music community.

At the same time, Israeli rock musicians who gained popularity were members of the dominant society, people not too radical, who incorporated traditional Israeli song elements into their rock productions. A small group of musicians forms the nucleus of this new Israeli musical expression, including artists Arik Einstein and Shalom Hanoch and groups such as Kaveret (Beehive) and Tammuz.[5] Einstein, a popular music performer, was credited with inventing Israeli rock due to his records *Poozy* (1969) and *Shablul* (1970), on which he sings in Hebrew with a rock band as backup. He collaborated with Shalom Hanoch, the Israeli artist most committed to the rock tradition on *Shablul*. Hanoch's work covers many rock styles: acoustic ballads, Beatles-influenced rock, and hard rock. Other artists, such as Matti Caspi, Shem-Tov Levi, and Shlomo Gronich, produced experimental or progressive rock recordings in the 1970s, while also working in the traditional *shirei eretz Israel* style. Kaveret, a seven-member band, with its catchy tunes, plays on words, and nonsense rhymes, was labeled "clever pop" by music critics.[6] The band's unprecedented record sales from 1973 to 1975 told another story.

These initial artists paved the way for the groups of the 1980s—bands such as Benzeen, Tislam, and Mashina and solo artists including Corinne Alal, Danny Sanderson, Gidi Gov, Yehudit Ravitz, Gali Atari, Si Hi-man, Rami Fortis, and Riki Gal. Yehuda Poliker and Ehud Banai produced rock albums that mixed in Mediterranean elements, their version of ethnic rock. *Ashes and Dust,* Poliker's 1988 album about growing up as the son of Holocaust survivors, achieved enormous critical acclaim. Other more traditional artists adopted electric instrumen-

Shalom Hanoch and Arik Einstein performing in 1979. Photo by Ya'acov Sa'ar. Courtesy of the Government Press Office, State of Israel.

tation and began to work with rock producers. Chava Alberstein and Shlomo Artzi both made this transition. Rock had arrived on the Israeli music scene.

In the 1990s, rock's face in Israel was Aviv Geffen. With orange hair, heavy makeup, extravagant unisex clothing, and an androgynous look, he stirred a national debate. Each of the albums he released in 1992, 1993, and 1994 went gold in Israel, selling more than 20,000 copies. His songs, mostly ballads, criticized militarism and spoke about betrayal and the meaninglessness of life. Geffen, son of poet Yonatan Geffen and nephew of famed Israeli Minister of Defense Moshe Dayan, did not serve in the Israeli army for reasons of conscientious objection. He became a national symbol of peace when Prime Minister Yitzchak Rabin was gunned down shortly after Geffen sang "I Cry for You" and embraced him on stage at a Tel Aviv peace rally in 1995.

Rap and Hip-Hop

The 1990s also saw hip-hop and rap become increasingly popular with Israeli audiences, first through American rap music and reggae and then through local hip-hop and rap, beginning with artists such as Mook E, Fishi Hagadol, and Shabak Samech. In 2002, hip-hop singles broke into the mainstream of Israeli music, topping the charts. In Israel, this music reflects and comments on the political conflict with the Palestinians—often from different sides of the political spectrum. Subliminal and the Shadow perform patriotic rap, such as "Divide and Conquer" on their album *Light and Shadow*, while Mook E criticizes Israel's occupation of Palestinian land in his song "Everyone Is Talking about Peace" from the album *Shema Yisrael*. Hadagnahash's single "Numbers" begins with the statement that one day there will be two states here, and it continues by protesting the huge salaries paid to economic leaders. Young and upcoming groups include Boyaka, Space Pioneers, and Shas. MC Shiri, Israel's first female rapper, started performing in 2000 and had to overcome a great deal of resistance. Her success paved the way for other female rappers, like Shorty (female rapper Hila Nisimov). Shorty's rap songs tend to be more personal, less political. She still deals with social issues in her music as she writes about battered women or warns women to care for their bodies. MC Jeremy Cool Habash is the leading Ethiopian Israeli rapper who is regularly featured on television and radio. A yeshiva graduate, his lyrics deal with love of Judaism and his pain at how his community has been treated in Israel.[7]

Rap has also entered Palestinian musical culture in Israel. MWR is a Palestinian rap group from Acre that began to sing together in 1999 at the Acre Alternative Theater Festival. Besides performances at Dinamo Dvash, a Tel Aviv club, they have appeared in Arab schools all over the country. They sing only in Arabic. One of their more popular songs, "Because I'm an Arab," includes lyrics about policemen arresting them because they are Arabs and about wanting just to live. Rap resonates deeply in the Palestinian community, facing as it does many of the social problems that spurred the creative work of African American rappers. Drugs, discrimination, poverty, dilapidated housing, unemployment, and police harassment are also the lot of young Palestinians in Israel, especially in the mixed cities like Acre and Lod. In 2001, a Nazareth rap festival drew thousands of people. Five other groups, with names that include Tammer and DAM, have joined the ranks of Palestinian rappers. The only known Arab female rappers in the world, Safa and Nahwa, who perform as Arapiot (Hebrew for "female Arab rappers"), sing about their struggles as young women in their community: "We have families that don't give us our freedom to determine our fate, to get an education, to go out with friends, to choose whom we will marry," says Arapiot's Safa. "In our songs we demand our freedom."[8]

Trance Music

Israel is known as a world center of trance music. The Israeli version of trance music combines Eastern musical influences with 1970s disco and 1960s psychedelia, in what is known as Goa trance. Trance music is characterized by its rhythmic beats—anywhere from 120 to 160 beats per minute. In the mid-1990s, trance raves enjoyed police protection and the support of antidrug organizations. One organizer was able to get a permit to hold a rave in 1996 at Rabin Square, where 30,000 people participated in the last mass rave held in Israel. Fears over drug use at raves, however, ended this brief period of public acceptance, and raves returned underground in Israel. The Israeli trance act Mystica hit the British charts twice in 1998. Another popular local performer is Ofaria.

House music at dance clubs is beginning to surpass the popularity of rock music for teens. Choopie, one of Israel's best-known disc jockeys, plays to more than 5,000 people every weekend at clubs in Tel Aviv's port area. Eyal Barkam's trance record, *Good Morning Israel* (1998), sold about 100,000 copies, making him the Israeli trance king and a household name there.

Musica Mizrakhit

A final major current in Israeli popular music is Middle Eastern music (*musica mizrakhit*), drawn from Greek, Turkish, and other Mediterranean styles. Although it accounts for 60 to 70 percent of the local music sold in Israel, this music has been marginal to the mainstream music culture. It circulates on low-budget cassette tapes, produced by the artists themselves and sold at the Central Bus Station in Tel Aviv: hence its other labels as *musica cassettot* or "bus station" music. It emerged in the 1970s and appealed to working-class Mizrahi communities, who were being urged to leave behind their Arab identities and assimilate into a Western, Israeli identity. These communities experienced their own ethnic awakening, as it became clear that no matter how Western they became, they would not be treated equally. *Musica mizrakhit* consists of Greek or Turkish songs, translated into Hebrew. Composers "build" songs and their repertoires.[9] They begin by listening to Turkish popular music to choose a song they like. Once they pick out a song, they send it to a lyricist to translate into Hebrew or rewrite. The musician then takes new text and melody and begins to work them together, to make the piece danceable. Singers graft ethnic colorings onto the songs to appeal to people from different Middle Eastern backgrounds. It is Western music overlaid with Middle Eastern styling—just as Middle Eastern Jews are supposed to be Western at heart and retain their ethnic heritage only as an overlay. Popular singers include the late Zohar Argov, Haim Moshe, Eli Luzon, Jackie Makayton, and Benny Albaz. Argov and Moshe became so popular that they were able to cross over to the mainstream music market. Despite its popularity, this music continues to be largely absent from radio and television music broadcasting in Israel.

Palestinian Music

Classical Arabic music makes use of quarter tones, notes halfway between the notes in the Western chromatic scale, which has 13 notes to the octave (e.g., from middle C on the piano to the C above middle C). Arabic music can thus be played with 17, 19, or 24 notes in an octave. This style of music also does not use harmony in the same sense that Westerners are used to. The music is sung or played by a single musician while the rest of the group repeats the music, or it is sung or played solo. The music is monophonic (one line of sound) with complicated rhythmic patterns (there are at least 32 different "beat styles"). Musicians improvise and change the music each time they play or sing it, which makes it difficult to document or write down a musical score for the piece.

Before 1948, the cultural life of Palestine was open to the Arab world. Performers would come from Egypt, Syria, and Lebanon. A look at Wasif Jawhariyyeh, whose playing has survived in several recordings, can provide insight into the musical culture of Palestine prior to 1948.[10] Jawhariyyeh, born in

Jerusalem in 1887, grew up in a musical household. He learned to play the oud (a short-necked, half pear-shaped, plucked lute) by working with the greatest players in Jerusalem and then studying with the Syrian master Omar al-Batsh, then stationed in Jerusalem as part of the Turkish army military band. Jawhariyyeh absorbed the playing of Egyptian masters such as Sayyid Darwish and Dawood Husni. Café Jawhariyyeh opened near the Russian Compound in 1918 and became the performance home for the best singers and artists in the country. Very little is recorded from this time period due to the disruption of the 1948 war and the destruction of Palestinian society in Israel that it produced.

Until recently, Palestinian music has been absent in the Israeli musical mainstream. Palestinian music is not played on Hebrew radio stations. "Arab music is largely absent from their [leading Israeli cultural organizations] products."[11] When one considers that until the Russian immigration changed the demographic balance, more than half of Israel's population came from Arab countries, there was no lack of an audience for the music. Instead, it is clear that Palestinian music suffered marginalization just as *musica mizrakhit* did because it was Arab music.

So what did Palestinians listen to in those years? Music from elsewhere in the Arab world could be picked up on the broadcasts of Egyptian, Lebanese, Syrian, and Jordanian radio stations, as well as Radio Monte Carlo. People listened to Mohammed Abdel Wahab, Umm Kulthum, Farid Al Atrache, and Warda (from Egypt), Fairuz and Wadi A-Safi (from Lebanon), and Sabah Fakhri from Syria. They purchased music cassettes, imported from Egypt and Lebanon. In some ways, it was a continuation of the pre-1948 situation, where Palestinian musicians were connected to a larger world of classical Arabic music making. However, local musical composition and innovation stagnated because musicians were expected to play songs of the great Arab tradition or more recent Arab pop music at weddings and other celebrations. With the Israeli school system ignoring most forms of Palestinian culture and identity, music education suffered neglect as well. Palestinian musicians cannot participate in important regional conferences because of the ongoing political conflict and are cut off from their natural audiences in the surrounding Arab countries.

Despite these difficulties, some Palestinian Israelis have made names for themselves with their music. Amal Murkus, for example, is a Christian from Kfar Yasif in the Galilee. She sings original compositions featuring the work of Palestinian poets (Mahmoud Darwish and Tawfiq Zayyad) and classical Arab songs and Palestinian folk songs. The small Highlights label released her debut compact disc, *Amal*, after major Israeli record companies turned her down, claiming there is no market in Israel for Arabic music. She received international attention as a new world music artist. Rim Banna, another prominent Nazareth singer, received her musical education in Moscow. While there, she produced two albums: *Jafra* (1985) and *Your Tears, Mother* (1986). Married to a Ukrainian musician, she lives in Nazareth and performs duets with her husband. Banna specializes in Palestinian folk songs and popular lullabies. She has produced a collection of children's songs that she composed and that have been featured at children's festivals around the country. She now has six albums and compact discs out and has performed both locally and internationally.

Kamilya Jubran, born in Acre and raised in Al-Rameh in the Galilee, was the main vocalist and qanun (a kind of dulcimer with 81 strings, stretched in groups of 3) player for the ensemble Sabreen, formed in Jerusalem in the 1980s under the artistic direction of Samir Murad, an oud player and composer.[12] Sabreen combined folk songs with more modern innovative musical techniques. Their music is composed by Murad, with lyrics from poets such as Mahmoud Darwish, Husayn al-Barghuthi, and Samih al-Qasim. Jubran has since begun her own career as a soloist and in a new ensemble with European musicians in a production *Mahattaat* (Arabic for "stations"). Her father, Elias Jubran, a musician and maker of traditional Palestinian instruments, was her principal music teacher. Jubran was the only female singer in her father's musical groups that performed at weddings and other celebrations.

Among the better-known instrumentalists are Samir and Wassem Joubran, Samir Shukri, and Simon Shaheen. Samir Joubran, born to a Nazareth family of oud makers, graduated from the prestigious Abdul-Wahab Conservatory for Eastern Music (Cairo) in 1993. He specializes in the musical genre known as *taqsim*, free-form melodic improvisation that serves to establish the mood of a piece. He often plays with his younger brother, Wassam, also a talented oud player and a master instrument maker. Samir Shukri, from Acre, learned music from his father, who played oud for the Israel Broadcasting Corporation. Samir is an accomplished violin player who crossed over with his song "Rona," which appealed to the *musica mizrakhit* crowd. Simon Shaheen was born in Tarshiha.[13] His father, Hikmat, was a professor of music at the Haifa Conservatory and was a renowned oud player. Simon Shaheen completed a degree at the Academy of Music in Jerusalem and taught music until he left Israel for New York in 1980. He remained in the United States, where he could more freely pursue his musical interests. He established the Near Eastern Music Ensemble in New York in the early 1980s. In the late 1990s, he created the band Qantara ("bridge" or "arch" in Arabic), which performs a fusion of Arabic, jazz, Western classical, and Latin music. He has achieved international acclaim on the oud and violin, playing Carnegie Hall and the Kennedy Center and appearing at the Grammy Awards with Sting in 2000, on his rendition of *Desert Rose*.

DANCE

Dance as celebration and a sign of joy has been an important part of Jewish religious ritual and communal life since biblical days, when Miriam led the women in dance following the crossing of the Red Sea to freedom. Dance became an institutionalized part of religious ritual as the temple service developed. Dancing occurs in many Jewish holiday celebrations, including the all-night festivities of Sukkoth (harvest festival) and Simchat Torah (which celebrates the end of the yearly Torah reading), where rabbis dancing with the Torah scrolls might take their congregants out into the city streets, and the festivities of Purim, to celebrate Esther's rescue from death of the Jews in Persia. It is at weddings, however, that dance has been most prominent because the Talmud requires Jews to dance at weddings. Dance has not always been permitted, however, as rulers or the Christian Church attempted to prevent the Jewish community from holding celebrations. And Jewish communities have often battled with their own rabbinical authorities over how they could dance—what was acceptable, what was seductive, what was impermissible. A number of conflicts arose between Sephardic communities and their rabbis over the question of "mixed" dancing between men and women. The rabbis often approached dance as being unclean, rather than seeing it as an integral part of a Jewish way of celebrating. They tried to impose restrictions on dance but often had to back down in the face of the community's refusal to abide by their restrictions.[14]

Within Islam, there are also different views about dancing and its appropriateness. Some religious Muslims strictly forbid dancing because it may cause people to sin. Others allow dancing as long as it is single sex and not done in front of the other sex. Here, women can dance but only in front of other women. In some Muslim countries, it is permissible to watch professional dancers (in some Muslim empires, non-Muslim women were trained as professional dancers), but no good Muslim woman would dance. Muslims attracted to the Sufi mystical practices use dance as a way to enter a heightened state of awareness and grow closer to Allah.

Folk dances were already present in many groups that later became Muslim, and Islam was not able to stamp these traditions out. Dance was a valued part of communal celebrations. It marked important life-cycle ceremonies (births, circumcisions, weddings), as well as major seasonal activities such as planting or harvest celebrations. In Palestine, every village had its own dance tradition that marked that village as unique from the others. In Israel, all these dance traditions converged and developed into two different tracks—a classical dance track, with professional performers, stages, and audiences, and a folk dance track that eventually spread out from Israel to Jewish (and non-Jewish) communities throughout the world.

Classical Dance: Modern and Ballet

New immigrants arriving from western Europe in the 1920s and 1930s brought classical dance to Israel. They favored the expressionist dance popular in Europe at this time. Rina Nikova, born in St. Petersburg, Russia, and trained in ballet there and in Berlin, immigrated to Israel and introduced classical ballet in 1924. Her Biblical Ballet (later, Yemenite Ballet) performed from 1925 to 1947. To form her company, Nikova recruited only Yemenite dancers and taught them classical ballet technique. She had to convince parents to allow their daughters to dance for her since the dances were being transformed from a religious purpose to a dramatic, theatrical performance. Gertrud Kraus settled in Tel Aviv from her native Vienna in 1933. She created original works from her arrival to the 1950s for her own company, as well as for the Palestine Folk Opera (1941–1947), Habimah, and others. A student who studied with Kraus notes that she "made a conscious effort to link our movement to the place where we lived."[15] Yardena Cohen, Israeli born (1910) but trained in modern dance in Vienna and Berlin, introduced dance therapy to Israel. Cohen used an orchestra of Arab and Jewish musicians to provide musical accompaniment for her dances. She employed large, open spaces, using tents or the natural landscape as a backdrop. In her zest for dance, she used classical ballet, modern dance, and folk dance styles woven together into her own unique style and inspired the generation of dancers and choreographers that followed her.

Inbal Dance Theater, founded by Sara Levi-Tanai in 1949, remains Israel's oldest professional dance company. The repertoire of this ensemble is based on movement material suggested by traditions of the Mizrahi Jewish communities. The pieces are built around biblical themes, such as the Song of Songs or the story of Ruth. Others deal with the conflict between tradition and modernity. The troupe also celebrates the many ethnic cultures that make up Israel's social fabric.

After World War II, Israeli dance professionals turned from Europe to the United States for their inspiration. Temporary visitors, such as Jerome Robbins, Anna Sokolov, and Talley Beatty, and new immigrant dancers who had trained in the United States, such as Rina Shaham and Rena Gluck, brought a new vision of modern dance to Israel. Heavily influenced by the theatrical performances of Martha Graham, these dancers and choreographers attempted to introduce new discipline into Israeli modern dance. The Israeli dance community was electrified by the 1955–1956 Graham Company tour of Israel. Anna Sokolov, wanting to do more than coach Inbal or occasionally choreograph, created her own short-lived dance company, The Lyric Theatre, in 1962.

Modern Dance

Modern dance exists in Israel due to the patronage of the Baroness Batsheva de Rothschild. In 1964, she founded the Batsheva Dance Company, which began its life as a troupe patterned after the work of Martha Graham, whom de Rothschild supported and admired. Graham herself was brought to Israel to train the dancers. She permitted them to perform her choreographies *Errand into the Maze*, *Embattled Garden*, and *Diversion of Angels*. With these dances as their foundation, the company attracted new choreographers including Glen Tetley and John Cranko. Batsheva introduced a new concept for a dance company to Israel—a repertory company based around the dancers and not the choreographer.

The baroness founded a new repertory company and school, Bat-Dor, headed by Jeanette Ordman in 1967. Bat-Dor also functioned as a repertory company and has worked with a long line of choreographers, including Paul Taylor, Alvin Ailey, Lar Lubovitch, and John Butler. The school has served to train new

The Batsheva Dance Company performing "Song of My People." Photo by Moshe Milner. Courtesy of the Government Press Office, State of Israel.

dancers for both repertory companies. A number of Bat-Dor dancers have also choreographed for the company. Some of them went on to start their own dance companies, thus further enriching modern dance in Israel.

The Kibbutz Contemporary Dance Company (KCDC) started in 1970, growing out of the Regional Western Galilee Dance Group, founded and directed by Yehudit Arnon. From 1970 to 1996, Arnon served as artistic director. Born in Czechoslovakia, she survived the concentration camps and went to Budapest at her release, where she became involved with the Hashomer Hatzair youth movement. She immigrated to Israel with her husband in 1948 and joined Kibbutz Ga'aton. There she established a dance center and devoted herself to dance education. The current artistic director, Rami Be'er, trained with the KCDC as a young adult. He joined the company in 1980 as dancer and choreographer. Under his direction, the KCDC has expanded its outreach to young children, with special dance choreographies especially for young people since 1994.

In 1978, Yakov Sharir and Moshe Efrati left Bat-Dor to found Kol U'Demama (Sound and Silence). The company has both deaf and hearing dancers. Efrati uses methods that allow deaf persons to sense vibrations transmitted through the floor to help them dance in the absence of being able to hear the music. The company has made a major contribution to allowing hearing-impaired individuals to participate and has earned an international reputation for its artistic merit.

Two companies that started performing in the 1990s express the current spirit of modern dance in Israel. Noa Wertheim and Adi Sha'al started Vertigo Dance Company in 1992. Their first professional collaboration, a short duet called *Vertigo*, led to the establishment of their company. They built the duet around the experience of spinning out of control, not just in the air but in relationships as well. The company provides performances, master classes, workshops, and coproductions with other companies from around the world. Their choreography *The Power of Balance*, created by British choreographer Adam Benjamin, brought together seven Company dancers with five disabled dancers in wheelchairs. This is in keeping with the company's commitment that dance is for everyone. Its dance school enables everyone to study dance, while the Vertigo Dance Workshop provides the necessary framework for training dancers.

In 1996, Eylon Nuphar and Boaz Berman founded the dance company Mayumana (derived from the Hebrew word for "skill"). They selected 19 dancers from more than 700 candidates and trained them in drumming, yoga, hip-hop, African dancing, acting, improvisation, and rock climbing. Their performances are explorations of movement, percussion, and rhythm. They began performing in Tel Aviv in 1998 at the Tzavta to rave reviews and a sold-out theater. The show has since moved to its own hall, Mayumana Hall, located in a hangar at the harbor in Jaffa. The troupe has put together a special program for children up to the age of 12 that allows them to be part of the show.

That same year, a new ethnic-inspired troupe began to perform. Led by Ruth Eshel, who performed solo and with Batsheva for 20 years, Eskesta Dance Theater presents artistic choreographies of Ethiopian movements to Israeli and international audiences. The troupe started with 11 members, 5 women and 6 men, studying at University of Haifa. *Esketa* refers to a brisk shoulder movement that is a prominent and unique feature of Ethiopian dancing.

Ballet

The Israel Ballet, Israel's only world-class classical ballet company, was founded in 1967 by the wife-husband team of Berta Yampolsky and Hillel Markman and four other dancers. Yampolsky and Markman had previously directed the Israeli Opera Ballet. To start the company, they used their own money and began to lobby for other funding. It was not until 1993 that the company achieved parity in financing with the country's modern dance companies. To begin, the company limited itself to re-creating dances they had danced with other companies. They commissioned their first work in 1974, Tod Bolender's *Still Point.* Yampolsky began her own career as a choreographer that year and to date has choreographed more than 20 ballets, including classics such as *Romeo and Juliet, Sleeping Beauty,* and the *Nutcracker* and shorter works such as *Harmonium* and *Gurrelieder.* Ballanchine's *The Four Temperaments, Serenade, Symphony in C,* and *Square Dance* have taken their place in their repertoire. Today the company boasts 35 dancers (native Israelis and Russian, European, and American immigrants) and is supported by the Ministry of Science, Culture, and Sport and the City of Tel Aviv. The ballet currently performs at the Tel Aviv Performing Arts Center. Besides the schools connected to ballet or modern dance companies, students can also study dance at the Jerusalem Academy of Music and Dance (formerly the Rubin Academy). The Suzanne Dellal Center in Tel Aviv has become a center for dance activity in the country.

Israeli Folk Dance

The early immigrants trained in modern dance in Europe also put their talents to creating a new dance form in Israel—Israeli folk dance. To do this, they drew on the folk traditions of their countries of origin, on the traditions and rituals of Judaism, and on indigenous Palestinian traditions. Israeli folk dance is an excellent example of combining elements from two or more cultural traditions to create something totally new. It is not really "folk" in the sense of a cultural tradition developed over hundreds of years, the origins of which are shrouded in the mists of time. Instead it represents an "invented" tradition, developed out of the particular images and ideals that its founders thought best represented Israeli national culture. Israeli folk dance is also unique in that, once created, it traveled back overseas to Diaspora communities, where it was enthusiastically seized upon, learned, taught, and enjoyed by Jews and non-Jews alike. There are Israeli folk dance clubs in 37 different countries—from the United States to Australia and Japan. The synergy between dancers in Israel and dancers overseas helped this form of dance become "folk" over the last 80 years.

The founders of Israeli folk dance were mainly women—Gurit Kadman (born in Leipzig, Germany; immigrated in 1920), Rivka Sturman (also born in Leipzig; immigrated in 1929), and Leah Bergstein (born in Vienna; immigrated in 1925)—and one man, Baruch Agadati (born in Serbia; immigrated in 1885). Native-born Yardena Cohen and Sara Levi Tannai, better known for their contributions to Israel's modern dance traditions, were also involved early on with the folk dance movement. Agadati, the first male Israeli dancer, went on to establish himself as an artist and filmmaker, best known for his film *This Is the Land* (1934) which details the founding of Tel Aviv and other events occurring in the Jewish community in Palestine. The dance that takes his name, *Hora Agadati,* dates to 1924.

Gurit Kadman and Rivka Sturman are generally recognized as the major creators of Israeli folk dance. Kadman and Sturman both came from Germany, which at the time they immigrated was undergoing a surge of popular interest in returning to nature and the simpler life. Kadman participated in the German Wandervogel youth movement, through which she visited the countryside and learned about German folk cultural traditions. She and Sturman also belonged to Zionist youth groups in Germany that prepared them as pioneers to immigrate to Palestine and to live on kibbutzim. Kadman helped co-found Kibbutz Hefztiba with other German and Czech immigrants. At night, young people would dance the Polish *krakowiak*, Romanian hora, the polka, *sherele* (a wedding dance), or rondo as a form of relaxation and amusement. The settlers decided to develop specific dances to help them celebrate seasonal agricultural festivals (sowing, harvesting) as these began to occur. These festivals had special meaning for them because farming was not a typical Jewish occupation in the Diaspora and thus they were part of a new phenomenon—Jewish farmers. On the kibbutzim in the 1920s, a tradition of festival dances began for the spring Festival of the First Fruits and the fall harvest of Sukkoth.

The birth of the organized Israeli folk dance movement occurred at Kibbutz Dalia in 1944. Gurit Kadman was asked by the kibbutz members to choreograph dances based on the Book of Ruth from the Hebrew Bible for their Shavu'ot celebrations.[16] She and other dancers used the occasion to also call a folk dance meeting there, and they began to plan a dance festival. Two hundred dancers gathered at "Dance Village" for two days and nights to dance, sing, and learn. More than 3,500 spectators gathered to watch the event. Most of the dances performed were from other countries. Israel was represented by a single Tu Bishvat suite of three dances, choreographed by Sara Levi-Tannai and Gurit Kadman. Yardena Cohen's dance drew on Arab movements, and Rivka Sturman staged a dance based around the movements of threshing. Yemenite singers, drummers, and dancers also made an appearance.

The Dalia Festival brought to light the absence of an Israeli folk dance repertoire. It became clear that if Israelis wanted dances of their own, they would need to create them. The festival sparked a creative urge in those who had participated. They returned home and began to create Israeli folk dances, drawing elements from European folk traditions, indigenous Arab dance styles, and even modern Latin dances. A popular couple dance, "Dodi Li," for example, owes its existence to Rivka Sturman's desire to create an Israeli version of the tango.

A number of steps are incorporated into many Israeli dances. One step, the *mayim*, is a basic "grapevine" step, with one foot crossing in front of the other, the back foot moved to the side, then the free foot passing behind the other foot, which completes the step by again moving to the side; this step can be done moving right or left. The *Yemenite* is a step that involves balancing to the right, putting weight on right foot, transferring weight back to left foot, and crossing over the left foot with the right foot. One repeats this sequence to the left to complete the step. The hora refers to a type of circle dance (originating in Romania), while the *debke* is a native Palestinian village dance performed in a line. The simplest *debke* rhythm is a straight march and stamp, but it can become quite com-

The Negev Folk Dance Troupe performing for Shavu'ot at a kibbutz. Photo by Ya'acov Gefen. Courtesy of the Government Press Office, State of Israel.

plex and syncopated. Forward stamps, simple progressive steps, knee bends endlessly repeated, combined leaps and kicks, and the beating out of a rhythmic pattern with one foot may all be interwoven into a single dance.

As dances were choreographed, they circulated throughout the country in pamphlets, with photographs, music, and descriptions. The Second Dalia Festival in 1947 drew 500 dancers and 25,000 spectators. This festival featured Palestinian and Druze dances as well as Israeli dances. The Dalia Festivals continued to grow in popularity. By 1968, there were 3,000 dancers and 60,000 spectators. Today, aficionados of Israeli folk dance flock to Israel in the month of July for the Carmiel Dance Festival, initiated in 1988. The three-day event is truly international, attracting performing groups and spectators from around the world. For 2003, the organizers of this event hosted 5,000 dancers and 250,000 spectators in Carmiel.

Israeli folk dance today is managed through a folk dance Choreographers and Instructors Association. The national union, the Histadrut, ran a department for folk dance from 1945 to 2000 that trained teachers of folk dancing. Today, there are two courses for training teachers, one at the Wingate Institute and one at the College of Givat Washington. There is a periodical dedicated to Israeli folk dancing, *Rokdim* (http://www.rokdim.co.il/). More than 300 groups meet throughout the country, reaching out to more than 300,000 people. Up to 100 new dances join the ranks of the 3,000 documented dances each year as the dance market requires that choreographers come up with newer and fresher material to feed the dancers' demand. Some long-time dancers fear that folk dance is quickly disappearing to be replaced by a more aerobic, mechanical, MTV-style of dance to popular radio tunes. Many dancers no longer connect to those around them but dance as individuals. With 800 to 1,000 people turning out to dance in a rented hall, the intimate family atmosphere of the early days has been lost. Because choreographers cannot protect their intellectual rights to their dances, the competition can get fierce as instructors try to prevent others from disseminating the dances they have developed.

NOTES

1. Peter Gradenwitz, *The Music of Israel: From the Biblical Era to Modern Times* (Portland, Ore.: Amadeus Press, 1996), 387–389.

2. Gradenwitz, *Music of Israel*, 351–352.

3. Regev, "To Have a Culture of Our Own," 230.

4. Motti Regev, "Musica mizrakhit, Israeli Rock, and National Culture in Israel," *Popular Music* 15, no. 3 (1996): 279.

5. Motti Regev, "Israeli Rock, or a Study in the Politics of 'Local Authenticity,'" *Popular Music* 11, no. 1 (1992): 1–14.

6. Regev, "Israeli Rock," 5.

7. Loolwa Khazzoom, "Israeli Rappers Prove Hip-Hop Will Translate to Any Language," *Boston Globe*, 4 January 2004.

8. Loolwa Khazzoom, "Hip-Hop Breaks Out in the Middle East," *Baltimore Sun*, August 10, 2003.

9. Jeff Halper, Edwin Seroussi, and Pamela Squires-Kidron, "Musica mizrakhit: Ethnicity and Class Culture in Israel," *Popular Music* 8, no. 2 (1989): 135.

10. Downloadable clips of Wasif Jawhariyyeh recordings can be found at www.orientaltunes.com/tunes.html, under the link for his name. For more on Wasif Jawhariyyeh's life, see Salim Tamari, "Jerusalem's Ottoman Modernity: The Times and Lives of Wasif Jawhariyyeh," *Jerusalem Quarterly File* 9 (2000), 5–34. http://www.jqf-jerusalem.org/2000/jqf9/tamari2.html.

11. Motti Regev, "Present Absentee: Arab Music in Israeli Culture," *Public Culture* 7, no. 2 (1995): 435.

12. Jubran has her own Web site at http://www.kamilyajubran.com/.

13. More information on Shaheen is available at http://www.simon-shaheen.com.

14. Judith Brin Ingber, "Is Sephardic Dance Too Sexy?" (paper presented at the meeting The Jews of Sepharad: 1300 Years of Crisis, Identity and Assimilation, University of Northern Iowa, Cedar Falls, Iowa, October 11, 1993).

15. Judith Brin Ingber, "Shalom: Hello or Goodbye to Israeli Modern Dance after the American Invasion?" In *American Dance Abroad: Influence of the United States Experience*, ed. Christena L. Schlundt. *Proceedings of the Society of Dance History Scholars, Fifteenth Annual Conference, 14–15 February 1992* (Riverside: University of California, Riverside. 1992), 245.

16. Ruth was a widowed, childless Moabite woman who refused to leave the side of Naomi, her Israelite mother-in-law when the latter decided to return to Bethlehem. Ruth told Naomi that she would take Naomi's people and god as her own. She married Boaz, a wealthy man, and was great-grandmother to King David.

Glossary

'Abayeh Sleeveless cloak of wool (Arabic).

Aliyah (pl. aliyot) To immigrate to Israel.

Ashkenazi (pl. Askenazim) Jews in Israel from Europe, the United States, and Latin America.

Diaspora Exile; term used to refer to Jews who live outside Israel.

Druze A religious sect within Islam (an eleventh-century offshoot from Shiite Islam) whose followers are found in modern times in Lebanon, Israel, and Syria.

Falafel Deep-fried chickpea balls.

Gemara Legal and philosophic debates and stories that form the second part of the Talmud.

Hadith The collected record of the body of sayings and customs attributed by Muslims to the prophet Muhammad and his companions.

Haganah The pre-state defense force of the Jewish community in Palestine, which became the IDF (army) after the state of Israel was founded.

Halakha The body of Jewish law.

Hallal Lawful or permissible (Arabic).

Halutz (pl. halutzim) Pioneer.

Haram Unlawful or not permitted (Arabic).

Haredi Ultra-Orthodox Jewish groups.

Hasid (pl. Hasidim) Member of a Jewish mystical sect founded in Poland about 1750 in opposition to rationalism and ritual laxity.

Hegira Flight of Muhammad from Mecca to Medina in A.D. 622 (Arabic).

Histadrut National Federation of Labor Unions formed in Palestine in 1920.

Hummus Dip made of ground chickpeas and sesame paste with lemon.

IDF Israel Defense Forces, Israel's army.

Imam Prayer leader of a mosque or a ruler that claims descent from Muhammad and exercises leadership over a Muslim region.

Intifada Uprising (Arabic); refers to Palestinian revolts since the 1980s.

Irgun Jewish right-wing underground movement founded in 1931.

Kashrut Jewish dietary laws.

Keffiyeh Square head cloth worn by Palestinian men (Arabic).

Kibbutz (pl. kibbutzim) Collective settlement whose residents pool labor and resources and share equally in profits.

Kippah Skull cap worn by Jewish men.

Knesset Israeli parliament.

Levirate Practice of marrying a childless widow to the brother of her deceased husband. The brother can formally refuse to wed her, in which case she is released to remarry someone else.

Matzo Unleavened bread eaten by Jews at Passover.

Millet system Under the Ottomans, a form of self-government by which each non-Islamic religious community was allowed autonomy to run its own communal affairs under a recognized community leader.

Minaret Slender tower of a mosque from which the call to prayer is given.

Mishnah Rabbinic commentary on the Torah laws compiled about A.D. 200 and made the basic part of the Talmud.

Mizrahi (pl. Mizrahim) Israeli Jews from the Middle East, Central Asia, and North Africa.

Moshav (pl. moshavim) Settlement whose residents individually own land but collectively purchase supplies and market produce.

Musica mizrakhit Pop musical tradition of Middle Eastern Jewish communities.

Palmach Elite branch of the Haganah, the pre-state Jewish defense force.

PLO Palestine Liberation Organization, formed in 1964 as the umbrella political movement for Palestinians throughout the world.

Pogrom An organized mob attack sanctioned by the authorities.

Purim Jewish holiday based on the book of Esther that celebrates the deliverance of the Jews from a massacre plotted by Haman.

Qumbaz An overdress (Arabic).

Quran The sacred book of Islam, composed of writings believed by Muslims to be the revelations of God passed through the angel Gabriel to the prophet Muhammad.

Rosh Hashanah Jewish New Year.

Sabra Native-born Israeli Jew.

Sephardi (pl. Sephardim) Jews whose ancestors lived in Spain and Portugal and who were expelled from there to the Balkans, the Levant, England, the Netherlands, and the Americas.

Shabbat Jewish day of rest and worship, observed from sundown on Friday to sundown on Saturday.

Shari'a Muslim religious law, based on the Quran.

Shavuot Jewish holiday that commemorates the revelation of the law on Mount Sinai and celebrates the wheat harvest.

Sukkoth Jewish harvest festival, that commemorates the booths in which the Israelites lived during their forty years wandering in the wilderness.

Talmud Codified oral law of Judaism.

Thob Plain long shirt or tunic (Arabic).

Torah Also known as Pentateuch; the first five books of the Jewish and Christian Scriptures.

Tzitzit Tassels or fringes on garments.

Ulpan Intensive language training program to teach Hebrew.

Waqf Muslim religious endowment (Arabic).

Yeshiva Jewish school for studying the Talmud and Torah.

Yom Kippur Jewish Day of Atonement, a day observed by fasting and prayer.

Zionism Jewish national movement to found their own state.

Bibliography

Abramson, Glenda. *Drama and Ideology in Modern Israel.* Cambridge, England: Cambridge University Press, 1998.

———. *Modern Hebrew Drama.* New York: St. Martin's Press, 1979.

Ahroni, Reuben. *Yemenite Jewry: Origins, Culture, and Literature.* Bloomington: Indiana University Press, 1986.

Ajzenstadt, Mimi, and Odeda Steinberg. "Never Mind the Law: Legal Discourse and Rape Reform in Israel." *Affilia* 16, no. 3 (2001):337–359.

Bargad, Warren, and Stanley F. Chyet, eds. and trans. *Israeli Poetry: A Contemporary Anthology.* Bloomington: Indiana University Press, 1986.

Ben-Ari, Eyal. *Mastering Soldiers: Conflict, Emotions, and the Enemy in an Israeli Military Unit.* New York: Berghahn Books, 1998.

Boullata, Kamal. "'Asim Abu Shaqra: The Artist's Eye and the Cactus Tree." *Journal of Palestine Studies* 30, no. 4 (2001): 68–82.

———. "Facing the Forest: Israeli and Palestinian Artists." *Third Text* 7 (1989): 77–95.

Boyd, Douglas A. "Hebrew-Language Clandestine Radio Broadcasting During the British Palestine Mandate," *Journal of Radio Studies* 8, no. 1 (1999): 101–115.

Brin Ingber. "Is Sephardic Dance Too Sexy?" Paper presented at the conference The Jews of Sepharad: 1300 Years of Crisis, Identity and Assimilation, University of Northern Iowa, Cedar Falls, Iowa, October 11, 1993.

———. "Shalom: Hello or Goodbye to Israeli Modern Dance after the American Invasion?" In *American Dance Abroad: Influence of the United States Experience,* ed. Christena L. Schlundt. *Proceedings of the Society of Dance History Scholars, Fifteenth Annual Conference, 14–15 February 1992.* Riverside: University of California, Riverside, 1992.

———. *Shorashim: The Roots of Israeli Folk Dance.* New York: Dance Perspectives Foundation, 1974.

Chazan, Naomi. "Politics and Women Go Together." *Jerusalem Post,* 12 March 1999.

Cohen, Erik, and Amnon Shiloah. "Major Trends of Change in Jewish Oriental Ethnic Music in Israel." In *Popular Music 5: Continuity and Change*, ed. Richard Middleton and David Horn, 199–223. Cambridge, England: Cambridge University Press, 1985.

Cozic, Charles P., ed. *Israel: Opposing Viewpoints*. San Diego, Calif.: Greenhaven Press, 1994.

Elad-Bouskila, Ami. "Arabic and/or Hebrew: The Languages of Arab Writers in Israel." In *Israeli and Palestinian Identities in History and Literature*, ed. Kamal Abdel-Malek and David C. Jacobson, 133–158. New York: St. Martin's Press, 1999.

El-Ghadban, Yara. "Shedding Some Light on Contemporary Musicians in Palestine." *Middle East Studies Association Bulletin* 35, no. 1 (2001): 28–34.

Elmessiri, Abdelwahab M. *The Palestinian Wedding: A Bilingual Anthology of Contemporary Palestinian Resistance Poetry*. Washington, D.C.: Three Continents Press, 1982.

Elon, Amos. *The Israelis: Founders and Sons*. New York: Penguin Books, 1971.

Esposito, John, ed. *The Oxford Encyclopedia of the Modern Islamic World*. New York: Oxford University Press, 1995.

Finkelstein, Israel, and Neil Asher Silberman. *The Bible Unearthed: Archaeology's New Vision of Ancient Israel and the Origin of Its Sacred Texts*. New York: Free Press, 2001.

Franks, Lynne. *Israel and the Occupied Territories: A Study of the Educational Systems of Israel and the Occupied Territories and a Guide to the Academic Placement of Students in Educational Institutions of the United States*. Washington, D.C.: American Association of Collegiate Registrars and Admissions Officer, 1987.

Fuhrer, Ronald. *Israeli Painting: From Post-Impressionism to Post-Zionism*. New York: Overlook Press, 1998.

Gerner, Deborah. *One Land, Two Peoples: The Conflict over Palestine*. Boulder, Colo.: Westview Press, 1991.

Glazer, Miriyam. *Dreaming the Actual: Contemporary Fiction and Poetry by Israeli Women Writers*. Albany: State University of New York Press, 2000.

Goodman, Susan Tumarkin. *After Rabin: New Art from Israel*. New York: Jewish Museum, 1998.

———. *Artists of Israel, 1920–1980*. Detroit, Mich.: Wayne State University Press, 1981.

Gradenwitz, Peter. *Music and Musicians in Israel*. 3rd ed. Tel Aviv: Israeli Music Publications Limited, 1978.

———. *The Music of Israel: From the Biblical Era to Modern Times*. Portland, Ore.: Amadeus Press, 1996.

Halper, Jeff, Edwin Seroussi, and Pamela Squires-Kidron. "Musica mizrakhit: Ethnicity and Class Culture in Israel." *Popular Music* 8, no. 2 (1989): 131–141.

Herzog, Hanna. "Homefront and Battlefront: The Status of Jewish and Palestinian Women in Israel." *Israel Studies* 3, no. 1 (1998): 61–84.

Hirshberg, Jehoash. *Music in the Jewish Community of Palestine 1880–1948: A Social History*. Oxford: Clarendon Press, 1996.

Iram, Yaacov, and Mirjam Schmida. *The Educational System of Israel*. Westport, Conn.: Greenwood Press, 1998.

Israel, Central Bureau of Statistics, Prime Minister's Office, The Authority for the Advancement of the Status of Women. *Women and Men in Israel*. Jerusalem: Central Bureau of Statistics, July 2000.

Israel, Central Bureau of Statistics. *Vital Statistics: Marriages and Divorces 1999*. Jerusalem: Central Bureau of Statistics, March 2003.

Kanaaneh, Rhoda. *Birthing the Nation: Strategies of Palestinian Women in Israel.* Berkeley: University of California Press, 2002.

Kaufman, Sheilah. *Sephardic Israeli Cuisine: A Mediterranean Mosaic.* New York: Hippocrene Books, 2002.

Khalidi, Walid. *Before Their Diaspora: A Photographic History of the Palestinians 1876–1948.* Washington, D.C.: Institute for Palestine Studies, 1984.

Khazzoom, Loolwa. "Hip-Hop Breaks Out in the Middle East." *Baltimore Sun,* 10 August 2003.

———. "Israeli Rappers Prove Hip-Hop Will Translate to Any Language." *Boston Globe,* 4 January 2004.

Kubovy, Miri. "*Inniut* and *Kooliut* Trends in Israeli Narrative Literature, 1995–1999." *Israel Studies* 5, no. 1 (2000): 244–265.

Lori, Aviva. "Brushed Off." *Ha'Aretz,* 13 August 2003.

Lowenstein, Steven M. *The Jewish Cultural Tapestry: International Jewish Folk Traditions.* New York: Oxford University Press, 2000.

Lustick, Ian, ed. *Triumph and Catastrophe: The War of 1948, Israeli Independence, and the Refugee Problem.* New York: Garland, 1994.

Massad, Joseph. "Liberating Songs: Palestine Put to Music." *Journal of Palestine Studies* 32, no. 3 (2003): 21–38.

Metz, Helen Chapin, ed. *Israel: A Country Study.* Washington, D.C.: U.S. Government, Secretary of the Army, 1990.

Nassar, Issam. "A Jerusalem Photographer: The Life and Work of Hanna Safieh." *Jerusalem Quarterly File* 7 (2000), 24–28.

Nathan, Joan. *The Foods of Israel Today.* New York: Knopf, 2001.

Neusner, Jacob, Alan J. Avery-Peck, and William Scott Green, eds. *The Encyclopedia of Judaism.* New York: Continuum, 1999.

Ofrat, Gideon. *100 Years of Art in Israel.* Boulder, Colo.: Westview Press, 1998.

Rajab, Jehan S. *Palestinian Costume.* London: Kegan Paul International, 1989.

Regev, Motti. "Israeli Rock, or a Study in the Politics of 'Local Authenticity.' " *Popular Music* 11, no. 1 (1992): 1–14.

———. "Musica mizrakhit, Israeli Rock, and National Culture in Israel." *Popular Music* 15, no. 3 (1996): 275–284.

———. "Present Absentee: Arab Music in Israeli Culture." *Public Culture* 7, no. 2 (1995): 433–445.

———. "To Have a Culture of Our Own: On Israeliness and Its Variants." *Ethnic and Racial Studies* 23, no. 2 (2000): 223–247.

Resh, Nura. "Track Placement: How the 'Sorting Machine' Works in Israel." *American Journal of Education* 106, no. 3 (1998): 416–438.

Roberts, D. S. *Islam: A Concise Introduction.* New York: Harper and Row, 1981.

Rosen, Claudia. *The Book of Jewish Food: An Odyssey from Samarkand to New York.* New York: Knopf, 1996.

Rubens, Alfred. *A History of Jewish Costume.* Rev. and enl. edition. London: Peter Owen, 1981.

Rubin, Joel. "Rumenishe Shtiklekh: Klezmer Music among the Hasidim in Contemporary Israel." *Judaism* 47, no. 1 (1998): 12–23.

Rueschemeyer, Marilyn. "Ethnic Place and Artistic Creation: Dilemmas of Sephardic Artists in Israel." *Journal of Arts Management, Law, and Society* 22, no. 4 (1993): 341–355.

Sachar, Howard. A History of Israel: From the Rise of Zionism to Our Time. New York: Alfred A. Knopf, 1979.

———. A History of Israel Volume II: From the Aftermath of the Yom Kippur War. New York: Oxford University Press, 1987.

Sandberg, Esther, and Oren Tatcher. "The White City Revisited." Progressive Architecture 75, no. 8 (1994): 33–34.

Segev, Tom. 1949: The First Israelis. New York: Free Press, 1986.

———. One Palestine, Complete: Jews and Arabs under the British Mandate. New York: Henry Holt, 1999.

Shaked, Gershon. Modern Hebrew Fiction. Bloomington: Indiana University Press, 2000.

Shapira, Anita. Land and Power: The Zionist Resort to Force, 1881–1948. New York: Oxford University Press, 1992.

Sharoni, Simona. Gender and the Israeli-Palestinian Conflict: The Politics of Women's Resistance. Syracuse, N.Y.: Syracuse University Press, 1995.

Shechori, Ran. Art in Israel. Tel Aviv: Sadan Publishing House, 1974.

Shohat, Ella. Israeli Cinema: East/West and the Politics of Representation. Austin: University of Texas Press, 1987.

Silver, Eric. "Bauhaus on the Mediterranean." World Press Review 41, no. 11 (1994): 43.

Slyomovics, Susan. The Object of Memory: Arab and Jew Narrate the Palestinian Village. Philadelphia: University of Pennsylvania Press, 1998.

Sofer, Barbara. "Growing Up in Style." Hadassah Magazine 79, no. 9 (1998): 14–18.

———. "Label Droppings: New Names in Israeli Fashion." Hadassah Magazine 78, no. 8 (1997): 28–31.

Swirski, Shlomo, Vered Kraus, Etty Konor-Attias, and Anat Herbst. Special Issue: Solo Mothers in Israel. Israel Equality Monitor 12 (2003).

Swirski, Shlomo, and Yaron Yechezkel. Women's Representation in the Legislature and the Executive in Israel and Worldwide. Tel Aviv: Adva Center, February 1999.

Tabory, Ephraim. "The Influence of Liberal Judaism on Israeli Religious Life." Israel Studies 5, no. 1 (2000): 183–203.

Tamari, Salim. "Jerusalem's Ottoman Modernity: The Times and Lives of Wasif Jawhariyyeh." Jerusalem Quarterly File 9 (2000): 5–34.

Tamir, Tally. "The Shadow of Foreignness: On the Paintings of Asim Abu-Shakra." Palestine-Israel Journal 6, no. 1 (1997): 111–119.

Tammuz, Benjamin, and Max Wykes-Joyce, eds. Art in Israel. New York: Chilton, 1967.

Torstrick, Rebecca. The Limits of Coexistence: Identity Politics in Israel. Ann Arbor: University of Michigan Press, 2000.

United Nations, Committee on the Elimination of Discrimination Against Women, Initial and Second Periodic Reports of State Parties: Israel, 8 April 1997, 240–241. http://ods-dds-ny.un.org/doc/UNDOC/GEN/N97/096/08/IMG/N9709608.pdf

Weir, Shelagh. Palestinian Costume. Austin: University of Texas Press. 1989.

Weiss, Shevach, and Yael Yishai. "Women's Representation in Israeli Political Elites." Jewish Social Studies 42 (1980): 165–176.

Index

About the Author

REBECCA L. TORSTRICK is Associate Professor of Anthropology at Indiana University, South Bend.